WHAT TO EXPECT

How adaptive is your organisation?
What does an adaptive organisation look like from the inside?
How do you build one?
Where do you start?

THIS BOOK PROVIDES THESE ANSWERS and many more. You could think of it as your *Complete Leader's Guide* to turning the organisation you have today, into one that holds an adaptive advantage over its rivals.

The Thrive Cycle, and its original framework, will enable you and your organisation to discuss, define, develop and measure adaptive capability in a meaningful way. It crystallises the lessons of twenty years spent influencing, cajoling and coercing large, complex organisations to adapt, and shares the insights from a career spent in-between the organisational silos. The result is a new, reality-based approach to one of the world's biggest challenges: CHANGE.

If you're a leader with the ambition, passion and strategic imperative to create The Adaptive Organisation, this book will show you how.

‘So many “a-ha” moments in *The Thrive Cycle* for any leader who has experienced major organisational change. This practical and engaging book provides a comprehensive and flexible framework, supported by a range of useful, easy to apply tools. A must-read!’

Gabrielle Prior

— Former International Director of Operations Quality, Nielsen/NetRatings (now Neilsen Online)

‘An extraordinary book from an author who possesses the unique combination of remarkable analytical and emotional intelligence, long-grounded experience in multiple businesses and a passion for people. It’s a masterpiece in what the classic philosophers call induction: creating a framework from the detailed observation of reality and not the other way round. Sadly, the latter is the case for so much of the management literature out there.’

Domènec Crosas

— Director General, Sanitas Mayores

UNLOCK
THE ADAPTIVE
ORGANISATION
WITHIN

Published by Handson Media, Melbourne.
First Published in Australia 2016
For further information, email enquiry@handsonmedia.com.au

The Thrive Cycle:
Unlock The Adaptive Organisation Within

Cataloguing-in-Publication entry is available from the National Library of Australia
http://catalogue.nla.gov.au
Dewey number: 658.406
ISBN: 978-0-9944751-0-7

Cover design: David Schembri
Internal design: Avril Makula
1st round editing: John Mapps
2nd round editing and proof-reading: Amanda Spedding
Cartoon illustrations: Hana Designer
Thrive Cycle infographic design: Natalya Kolyvayko
Cover photo: Rebecca Hughes

ABOUT THE AUTHOR

"I picture a world where change is something that is **embraced**, not feared; where the ability to adapt is **the norm** (and not the exception); and where change is something that **energises** people, rather than exhausting them.

That's why I do what I do."

KATE CHRISTIANSEN is an author, business leader and passionate change-advocate.

Kate has spent more than twenty years navigating the highs and lows of strategic change. She's worked extensively across Europe, South-East Asia and Australia and has held leadership roles in telecommunications, outsourcing, healthcare, financial services and the tertiary sector. In addition to operational leadership roles, Kate has led many mission-critical change initiatives including multi-country change programs; start-ups; entry-strategies for emerging economies; and has integrated multi-billion-dollar mergers.

Kate is the originator of The Thrive Cycle – a framework that enables adaptive capability to be discussed, identified, developed, measured and improved within an organisation. Kate is also the co-founder of The Adaptive Advantage. Her organisation empowers senior executives and their teams by enabling them to identify The Thrive Cycle within their organisation, then evolve it to create a sustainable, adaptive advantage.

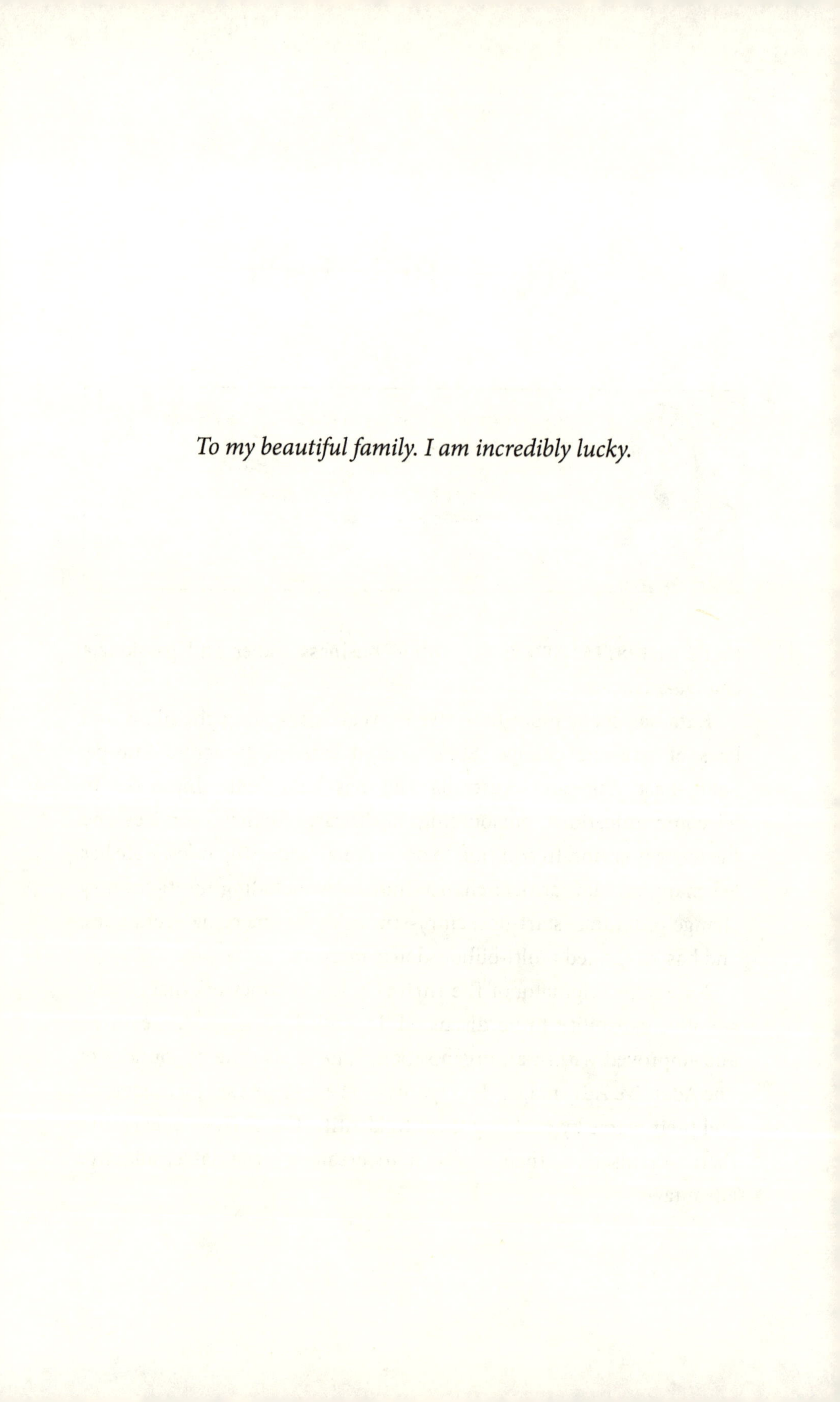

To my beautiful family. I am incredibly lucky.

ACKNOWLEDGEMENTS

SO MANY PEOPLE have provided guidance, support, feedback and encouragement throughout the process of writing this book. They've given their time freely and been generous with their contributions. To those who took me for a coffee (or something stronger), endured countless name-changes, shared ideas, tested concepts and waded through hundreds of pages of manuscript, I am incredibly grateful.

Also a huge thank you to Bo. You've been with me every step of the way and encouraged me to keep going when I said I'd had enough. I couldn't have done it without you.

CONTENTS

LIST OF APPLIED LEADERSHIP RESOURCES

Hands-on strategies to apply the ideas from this book within your organisation.

1

The Adaptive Dilemma

YOU ARE A LEADER IN A SUCCESSFUL organisation but you know it's caught in a rut. You know this because whenever it attempts strategic change, the outcome rarely lives up to expectations, and the process feels harder than raising the *Titanic*.

The world is changing at an accelerating rate and to succeed, you know your organisation must move beyond its linear, project-by-project approach. It must be able to holistically adapt, continuously evolve and change itself in order to stay relevant. This will be essential if your organisation is to deliver a superior customer-experience and consistently deliver superior performance.

Most leaders in your organisation know it's not as adaptive as it needs to be and there have been numerous attempts to change. Topics like innovation, agility, customer-focus and strategy execution have bounced around the executive table many times. Consultants have been engaged, processes have been re-engineered and systems have been bought. And while there have been some improvements, none have lived up to 'The Adaptive Organisation' that was promised.

I can help.

After 20 years adapting organisations to address strategically-critical changes in their environment, I know it's not easy. I've led many change-initiatives and have covered the spectrum from strategy development, change leadership to business analysis. I've led global change programs across multiple countries; integrated multi-billion dollar mergers; established several start-ups; led transformations; and developed entry strategies for emerging markets. I've worked extensively across Europe, Asia and Australia and held leadership roles in numerous sectors including telecommunications, outsourcing, healthcare, financial services and tertiary education.

Most of my career has been spent in 'organisational no-mans-land' – the unmapped territory between the vertical silos. It's from there that I've influenced, cajoled and wrangled with vertically-oriented organisations, convincing (even coercing) them to think and move in a horizontal, holistic way.

This experience has given me a unique, first-hand understanding of what *really* happens within organisations when they attempt to adapt. Why they miss game-changing opportunities; why organisational change always takes longer and costs more than expected; why so much resistance is encountered; and most importantly, why strategic change so rarely lives up to its promises.

If you're looking for these kinds of answers – this book is for you. You should also know that you're not alone.

A recent survey[45] found as few as 9 percent of organisations rated themselves as being 'excellent' at executing initiatives aimed to deliver strategic results. Similarly, only 56 percent of strategic initiatives met their original strategic intent. Another study[22] found that 88 percent of C-suite executives saw executing strategic change as being 'essential' or 'very important' to their organisation's competitiveness. And yet, 61 percent acknowledged that it was something their organisation found extremely difficult to do. A separate study revealed that 57 percent of organisations reported being unsuccessful at executing strategic initiatives during the previous three years[20].

Many CEOs of large, successful organisations will tell you that they see significant change on the horizon, yet they lack confidence in their organisation's ability to cope with it[45]. Their nervousness is not without cause. By 2020, it is predicted that 75 percent of organisations on Standard & Poor's Top 500 list, will have been established after the year 2000. This prediction is reinforced by the declining average lifespan of publicly listed companies, which has reduced from 67 years in the 1920s to 15 years today[49].

Of course, established organisations having difficulty adapting to change is not a new problem.

It was 1996 when John Kotter brought the topic of organisational change and change leadership to mainstream conversations[34]. It was the same year Michael Porter presented his thoughts in '*What is Strategy?*' and called for leaders to re-think their approach to market change[46]. Since then, NASA has successfully landed two Rover robots on Mars, we've cloned sheep, developed a map of the human genome and transitioned computing from a room full of mainframes into a device that can fit in your pocket.

So why, when we've made such progress in other areas, do organisations led by smart people still face the same issues? Why do companies like Kodak, Blockbuster and Borders fail when Fujifilm[29], Netflix and Amazon succeed? And why do former 'game-changers' like Nokia and Blackberry find themselves falling from former glory?

There are many theories.

Some put it down to complacency, others suggest what's needed is greater innovation or customer-focus. While all of these form part of the answer, you and I know from experience, it's not that simple.

So what is a modern-day leader to do?

How do you lead your *pre-millennial* organisation to secure a place in the remaining 25 percent of the Standard & Poor's Top 500? How do you ensure that it's the top 25 percent, not the bottom? And importantly, how do you do all of this while sustainably creating short and long-term value for your customers, organisation, and its stakeholders?

This is *The Adaptive Dilemma,* and this book solves it.

THE FUNDAMENTALS OF CHANGE

Experience has taught me many things. One of the most valuable lessons has been, that in order to successfully adapt to any change, you must begin by asking the right questions. Not only this, you must ask and answer them in the right order. This is true regardless of whether the change is big or small or affects us as individuals, our teams or our organisations.

Failure to answer the right questions is guaranteed to make the change harder than it needs to be, more costly, deliver a less valuable outcome and take a higher toll on your most valuable asset – your people.

I call these questions *The Fundamentals* and within the context of an organisational change they include:

- What are we trying to achieve?
- Why is change required?
- Why change now?
- What does the ideal outcome look like?
- Where are we today?
- What's the gap?
- What's causing the gap and where should we focus?
- Where do we start?

Notice that none of these early questions start with the words *how* or *when*. These come later because unless you know what you are trying to achieve, why it matters and where you want the change to take your organisation, you're guaranteed never to get there. Further, unless the people within your organisation know these answers, they will be unprepared for, or unwilling to take the journey and unlikely to reach the finish line.

Creating an organisation that is more adaptive than it is today is an organisational change and just like any other, it needs to start by answering the right questions. The irony is, of course, that in order to successfully transition from where your organisation is today, to where it needs to be, requires the same capability (i.e. being adaptive) that it is actually wanting to create. This makes creating The Adaptive Organisation one of the toughest changes of all and helps to explain why so few organisations succeed. It's also why starting with what I call *The Adaptive Fundamentals* is critically important.

The Adaptive Fundamentals and why they matter

In order to successfully create The Adaptive Organisation, your organisation needs to develop clear answers to eight questions. Each question fulfils a specific purpose and clears a path for the change to follow (Figure 1-1).

So now, let's come back to your organisation. Thinking about the eight questions I just described, take a moment to reflect on your own organisation.

- *How many of these questions have been satisfactorily answered?*
- *If you asked five of your leadership colleagues, how consistent would their answers be with yours, or with each other's?*

What happens when The Adaptive Fundamentals are missing?

When doing the above exercise, if you answered 'not many' and 'not very', then the following scenario may sound familiar.

A mission-critical project fails. People run for cover and work frantically to show why the disaster wasn't their fault. When the dust settles, the organisation decides that something has to change to prevent this kind of thing from happening again. It's urgent! The Executive Team want results! However, instead of starting with The Adaptive Fundamentals, the organisation scrambles to find a solution.

Unfortunately, when an organisation attempts to become adaptive without first addressing The Adaptive Fundamentals, the journey goes something like this.

The initial conversations tend to run around in circles. Most stakeholders find it too theoretical because there is no commonly-accepted language or reference point that enables people to connect,

FIGURE 1-1: The Adaptive Fundamentals – Eight questions that provide a solid foundation for The Adaptive Organisation

QUESTION TO ASK	WHY THE ANSWERS ARE SO IMPORTANT
1. What are we trying to achieve?	• **Establishes a shared benchmark** with which your organisation can compare itself.
2. Why should our organisation become more adaptive?	• **Aligns the hearts, minds and actions** of your leaders (and thus, their teams) and fosters the motivation, determination and resilience to succeed.
3. Why should we change now?	• **Creates a sense of urgency** and develops the appetite for action.
4. What does The Adaptive Organisation look like for us?	• **Creates a clear goal that is relevant** to your organisation's circumstances and makes sense to your leaders, customers, people and stakeholders.
5. Where are we today?	• **Creates a shared view of reality** and consensus as to how adaptive your organisation *really* is.
6. What's the gap between today and our desired future?	• **Develops a consistent understanding of the challenge** to be overcome and where the greatest attention is needed most.
7. What's causing the gap and where should we focus?	• **Ensures that interventions are targeted** and focus on the things that will drive the greatest improvement.
8. Where do we start?	• **Provides a clear way forward** and enables the organisation to move from talking about becoming adaptive, to actually making it happen.

understand one another or talk in 'concrete' terms. Everyone has their own opinion as to what the answer should be.

Engaging stakeholders becomes a long, painful process. While on the surface people will say the organisation needs to be more adaptive, not everyone is convinced it offers tangible benefits. And, because progress is so slow, even those who start out as believers can find it all too hard and eventually lose interest. 'Herding cats' is an image that frequently comes to mind.

Eventually, the organisational approach fragments and stakeholders, fed-up with the apparent lack of progress, start to implement their own solutions. However, because there is no overall design, none of the solutions fit together and instead of making the organisation *more* adaptive, they make it *less* so.

I could go on but there's no need. You've experienced this scenario first-hand, either in your own organisation or one you've previously encountered. It's like a three-legged-race with a thousand people tied together but no one knows which leg they should start with.

Is it any wonder that when the starter-pistol fires, everyone topples over?

So, why does this happen? Why don't organisations start with The Adaptive Fundamentals?

ALIGNMENT. EASY TO SAY, HARD TO DO

A bit like playing football, building The Adaptive Organisation is not a solo sport. Sitting in a room, writing up the answers then sharing them by email is not enough. The Adaptive Fundamentals must be underpinned by intellectual and emotional alignment between the senior leaders of your organisation. Without this foundation, there is no platform from which to cohesively and effectively lead the change.

Many business books talk about the importance of alignment. It sounds so simple on paper. Just get all the leaders in a room, have a workshop, agree on the answers and there you have it – *instant alignment.*

'Creating The Adaptive Organisation is like a three-legged race. Everyone needs to work together or the whole thing falls flat on its face.'

Yeah. Right!

So why is alignment so difficult to achieve? And, why is it particularly hard to achieve when you're trying to make your organisation more adaptive?

Many of the challenges can be traced back to human psychology.

As individuals, every experience and conversation we have is filtered by our own perspective, beliefs, values and understanding of the world. These individual filters influence what we think, the choices we make, what we say and how we behave.

Just imagine putting twenty people in a room and asking them 'where should we go for lunch?'

Immediately mental 'cogs' would start turning. Twenty individual filters would kick into action and use the information available to form opinions, make suggestions and assess the options. In fact, when viewed collectively, there would be hundreds of filter-combinations influencing the group's ability to agree where we should go for lunch.

If this is what happens when a group is dealing with a familiar concept like 'lunch', it's little wonder achieving alignment around a more complex and abstract concept (i.e. adaptiveness) poses a significant challenge.

WHY A NEW APPROACH IS NEEDED

Human beings have an innate drive to make sense of the world. 'Not knowing the answer' makes most of us feel incredibly uncomfortable and we'll often go to great lengths to understand and make that feeling go away.

One of the ways we do this is by creating frameworks. We develop language and create tools that help us to turn abstract concepts (i.e. stuff that's hard to get your head around) into something more concrete. We then use these frameworks to connect with each other, achieve shared understanding, and this enables us to create things together.

Consider the following example.

Imagine that you and I are going on a business trip. If I said I'd pick you up at midday, you'd know when I expected you to be waiting on the pavement with your suitcase. That's because there is a common framework for *time*, which includes terms like *minutes*, *hours* and *midday*. And, thanks to horology[a] we also have tools like clocks, watches, schedules and calendars that make the concept more concrete and thus, enable shared meaning to be easily created.

---

a The study and measurement of time

But what would happen if this common framework didn't exist? What if we had no way of talking about or telling the time? How would that impact our ability to catch a plane? How would the plane know when it was supposed to take off? How would we know what day we were leaving?

When you think about it, the impact would be profound. Without a clear concept of what time was and how to measure it, there would be no computers, cars, traffic lights, timetables, New Year's Eve and no birthdays. In fact, consider this scenario long enough and you'll quickly conclude that without a common *time* framework, we'd be back in the dark ages, relying on candles and oil-lamps.

So having a common framework is useful. It makes communication quicker and easier and enables us to connect and collaborate more effectively.

Let's explore what happens when we have multiple frameworks operating in the same space. How does this impact our ability to connect with one another?

To demonstrate, I'd like you to picture a scene of a 32-degree day in your local main street. What are people wearing? If you live in America you've probably pictured lots of overcoats, scarves and hats, because 32-degrees Fahrenheit is pretty cold. In Australia, however, we use Celsius to measure temperature and so 32 degrees is beach weather. If I were picturing my local street, I'd imagine people wearing light, cool clothing and sunhats. Therefore, if a friend asked both of us 'what kind of clothes should I pack to wear in 32-degree temperature?' we'd both give completely different answers. While we'd both technically be right it wouldn't help our friend with their packing.

So, even when we're using concepts that are quite familiar, without establishing a common framework first, shared meaning quickly dissolves.

Now let's come back to The Adaptive Organisation and the eight questions (i.e. The Adaptive Fundamentals) that need to be answered if we're to succeed.

When you read through the questions, they look straight-forward. However, if like me, you've ever brought a group of leaders together and tried to answer these questions, the conversation was probably harder than expected. That's because *being adaptive* (like *time*) is an abstract concept.

Without a common framework of language, measurement and tools that turn *adaptiveness* into something more concrete, there is no shared reference point through which to reach agreement. As a result, the conversation degenerates into a collection of firmly-held opinions fueled by past experiences and driven by personal ambitions. At best The Adaptive Fundamentals become half-answered or half-agreed and without this strong foundation, any momentum dissolves and you're soon back where you started.

But what if it didn't have to be this way? What if your senior leaders spent less time arguing over opinions and more time having reality-based conversations that made your organisation more adaptive? What if there was a framework that ensured *everyone* started *every* adaptive conversation on the same page? And, what if at its core, sat a concept that was so simple it could be explained and understood in less than ninety seconds?

Well, now there is. It's called The Thrive Cycle.

THE THRIVE CYCLE IN A NUTSHELL

The Thrive Cycle is an organisational capability. It exists within every organisation and determines the degree to which that organisation is able to holistically adapt to change. There's a whole chapter on it later so for now, I'll just give you a quick overview.

Some Thrive Cycles are stronger than others. When The Thrive Cycle is nurtured it becomes robust and the entire organisation becomes more adaptive. When The Thrive Cycle is neglected, it becomes weak and the organisation becomes less adaptive. It therefore follows that if we're wanting to create The Adaptive Organisation, we need to build a strong Thrive Cycle capability. However, like the concept of 'time', in order for The Thrive Cycle to be something we can work with and improve, we first need a way to talk about, recognise and measure it. That's where the Thrive Cycle Framework comes in, and it is this original concept that will *Unlock The Adaptive Organisation Within.*

ABOUT THIS BOOK

Any established organisation, no matter how big or how complex, can become adaptive. I'm not saying it's easy or that it can be achieved overnight.

This book is for experienced leaders who have the required ambition, courage and commitment to create an adaptive, organisational advantage and who wish to learn how it can be done.

The Thrive Cycle Framework and the ideas shared within this book have been developed using first-hand knowledge of what works, what doesn't, and why. At its core sit real-life lessons (my own and those shared with me by others) gained during years of satisfying successes, excruciating failures and those head-in-hands moments thinking 'Surely… you can't be serious'.

Once understood, The Thrive Cycle Framework will enable you (and your people) to identify, understand, develop, measure and continually improve your organisation's Thrive Cycle capability. It will:

- **Increase the adaptive consciousness** of your organisation, enabling it to have meaningful, structured conversations that create alignment.
- **Empower your organisation and its leaders** by identifying the organisational levers that drive Thrive Cycle capability, so that they can be systematically addressed.
- **Provide hands-on strategies** that enable you and your leaders to overcome the inevitable challenges of creating The Adaptive Organisation.

To achieve this, the book has been divided into three sequential parts.

PART 1 – UNDERSTANDING THE ADAPTIVE ORGANISATION

Part 1 focuses on building a foundation of knowledge and addressing some of the early Adaptive Fundamentals. It answers questions like 'what does it mean to be adaptive?' and 'why does being adaptive matter?'. We'll explore The Thrive Cycle and complete the Adaptive Audit to assess its status within your organisation. We'll also identify your Adaptive Profile and you'll be introduced to four very different organisations (the Surfers, Swimmers, Splashers and Sinkers) and understand how their attributes impact their ability to adapt.

PART 2 – THE SIX ELEMENTS OF ADAPTIVE SUCCESS

In Part 2 we'll start to look beneath your organisation's Adaptive Profile and examine some of the key drivers contributing to it. You'll be introduced to The Six Elements of Adaptive Success and learn how and why they make your organisation's Thrive Cycle stronger or weaker.

Starting with the first Element, *Enduring Commitment,* we'll explore the concept of adaptive advantage and consider what it means within the context of your organisation. This chapter also emphasises the importance of engagement and shows how you can build ongoing alignment across your leadership community.

The chapter on the second Element of Adaptive Success, *Adaptive Principles,* will show how putting customer-value first holds the key to building and sustaining an adaptive advantage. From there, we'll explore the third Element of Adaptive Success, the *Anchors of Certainty.* We'll examine the role of organisational purpose and how establishing Value-Creating Values enables confident decision-making during times of turbulent change.

When we reach the fourth Element of Adaptive Success, *The Vital Thread,* we'll explore how it can be used to predict and respond to change-opportunities in your organisation's internal and external environments. We'll meet Orion Healthcare and learn how a strong Vital Thread holds the key to remaining relevant to customers, leading disruption and creating maximum value from organisational change.

The fifth Element is *Thrive Cycle Leadership* which, quite literally, makes The Thrive Cycle go round. This chapter discusses the three leadership capabilities your leaders need to develop, and reveals the secret to applying the right leadership behaviour and mindset at the right time.

And then, in the last chapter of Part 2, we'll examine the sixth Element of Adaptive Success, a *Balanced Ecosystem*. Within any large, complex organisation, achieving the right balance between customer, people, process and systems can be challenging. It answers questions like:

- How do you continue to stay relevant to customers?
- What kind of organisational structure do you need?
- How do you measure and improve your adaptive capability?
- How do you get prioritisation right?
- What kind of leadership and people capabilities does your organisational environment need to support?
- How do you ensure your adaptive capability continuously improves?

This chapter explains why your organisation needs a Chief Adaptive Officer, what an Adaptive Advantage Team does, and shares practical ideas as to how to achieve the necessary buy-in from your leadership team. We'll also learn how Thrive Cycle Learning enables you to create an Adaptive Advantage Scorecard as a means of tracking and improving organisational adaptiveness.

PART 3 – UNLOCKING YOUR ORGANISATION

Part 3 consolidates everything we've talked about in the previous two sections and moves the conversation into 'action' mode.

We'll come full-circle and revisit the eight Adaptive Fundamentals. We'll go through each question – one by one – and show how you can apply what you've learnt to develop the answers. This chapter explores how you can do so in a way that achieves consistent and aligned agreement among your leadership community. In some ways, this chapter is like a quick reference guide. It summarises many of the key concepts from the book and can be used back in your organisation. There's also a roadmap to help you get things started.

The final chapter is entitled *You're it!* This brings the conversation back to you and your role as the *Driver* behind The Adaptive Organisation. It describes what it will take to successfully lead this change and introduces some practical ways to overcome some of the inevitable challenges like engaging the non-believers, being willing to take risks, and letting go of control.

◆◆◆

These are just some of the highlights. You'll also find over thirty 'Applied Leadership' sections that look like the following.

THESE SECTIONS HAVE been specifically designed to bring the ideas within the book to life within your organisation. They do so by either asking you to reflect or by sharing practical tools and guidance (e.g. checklists, step-by-step strategies, advice for tricky situations etc.). You may also like to keep a notebook close by to capture your thoughts.

You'll find a list of these Applied Leadership Resources at the front for future reference. **This book also provides exclusive access to the online Thrive Cycle Learning Centre (www.thethrivecycle.com). This includes the Adaptive Audit and other tools, templates and videos.**

Anyway, that's enough about what's coming up. I'm really excited to be sharing this journey with you so let's just sit down, grab ourselves a hot drink and make a start.

PART 1

Understanding The Adaptive Organisation

Part 1 focuses on building knowledge and establishing a common language that will enrich understanding. It also offers many opportunities to reflect and learn about your organisation and ask yourself 'how adaptive are we really?'

2

The Adaptive Organisation and why it matters

This chapter provides a definition of The Adaptive Organisation that clearly describes what we're setting out to achieve. We'll also explore the rationale for becoming more adaptive and why it's a case of 'now or never'.

LANGUAGE IS IMPORTANT. BEING CLEAR about the terms you use and what they mean will ensure others understand what you're trying to achieve from the very beginning.

AGILE, ADAPTIVE OR ADAPTABLE?

The words agile, adaptive, and adaptable are frequently used as though they mean the same thing.

The word 'agility' is commonly used to describe a core quality an organisation needs if it is to succeed in a changing environment. The dictionary[12] defines agile as 'being able to move quickly and easily'.

There are in fact, times when an organisation needs to move quickly and where this is the case, the concept of agility is helpful. There are also agile methodologies that use a test-and-learn approach and these can also be highly effective.

However, when talking about your organisation, using the word 'agile' as though it's synonymous with 'adaptive', can have unhelpful consequences. They include:

- assuming speed is always the right answer when sometimes going slowly will deliver greater adaptive success.
- underestimating, and under-valuing *thinking* as a leadership tool and showing a bias towards premature *doing*.
- assuming every part of the organisation needs to be fast when different capabilities may be needed in different parts.
- thinking 'we just need to do what we do, but do it faster' rather than considering a new way of doing things.

At some point you'll probably decide that *agility* is a key characteristic of The Adaptive Organisation you want to create. It's important to be very clear what you mean by the term and what makes it important within your organisational context.

Adaptable versus adaptive

Most of the time, the words *adaptable* and *adaptive* are used interchangeably. However, there is a subtle, yet important difference.

When something is *adaptable*, it means it *can be* easily *adapted* (generally by someone, or something) to accommodate a change. For instance, I have an adaptable dining table that can be extended to seat ten people, instead of the usual six.

Adaptive, however, means that something is consistently able to *change itself*, to accommodate change.

I draw a parallel with the natural world. When a species evolves particular traits that improve its chances of survival, it creates an *adaptive advantage*. When a species enjoys a significant adaptive advantage, not only does it survive, it *thrives*. Let's look at one group of lizards – the chameleons.

Chameleons' ability to change colour is often cited as an adaptive advantage, because it allows them to blend in to their environment. But this is not actually the case. Chameleons change colour to stand out to other chameleons and predators, and give warning of their current emotional state. For example, *black* means they are furious (telling enemies to beware), whereas other colours are used when they are looking for a mate.

They also possess another significant adaptive feature. A chameleon's eyes can look in two different directions at the same time, a big advantage when looking out for predators.

These and other adaptive features allowed chameleons to inhabit a host of environments from rainforests to deserts, and there are now dozens of species[37].

A CLEAR AND USEFUL DEFINITION

If we're going to create The Adaptive Organisation, we need to start with a clear definition of what that actually means.

An organisation can be defined as 'a group of people who work together in an organised way for a shared purpose'[12]. While these people are supported in their endeavour by systems and processes, ultimately the likelihood of achieving the shared purpose comes down to the people. Thus, when setting out to build The Adaptive Organisation, we are seeking to create:

A *purpose-driven* group of people that is able to:

- *change itself* (and the infrastructure that supports it) in order to *capture opportunities* that offer the *greatest potential value*; and
- *recognise* those opportunities, regardless of whether they occur inside or outside the organisation; and
- achieve all of the above *to a standard* and *at a pace*, that *creates value*; and
- gives the organisation *an adaptive advantage* over its rivals.

Using the outcome to create alignment

WHEN ATTEMPTING TO create The Adaptive Organisation there will be times when there is a lot of 'noise' (i.e. irrelevant activity and information that inhibits clear thinking). Keeping this definition constantly available will help to maintain focus by using it to:

- **help build alignment** by reminding people what you've set out to achieve and why.
- **help you to stay focused** by providing a checklist. You can use it to test whether the proposed approach is delivering an organisation that meets all four of the defined criteria. If it is, great! If not, then is it really the right approach?
- **help you to engage others** by providing a starting-point for conversations? Try sharing the definition and ask questions like:
  - *what do you think this means within the context of our organisation?*
  - *to what extent is this describing our organisation today?*
  - *what kind of advantage could be achieved?*

Okay. So now we've started to address our first Adaptive Fundamental question by being clear about what we're wanting to achieve. However, we still need to establish the benefits of creating such an organisation and why now is the time to do it.

THE POSITIVE CASE FOR CHANGE

Drive superior performance

Intuitively, creating an adaptive organisation feels like a good thing to do. However, doing so requires considerable focus, investment and commitment. But what's the evidence to show being adaptive improves economic performance?

One study examined the financial performance of 243 large firms in 17 industries[54]. Looking across a 30-year period, the authors found in every industry there were two or three so-called 'out-performers'. These companies achieved above-average profitability for their industry, for more than 80 percent of the study period. These made up 18 percent of the organisations sampled. Similarly, 18 percent of the sample were 'under-performers' (i.e. achieved a below-average performance for 80 percent of the time). The remaining 66 percent of organisations were labelled in the research – 'Thrashers'. These 'middle' organisations were consistently inconsistent, with their profitability fluctuating between under and over-performance.

In the same study, 4700 executives were then surveyed from 56 companies. They questioned them as to how they went about developing strategy, designing their infrastructure, approached change and innovation and so on. They found the 'out-performers' had the ability to anticipate and respond to change, solve problems and implement change better than the 'Thrashers'[54]. Further, 'out-performers' were consistently able to:

- develop their strategy in a dynamic way
- accurately 'see' changes within their environments
- test potential responses
- implement new capabilities as a whole organisation.

An IBM study compared the features of industry 'out-performers' and 'under-performers' (as measured by profitability and revenue growth). It found that 73 percent more 'out-performers' said they excelled at managing change, than 'under-performers'. Similarly, 84 percent more said they were able to turn 'insights into action' better than industry peers[32].

Create a sustainable advantage

The term 'sustainable competitive advantage' is often used to describe an edge that an organisation has over its rivals, and one that is difficult to imitate.

Harvard Professor Michael Porter described several bases upon which competitive advantage could be created, including cost, differentiation, innovation or operational-effectiveness[46]. When you think about it, no organisation is able to effectively conceptualise or deliver any of these strategies, unless it is able to adapt.

While the outside world can see an organisation is adaptive, the capability itself is something that comes from within. Therefore, when The Adaptive Organisation is created, it offers an advantage that is less vulnerable to imitation and thus, sustainable.

WHY IT'S NOW OR NEVER

Many years ago my boss used to say 'When change arrives, you're either on the bus or you're under it'. This phrase is equally pertinent when talking about modern organisations and the wave of change they now find themselves facing.

It's no longer a case of *if* disruptive change is coming, it's *when*.

Of course, for most established organisations change is not something new. In fact, quite the contrary. While new super-agile, post-digital organisations receive a significant amount of publicity, most of us still work in organisations that have been around for decades or even centuries. Such longevity is only possible if an organisation has developed some form of adaptive capability.

So what is it about change today that is different?

The 'new normal' no longer exists

It's not that long ago that the phrase 'the new normal' was coined to describe how change influences our perceptions of what we consider to be 'normal'. It refers to a time when the impacts of change become no longer note-worthy and an expected part of 'the everyday'.

When thinking about change in this context, the journey tends to resemble a series of steps in which significant disruption is followed by a period of stability, followed by more disruption and so on. This kind of thinking works in an environment where stability dominates.

In today's environment however, this ratio is being reversed, with many organisations experiencing few, if any, periods of stability. The steps of the 'new normal' have become a single increasing line of constant change. Not only that, its gradient is intensifying at an exponential rate. This is being driven by many factors.

The Industrial Age has long since given way to the Information Age

It's been almost two centuries since the use of coal and steam enabled machines to do jobs once done by human labour. Autonomous cars are on the streets of New York and London. From here, it is a relatively small step to the world of 'autonomous everything'.

Digitisation is creating and dissolving industries on a regular basis

Digitisation is increasingly turning physical things into digital, electronic formats[25]. This is opening up significant opportunities by removing physical constraints. For example, the digital world is unconstrained by the requirements of physical transport, waiting for delivery, storage, physical location and so on. For those on the digital wave of change, this offers almost limitless opportunity. For those still living in the analogue world, it spells potential disaster.

Ever-changing consumer preferences make it hard to keep up

Keeping up with the voracious consumer appetite for technology constitutes a major challenge for organisations in every sector. This trend is showing no signs of slowing. Boston Consulting Group surveyed thousands of consumers – in 13 countries – to ascertain the degree to which respondents were willing to give up a lifestyle habit for a year, in favour of the Internet. 75 percent of respondents said they'd give up alcohol, 27 percent said they'd give up sex and 22 percent said they'd give up daily showers[15].

Barriers to entry aren't as robust as they used to be

Large organisations are no longer safe behind the high-cost-of-entry barrier[47]. Cheaper more accessible on-demand technologies are empowering a new breed of leaner, faster and yet equally powerful competitors. While scale still has its benefits, many of the traditional barriers in many established industries (finance, manufacturing etc.) are being called into question. This trend is set to increase as advances in 3D printing, artificial intelligence and 'the internet of things' make capabilities that have historically required significant capital investment available to the ambitious entrepreneur.

Organisations are drowning in data

In 2013, the world had 250 million websites, 150 million blogs, 25 million tweets and 4 billion Flickr images[33]. In fact, the amount of new digital content created back in 2011, was several million times more than the amount of information contained within every book ever written[2].

It seems that data is now collected by almost everything: sensors, cars, supermarket checkouts, mobile devices, and the list goes on. There are no signs of it slowing down anytime soon. It's predicted that the number of devices collecting then storing data is going to increase from 9.1 billion installed devices in 2013 to 28.1 billion by 2020[24].

There is more 'big-change' with even bigger implications

When things aren't connected to each other, change causes a ripple effect. The areas close to the change-event are severely affected, but those further away hardly notice the ripples. However, in a global economy where everything is connected to everything else, a single event in one country is enough to cause a global recession.

The economic dynamics of the world are changing too. The rise of the emerging economies, the shift in economic power to China, and the increasingly volatile nature of certain geographies have changed the world so that nothing seems to be contained any more.

Workforce dynamics are changing

The different generations of employees expect different things, creating a challenge for employers to 'keep everyone happy'. Attracting the right 'talent' already looms large on CEOs' top three concerns[28]. Then there are the big future changes which everyone (employers and employees alike) has yet to get their heads around. While many organisations may see robotics and advanced automation as being something for future generations to work through, those advances may become reality sooner than expected. Already, a factory in China has replaced 1800 workers with 1000 robots[11].

◆◆◆

Alright, so there's more change than there used to be. But why can't your organisation just 'ramp-up' the same adaptive capabilities that have served it well in the past? Why is a different approach needed?

Volatility, uncertainty and complexity are here to stay

Leaders often say to me they are concerned about the volume and speed of change. When they do, I remind them that it's not the change itself that matters. What's more important is the *affect it has on their organisation's environment and the ability to create value for customers.*

It wasn't the tip of the iceberg that caused the Titanic to sink[6]. Thus, it doesn't matter if a change looks small, it's the size and nature of the implications. You've probably experienced this first hand where the slight change in the wording of a regulation has meant you've needed to turn your organisation inside-out just to stay in business.

Within this context, one of the biggest challenges for today's organisations is that it's difficult to predict what the effects of change will be. This makes decisions slower and less clear, leadership more difficult and the risks far greater than they were before. Further, the following environmental forces will ensure that these organisational challenges will intensify over time.

Increased volatility

Volatility will make change increasingly dynamic. It will arrive even more quickly than it does today and rapidly escalate from being inconsequential to significant.

If your organisation is adaptive, it will see the changes coming and be ready to act. It will look for the opportunity and respond in a way that creates a superior competitive position. If however, your organisation is not adaptive, it won't see the changes. When your organisation eventually responds, if it's lucky, it will stumble through them. If it's not lucky, well…?

Greater uncertainty

Uncertainty will bring with it a growing element of surprise. This will make your environment even less predictable than it is today. Across your organisation, this will perpetuate an underlying discomfort caused by never quite knowing where you stand. For your people, it will feel like floating on a turbulent sea with no anchor and no sense of where the next wave might be coming from. Unless your people are ready for it, uncertainty will erode their confidence, reduce their willingness to step outside comfort-zones and deter them from taking personal and professional risks.

Also, changes that affect your organisation will rarely have a clearly identifiable catalyst. Changes are more likely to come out of nowhere, making them harder to see and making an appropriate response harder to define and deliver.

Layered complexity

Multiple change-forces converging on one another will drive increasing complexity in the internal and external organisational environment.

It is here many organisations already find themselves caught in a vicious cycle. The faster change occurs on 'the outside', the more complexity it creates on 'the inside' of the organisation. The greater the complexity, the more difficult each organisational change becomes, and the less successful it is likely to be. This creates even more complexity and makes the organisation even less ready for the next change.

◆◆◆

All of these factors combined create the most powerful force of all. Ambiguity. As human beings, accepting there are things we can't change, doesn't come easily. Unlike most animals that adapt to fit-in with their environment, we are environmental engineers. We expect to be able to change the environment to suit our needs. Thus, when we find the environment is not within our control, it comes as a bit of a surprise.

I suspect in your organisation there is already a growing sense that things never seem to be 'locked in position'. You can no longer assume 'what-you-see-is-what-you-get', and straight answers have been replaced by 'it depends'.

Further, organisations like yours will increasingly find themselves layering new change on top of already changing operations. In fact, at any one time, approximately 75 percent of companies are already undertaking some form of transformation[39]. If not handled effectively, this will increasingly encroach on business performance as leaders and teams try to perform an operational juggling act. As a result, your operational leaders and their teams will face increasing ambiguity. They will need different skills as they are expected to achieve standardisation, efficiency and scale, while also being flexible, innovative and responsive.

The costs of failure are high

Most organisations know change is difficult and costly but the true costs (i.e. financial, reputational, competitive etc.) are often invisible.

In 2008, an Economist Intelligence Unit report found that UK companies were losing an average of £1.7 billion a year as a result of failed organisational change[21]. The figure for global organisations was

'Operational leaders will face increasing ambiguity as the line between business-as-usual and change activity becomes increasingly blurred.'

even more staggering, with estimates of £7.8 billion per year. There are few signs to suggest things have improved in recent years. Another 2014 study[45] found that for every US$1 billion spent on organisational change, US$109 million was wasted. That's almost 11 percent!

Then of course, there is the personal and professional cost for the leaders and Board members whose organisations fail to adapt.

Think about Kodak and more specifically, its Executive Team. Will they be remembered for the incredible industry leadership their organisation achieved for over a century? Or, will they be remembered for Kodak's failure to change with the times?

Being adaptive is no longer a 'nice-to-have'. Company Boards are expecting their organisations to be more adaptive and they're holding CEOs and Executive teams accountable for making it happen.

A study of 280 organisations revealed the top reason for CEOs being fired was not short-term performance or a reduction in the share price. At the top (in 32 percent of cases) it was the CEO's mismanagement of change that led to their dismissal. This was followed closely by 'Ignoring Customers', at 28 percent[31]. Later, we'll look at how both these factors are inextricably linked.

CHAPTER CONCLUSION

All of the environmental changes described in this chapter create a pretty confusing and uncertain picture for business leaders. The days of planning on an annual basis and delivering strategy via a series of relatively unconnected projects are gone. We're no longer talking about linear, sequential change. Instead, if your organisation is to succeed in a world of exponential change, it needs to be able to *evolve*.

So now we've started to build the case for creating The Adaptive Organisation and have gathered some of the ingredients. However, we're not there yet. We need to create a collective 'lightbulb moment' within your organisation that brings the real opportunities and threats to life and creates a laser-like focus.

We'll start to do this in the next chapter where you'll complete an Adaptive Audit of your organisation. We'll use the results throughout the remaining chapters.

KEY POINTS TO REMEMBER

- While agility has its place and is often part of adaptive capability, the term needs to be used in the right context.
- Being adaptive is about responding to the changes that are relevant and matter to us, our customers, and our organisation.
- Use the definition of The Adaptive Organisation as a check-list and a way to engage others in conversations.
- Being adaptive drives business performance and creates an advantage that is difficult to imitate.
- While your organisation is no stranger to change, the nature of it is now different. Just doing what it's done in the past, faster and on a grander scale, won't deliver the required outcome.
- The inability to adapt already costs organisations much more than most realise. It's not just the immediate consequences of failed change, it is the internal complexity and rigidity that makes change even harder next time.

3

Your organisation's Adaptive Profile

If we're going to create The Adaptive Organisation described in the last chapter we need to know where we are today. In this chapter we'll explore your own organisation and follow a series of steps to develop a picture of its Adaptive Profile today. I encourage you to take some time to reflect on the questions being asked. The more thinking you do in this chapter, the richer the insights will be later on.

WHEN WE WANT TO IMPROVE SOMETHING about ourselves, our lives or our organisation, we frequently start by trying to understand others and then copy what they do. And yet so often, the real insights and answers we need can be achieved through a better understanding of ourselves.

Creating The Adaptive Organisation requires *self-awareness* and starts with understanding how adaptive your organisation is today. In the following pages you'll complete an Adaptive Audit. **This can also be done online by registering at www.thethrivecycle.com**

I always like to do this before we've covered too much of the detail because I've found it enables you to answer in a more objective way.

We're going to follow a series of steps and end by plotting an Adaptive Profile for your organisation. This won't mean much to you at this stage. In the following chapters however, all will be revealed.

DEFINE YOUR CORE ORGANISATION

The definition of The Adaptive Organisation can be applied to *any* group of people working together to achieve a common purpose. It is equally applicable to public and private companies, non-government organisations, business teams, educational institutions and so on.

When you think about creating The Adaptive Organisation, which entity do you have in mind? Is it the entire corporate group, your local division or business unit? Or, is it your function? Defining your *Core Organisation* simply means drawing a circle around your business to show which part you want to make more adaptive (Figure 3-1).

If your organisation has four hundred employees and you only do business in the UK, then the Core Organisation probably encompasses the entire company.

If, however, you work in an international company that has its head office in Toronto, but business units spread across 12 countries, under three regions, the Core Organisation may be less clear.

Trying to make a corporate group adaptive, versus, say, its Australian Business Unit adaptive, are two very different challenges. Where possible, align the Core Organisation with your professional sphere of influence, and remember, the wider the scope, the more commitment you will need to succeed. That said, if you are highly influential (e.g. a CEO) and the potential for an adaptive advantage is significant, then using a wider definition could be the best option.

What's important is that the size and nature of the ambition is clear and that's why the Core Organisation needs to be decided in advance.

From now on, when I talk about *your organisation*, I am referring to the 'purpose-driven group of people (and the supporting infrastructure)' contained within your Core Organisation.

FIGURE 3-1: Defining The Core Organisation

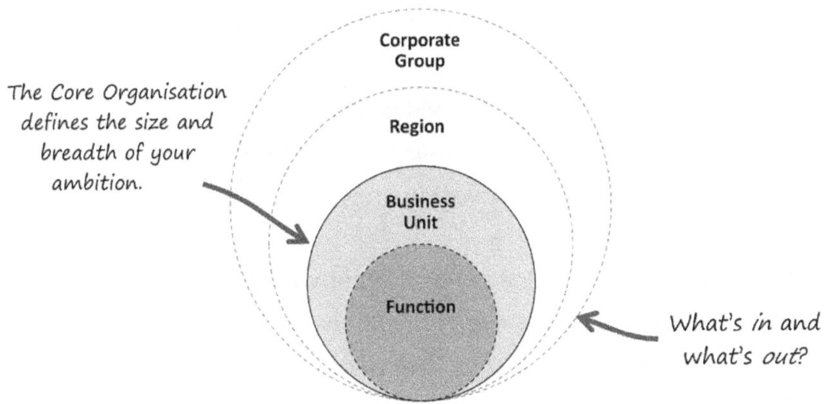
Corporate Group
Region
Business Unit
Function
The Core Organisation defines the size and breadth of your ambition.
What's in and what's out?

REFLECT UPON THE PAST

Take a few moments to think about your organisation. Over the last three to five years, what are the most significant change-opportunities your organisation has attempted to respond to?

Now reflect upon the type of factors that triggered those opportunities to occur. For example, they may have been the result of:

- changing customer needs
- competitor activity
- regulatory change
- broader socio-economic or technology changes
- efficiency improvements
- short-term performance pressures

What was the primary motivation behind these changes? Was it to deliver more value to customers or protect the value they were already experiencing?

Or was there another value driver? And, in the end, was the expected value realised? Did your organisation ultimately create or protect the value it expected?

You may find it useful at this point to briefly note down your thoughts as shown in Figure 3-2.

Let's pause for a moment and reflect on the process you've just gone through.

- *How easy was it to answer these questions?*
- *Does this provide any insight as to the types of change-opportunities your organisation pursues, or why it pursues them?*

Now, let's think about some of the content you've put down.

- *What do you notice as you run your eye down the list?*
- *What insights can you start to develop?*

For example, are there particular themes that come through, or do some triggers appear more often than others? Has most of the change delivered the value that was expected?

Ideally, take a minute or so to write down some of your key thoughts. This will provide useful background for the next step.

FIGURE 3-2: What drives change in your organisation?

Internal name used to identify the opportunity or threat	Description of opportunity or threat	What was the main trigger?	Was it attempting to protect or create value?	Within what timeframe was value expected to be created or protected?	Was expected value realised?
Operation Elroy	Customers opting out of industry due to loss of perceived product value	Removal of existing customer tax incentives (threat)	Protect existing value	Medium term	Yes
Operation Bluebird	Growth via new business acquisition	Financial performance/ Growth (opportunity)	Creating new value	Short term to medium term	No

COMPLETE THE ADAPTIVE AUDIT

Think about the change-opportunities you identified in the previous exercise. Then, answer the following questions by placing a number from 1 to 5 in the box provided.

1 = Never 2 = Rarely 3 = Sometimes 4 = Usually 5 = Always

Where the questions refer to 'we' or 'our', think holistically in terms of the *Core Organisation* you just defined.

SECTION A	**SCORE (1–5)**
1. We are constantly on the alert, looking for change-opportunities both inside and outside our industry	
2. We place equal importance on opportunities coming from outside and inside our organisation	
3. When identifying opportunities, we start by asking how will this create value for customers	
4. When a change-opportunity occurs, we see it, and take action before our rivals	
AVERAGE SCORE	

SECTION B	**SCORE (1–5)**
1. Our leaders clearly understand how our organisation creates value for customers today	
2. Improving the value experienced by customers is the primary driver of change within our organisation	
3. New ideas are welcomed, even if they are contrary to long-standing organisational beliefs	
4. We take the time necessary to truly understand change-opportunities before we start looking for solutions	
AVERAGE SCORE	

1 = Never 2 = Rarely 3 = Sometimes 4 = Usually 5 = Always

SECTION C	**SCORE (1–5)**
1. We effectively prioritise all activities (not just change) using the same customer-driven metrics	
2. When setting priorities, we maintain a balance between short and long-term value creation	
3. We look at change holistically and consider the combined effects of all change on customers and the organisation	
4. Our stated organisational priorities are consistent with the actual allocation of funding and other resources	
AVERAGE SCORE	

SECTION D	**SCORE (1–5)**
1. When designing solutions to change-opportunities, we focus on customer needs, not our products or services	
2. We are clear about the type of future we want to create for our customers and the organisation	
3. When faced with a change-opportunity, we explore many options and engage the right people when doing so	
4. Our solutions achieve the optimum balance between the ideal design and what can actually be delivered	
AVERAGE SCORE	

SECTION E	**SCORE (1–5)**
1. We understand the nature of change and match our approach with the type of change and its degree of difficulty	
2. We understand the value that each change initiative is expected to deliver, and plan to deliver that value, not just milestones and budgets	
3. For any given change-opportunity, the right resources are usually available at the time they are needed	
4. Our planning maintains a healthy balance between speed, process and pragmatism	
AVERAGE SCORE	

1 = Never 2 = Rarely 3 = Sometimes 4 = Usually 5 = Always

SECTION F	**SCORE (1–5)**
1. We are effective at managing organisational change, even when it's complex and difficult	
2. Taking into account the effort involved, organisational change creates more value than it erodes	
3. Once an organisational change has finished, the new state is usually sustained	
4. Our people and leaders are energised by change, and embrace it, regardless of the challenge	
AVERAGE SCORE	

SECTION G	**SCORE (1–5)**
1. We aspire to having an adaptive organisation and focus on continually improving this capability	
2. We review each organisational change, starting from when the opportunity was first seen, to learning from implementation.	
3. When capturing learnings holistically, we consider many factors including the type of change, organisational capability, circumstances, process execution etc.	
4. When it comes to responding to change-opportunities we rarely make the same mistake twice	
AVERAGE SCORE	

PLOT YOUR ADAPTIVE PROFILE

Every organisation has its own *Adaptive Profile*. This provides a picture of what happens within the organisation when it attempts to adapt to changes in its environment. Once it has been agreed, an Adaptive Profile is also useful across the organisation because it provides a baseline against which future aspirations can be set.

When I develop an Adaptive Profile for an organisation, I tend to use a comprehensive process of interviews and capture feedback from a representative cross-section of the organisation. For our purposes, however, your own feedback will provide a useful starting point from which to develop an initial understanding.

Sometimes it can be disconcerting to only have letters, rather than categories across the horizontal access. As you've probably guessed, each of the sections corresponds with a stage of The Thrive Cycle so fear not, in the next chapter, all will be revealed.

For now however, use Figure 3-4 to plot the average scores you gave in each section of the questionnaire, and plot them against each relevant 'label' on the horizontal axis (shown in Figure 3-3). For example, if you had an average score of 2.5 in Section A, you would put a dot at the 2.5 mark of the vertical axis and above the (A) on the horizontal axis.

CHAPTER CONCLUSION

Now we have a picture of your organisation's Adaptive Profile, we can refer to it as we progress through the remainder of the book. In the next chapter we'll use The Thrive Cycle to reveal what each of the letters on the horizontal axis represent. More importantly, we'll explore what they might be telling us about your organisation's adaptive capabilities today. Then, in Chapter 5 we'll start to interpret your organisation's

FIGURE 3-3: How to plot your Adaptive Profile

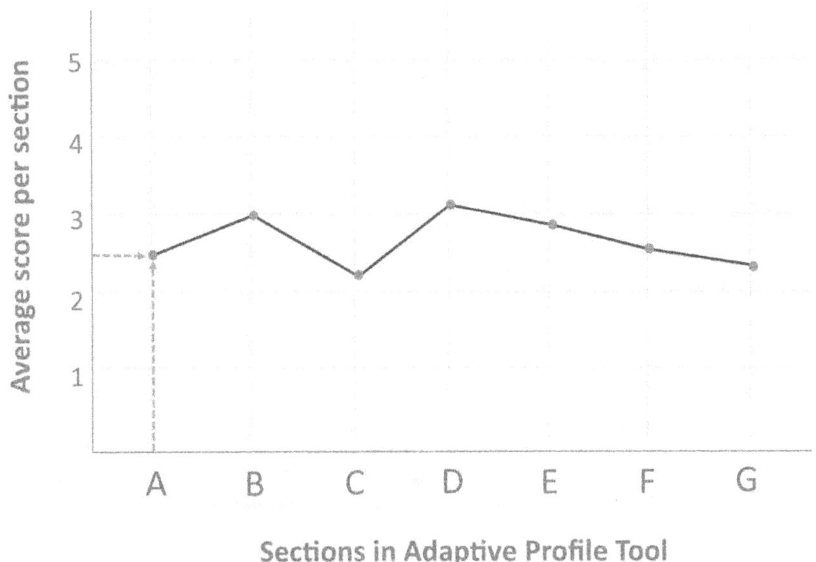

FIGURE 3-4: Adaptive Profile – your organisation

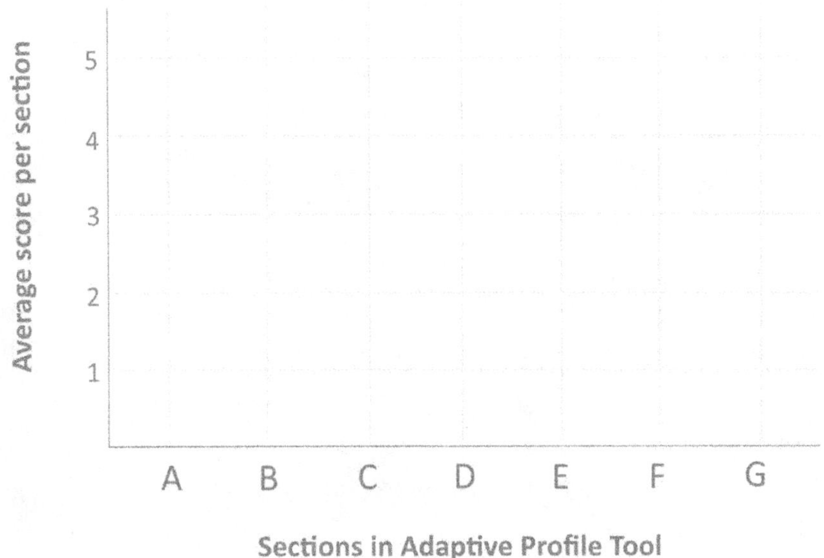

Adaptive Profile and see how it compares to the four *Adaptive Archetypes*: the Surfers, Swimmers, Splashers and Sinkers.

KEY POINTS TO REMEMBER

- In order to create The Adaptive Organisation, we need to develop a clear picture of where your organisation is today.
- Start by defining the Core Organisation. In other words, which entity do you want to make more adaptive?
- Take time out to objectively reflect on your organisation and how it has responded to change in the past. What drives it? Does it achieve the value that is expected?
- The Adaptive Profile is a simple way of depicting what happens within your organisation when it attempts to adapt to change-opportunities. Keep this assessment close by, because we will refer to it throughout the following chapters.

4

The Thrive Cycle

This chapter introduces The Thrive Cycle capability and The Thrive Cycle Framework that will bring it to life in your organisation. It illustrates how The Thrive Cycle overcomes many of the obstacles that prevent organisations from becoming adaptive.

AS A CONCEPT, *being adaptive* is applicable to many contexts: our personal lives, in nature, and in organisations.

As individuals, being adaptive is about responding to the changes that *matter to us*, because they are both relevant and important. This sub-set of changes (i.e. those specifically relevant *to us*) is called *change-opportunities* and they can be defined as:

> *any event (or events) in which the potential*
> *consequences could alter the rhythm, or balance,*
> *of our world and thus, our future chances of success.*

We encounter potential change-opportunities every day, often without giving them a second thought. A friend leaves a voicemail message about a job opportunity; a critical system in your business fails; a new technology appears on the edge of your industry; your local supermarket no longer stocks your favourite breakfast cereal.

All of these are potential change-opportunities. However, whether or not we actually *realise* that potential and take action, depends upon our ability to navigate a simple sequence.

THE THRIVE CYCLE

Consider the example of a friend calling you about a potential job opportunity. This is a change-opportunity for you, because the potential consequences could alter the rhythm, or balance, of your world and thus, your future chances of success.

In order to successfully *adapt* to this opportunity, you would need to complete the following seven-stage sequence.

SEE IT – *See the change* (or in this case hear the voicemail message) and recognise it as being relevant and important enough to take some form of action.

UNDERSTAND IT – *Understand the opportunity*, without yet trying to solve it. You might meet your friend for a coffee, or research the company that they're referring to. You'd want to find out whether this *really is* an opportunity, and if so, what kind of opportunity it is.

PRIORITISE IT – *Make the choice to do something* about it, or alternatively, not to take action at all. You might ask questions like:

- 'Is this opportunity better than the job that I already have?'
- 'Would I be prepared to give up being close to work in order to receive higher pay?'

Of course, prioritisation is rarely a one-and-done activity. As you learnt more, and gained a clearer picture of the change-opportunity, you would regularly ask yourself 'Is this still worth pursuing?'

DESIGN IT – Assuming you believed the opportunity was worth responding to, you'd need to *design a solution.* I say design it because to make the best choice, it would help to be clear about what it was you were looking for in a job. Then, you could use these design criteria to explore whether this job offered the best-fit.

PLAN IT – Having decided to take the job, you'd need to *plan* some of the practical details. Success would come from being able to consider the various activities, including the who, what, where, when and how of what needed to happen to ensure a positive outcome.

MOVE TO IT – Now, it would be crunch-time. You'd need to *make the move* from where you are, and start working somewhere else. This would involve resigning, tying up loose-ends and walking out the door of your old workplace for the last time. Then, you'd reach your new job and encounter the learning-curve. Focusing on the basics like getting to know your team, understanding how the organisation works and deciding where to buy the best coffee.

And, as the world doesn't stop just because a change comes along, you'd need to take this journey, while still keeping other aspects of your life intact. Things like taking the kids to swimming lessons, coaching weekend basketball and making sure that the car had been serviced.

LEARN FROM IT – Having settled into your new job, there would be an opportunity to reflect and *learn from your experience.* What would you repeat and what would you do differently? Was taking the job the right thing to do? Then, you could successfully apply what you'd learnt the next time a similar change-opportunity came along.

◆◆◆

While the above sequence may seem relatively straightforward, you would have relied upon two factors to successfully adapt to the change-opportunity.

First, before the change came along, you needed to have developed the core capabilities necessary to complete each of the seven stages. This meant that when the opportunity came along you were able to *See* it; *Understand* it; *Prioritise* it; *Design* a response; *Plan* for it; *Move* to it; and then *Learn* from it.

Second, you also needed to be able to *apply* these capabilities effectively, in the right sequence and with the right timing, such that you moved the specific opportunity forward.

These two factors, when combined, create The Thrive Cycle (Figure 4-1). In the above example, the strength of your Thrive Cycle would determine whether you were able to successfully adapt to the change-opportunity.

The Thrive Cycle is equally relevant for organisations.

HOW THE THRIVE CYCLE WORKS

Every organisation, no matter where, how big or what industry, has a Thrive Cycle within it. In some organisations it is strong and effective while in others it is weak and barely recognisable. Regardless of its current status, The Thrive Cycle is *always* there – you just need to look for it.

The Adaptive Organisation nurtures its Thrive Cycle as a core capability and as a result, is able to navigate it better than any of its rivals.

FIGURE 4-1: The Thrive Cycle is underpinned by the ability to consistently navigate and complete seven sequential stages

1
See the change and recognise it as being relevant/ worth noticing

2
Clearly **understand** the *real* opportunity or problem

3
Prioritise the opportunity and make the necessary trade-offs

4
Set **design** criteria and use them to explore and choose options

5
Define the destination and **plan** how to get there

6
Move from where we are today, to where we need to be

7
Learn from experience and improve next time

THE THRIVE CYCLE™
SEE
UNDERSTAND
PRIORITISE
DESIGN
PLAN
MOVE
LEARN

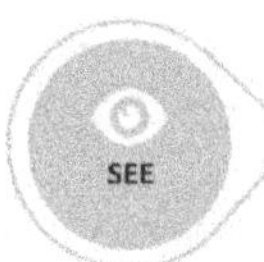

The Adaptive Organisation is constantly on the alert, sees change-opportunities sooner than its rivals and takes action at the best possible time. It has better insight and uses this to create new opportunities. A study in 2010 found that 49 percent of the top financially performing organisations were able to anticipate and initiate change effectively, compared to only 20 percent in the lowest performing organisations[11].

The Adaptive Organisation takes the time to thoroughly understand what it is dealing with, and proactively avoids unhelpful, knee-jerk reactions. It never panics. New ideas are welcomed and given due consideration, even when they are contrary to popular organisational beliefs.

Priority choices are consistent and balance short and long-term considerations. They are also constantly monitored to ensure the right focus is being maintained, and there's a willingness to refine them as new information comes to light. Importantly, there's consistency between the priority choices being made, and the corresponding allocation of resources and management focus.

When deciding on the best response, The Adaptive Organisation starts with a clear understanding of the problem or opportunity[9]. It never accepts the first option as being the right answer. The people who are involved in the design process are there because they have something to offer (not merely to keep them happy). Above all, when designing the response, The Adaptive Organisation remains 100 percent focused on delivering value, and never embarks on change for any other reason.

Plans are developed in the full knowledge they will be wrong and, as such, will require constant renewal. There's a healthy amount of pragmatism that emphasises the outcome, ahead of the journey. Plans are also contextually relevant, with a full knowledge of the landscape and not just the road the organisation will travel. Because of this, the right resources are available when needed and the people of the organisation always know where they are along the journey.

When The Adaptive Organisation moves to a new way of working, it is seen as a positive challenge, regardless of the type of change. When they make mistakes, they recover quickly and their people feel empowered and energised. Importantly, when these organisations move to a new state, the changes are long-lasting and create sustainable value.

The Adaptive Organisation is better than its rivals because it learns. As a result, it rarely repeats its mistakes, always builds on its successes and is constantly looking for ways to do things better. Further, it monitors trends over time and uses these insights to identify and address the cause (not the symptom) of poor adaptiveness.

And what makes these organisations really stand out is that they are able to do all of the above, consistently well, for many change-opportunities, in parallel.

◆◆◆

We'll repeatedly come back to The Thrive Cycle during the ensuing chapters. For now, let's look at how this simple concept will reveal hidden opportunities within your organisation.

HOW THE THRIVE CYCLE UNLOCKS YOUR ORGANISATION

I took my family to the Planetarium to see an exhibition about the Universe. As we lay back in the reclining seats looking up at the domed screen, the presenter introduced an astronomical concept that was equally relevant to organisations.

When viewed from space, our galaxy (the Milky Way) looks a bit like a flat, disk-like spiral. So, while it measures about 600 million light-years across, it is very thin (like a plate viewed from the side) and it measures only a couple of light-years from top to bottom.

Now, imagine that you are standing in the centre of our galaxy.

You would have a clear view of the areas of the universe that were above, or below you, because there is very little debris from our own galaxy getting in the way. This means you can see further and potentially gain a better understanding of what's out there and how the universe hangs together.

However, if you tried to look either left or right, it would be a completely different story. It's difficult to see beyond our own galaxy, there being so many nearby stars, asteroids and planets in the way. This creates a blind spot in which our understanding of the Universe lying beyond our galaxy is limited. Scientists call this blind-spot The Zone of Avoidance (Figure 4-2).

It's a great term isn't it?

As an organisation increases in scale and complexity, it can develop its own *Adaptive Zone of Avoidance.* So much clutter in the day-to-day can make it difficult to see and understand the factors that are inhibiting your organisation's ability to adapt. Without this kind of self-awareness, and knowing how adaptive the organisation *really* is, it is difficult to change the way things are.

FIGURE 4-2: The Zone of Avoidance is the area of the Universe obscured by the debris of our own galaxy, The Milky Way.

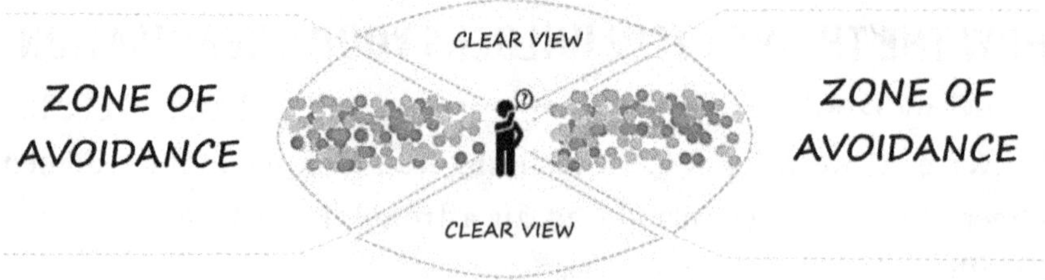

And so, they stay the same. Locked in place, with everyone complaining the organisation is not as adaptive as it needs to be but no one knowing what to do, or having the language to talk about it.

In this way, it's the Adaptive Zone of Avoidance that prevents your organisation from answering the eight fundamental questions (i.e. the Adaptive Fundamentals) required to bring about effective and sustainable change.

So here's the good news.

As soon as your organisation recognises that it *has* a Thrive Cycle (regardless of the state it's in) it can start to break down the Adaptive Zone of Avoidance (Figure 4-3). In fact, I'm confident that now *you* know about it, you'll see your organisation with a greater level of adaptive insight than you've had in the past.

So, how does having the concept of The Thrive Cycle (and a framework that supports it) release your organisation from the Adaptive Zone of Avoidance?

Seeing the real problem, not just the symptoms

The Matrix[51] is one of my favourite films. If you've seen it, you will remember the scene in which Keanu Reeves' character, Neo, *sees* 'The Matrix' for the first time. Instead of people and buildings to which he

FIGURE 4-3: The Thrive Cycle breaks-down the Adaptive Zone of Avoidance and enables the eight Adaptive Fundamentals to be answered.

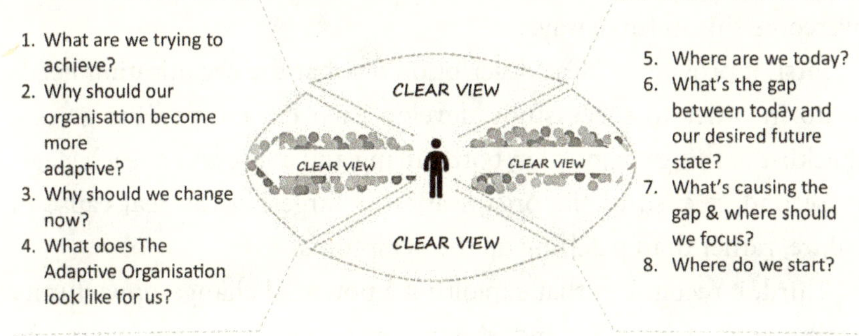
1. What are we trying to achieve?
2. Why should our organisation become more adaptive?
3. Why should we change now?
4. What does The Adaptive Organisation look like for us?
CLEAR VIEW
CLEAR VIEW
CLEAR VIEW
CLEAR VIEW
5. Where are we today?
6. What's the gap between today and our desired future state?
7. What's causing the gap & where should we focus?
8. Where do we start?

has become accustomed, he sees the millions of lines of computer code that is determining what he sees.

Many organisations when they attempt to understand *why* they lack adaptive ability, focus on the things they can see. As a result, they focus upon what happens when the organisation actually starts to 'move'. They make the assumption that what they can see *is* the problem that needs to be solved. This tends to lead to what I (unimaginatively) call The List, which describes the *perceived causes* of failure. Those causes include:

- insufficient communication
- resistance to change
- poor alignment
- insufficient resources
- poor accountability
- unclear priorities.

Then, having created The List, the organisation proceeds to implement one or two tactical improvements. It might implement a new methodology in IT, or put a program-office in place. And yet, it still finds itself creating The List once again, the next time around.

So why is that?

The simple truth is that most senior leaders don't really know *why* their organisation finds organisational change so difficult. Most know something isn't right and they have some theories, but they are unable to narrow the problem down enough to address it effectively.

Recognising The Thrive Cycle within your organisation helps to overcome this in three ways.

First, it provides a clear description of what the organisation needs to do in order to successfully develop each capability. This gives a checklist of things to look for, both during and at the end of each stage.

Second, it ensures the organisation is targeting the real cause of failure, rather than patching up the symptoms.

Third, it recognises that exploiting a potential change-opportunity begins with *Seeing* it, and doesn't just get underway when the organisation starts *Moving* to the new state. As a result, the challenge can be addressed holistically and target the root cause.

Overcoming structural boundaries and seeing the horizontal picture

Many organisations that have been pursuing growth for some time have developed a fairly ingrained functional structure, which divides accountabilities vertically. Because of this, few organisations have a holistic concept like The Thrive Cycle in which there is direct executive accountability for ensuring their organisation:

a) develops, then continually evolves the capabilities required to complete each stage of The Thrive Cycle.
b) is able to maintain a level of consistency and continuity as individual changes attempt to move from one stage in The Thrive Cycle, to the next.

It could be argued that ultimately the CEO is accountable for The Thrive Cycle within an organisation, but he or she usually delegates responsibility to their team.

Many traditional executive structures have a series of separate Thrive Cycle-*like* activities distributed across various C-suite roles (Figure 4-4). Often when this happens, The Thrive Cycle, both as a concept and a capability, ceases to be visible within the organisation. The organisation then becomes caught in a never-ending loop. No one is responsible for creating a strong Thrive Cycle, no one even knows about it and so, no one holistically takes action to initiate positive change. Thus, the Thrive Cycle remains weak and fragmented. And so the loop goes on.

By way of contrast, if your organisation (and your Executive Team) have a shared appreciation of what The Thrive Cycle is, you can start to make an informed choice regarding its importance, and whether it is something that could provide an advantage.

The Thrive Cycle is also functionally agnostic and continuous. This means that once an organisation has defined what its Thrive

Cycle needs to look like, it enables functional teams to work together, without them owning any part of it.

Seeing beyond the myth of 'the perfect' organisation

As the saying goes, 'the grass is always greener on the other side'. As a leader sitting in a large, sometimes cumbersome organisation, it's tempting to look at the nimble, digital entrepreneurs and yearn to be like them. In some ways, it can appear that many of them are perfect and thus, in order to become adaptive, and nimble like them, your organisation needs to also be perfect.

This kind of thinking can make the task of creating an adaptive organisation seem insurmountable. Further, because of this belief, the magnitude of change can feel 'all too hard', leading back to a more tactical approach.

I firmly believe the *perfect organisation* is an unhelpful myth. Even the most adaptive organisations get it wrong, but when they do,

FIGURE 4-4: The traditional design of senior executive teams[a] tends to fragment the concept of, and capabilities required within, The Thrive Cycle.

The seven organisational capabilities required to successfully navigate The Thrive Cycle

Traditional C-Suite Executive Accountability for developing Thrive Cycle 'like' capabilities

	SEE	UNDERSTAND	PRIORITISE	DESIGN	PLAN	MOVE	LEARN
CEO	*Accountable for overall adaptiveness but delegates responsibility to C-suite*						
CFO	-	-	✓	-	✓	-	-
COO	-	-	✓	✓	✓	✓	-
CCO	✓	✓	-	✓	-	-	✓
CSO	✓	✓	✓	✓	✓	-	-
CTO	-	-	-	✓	✓	✓	✓
CRO	✓	✓	-	-	-	-	-
CMO	✓	✓	-	✓	-	-	-
CIO	-	-	-	✓	✓	✓	-
CHRO	-	-	-	-	✓	✓	✓

a *CFO – Chief Finance Officer; COO – Chief Operating Officer; CCO – Chief Customer Officer; CSO – Chief Strategy Officer; CTO – Chief Transformation Officer; CRO – Chief Risk Officer; CMO – Chief Marketing Officer; CIO – Chief Information Officer; CHRO – Chief Human Resources Officer.*

they pick themselves up, learn from it and move on. The Thrive Cycle therefore enables your organisation to approach what may, historically, have been perceived as an impossible task. Not only that, it will enable it to incrementally try, fail, learn and evolve, rather than aspiring to an unrealistic benchmark of perfection.

Overcoming the barriers created by common business language

Every day, people in business will use words like strategy, delivery, project management and change management as part of normal business conversations. When doing so, however, they are unlikely to be aware of the mindset and implicit value judgements that have attached themselves to these words over time.

Strategy has its origins in universities like Harvard and MIT. *Delivery* and *project management* emanate from task-driven engineering projects. And then, there is 'change management', which came on the scene much later, to take care of the people stuff that project managers historically ignored.

So from the very beginning, the professions that have inherited many aspects of The Thrive Cycle came from very different philosophical positions. Over time, these differences have developed into an inherent inability to 'get' one another. The doers do the doing, and complain about how the strategists don't understand the business. In turn, the strategists complain about the business and wonder why their strategies never seem to be realised.

This kind of conflict exists in many professions. Doctors versus nurses; architects versus builders and so on. So why is it particularly a problem when it comes to being adaptive?

Words like strategy, innovation, project management and so forth, now create unconscious barriers in the minds of the people who use them. They define which aspects of The Thrive Cycle a professional is likely to focus on. For example, it is not the job of a strategist to deliver change, and it is not the job of the project manager to see organisational opportunities[4]. These mental barriers once again fragment The Thrive Cycle and remove the continuity upon which it depends for success.

Having a way to understand and improve adaptive performance

In the words of Peter Drucker 'What gets measured gets improved'[18]. If your organisation doesn't have a clear understanding of what being adaptive means and doesn't know how adaptive it is today, how can you possibly measure and improve it?

The truth is, you can't. Looking at project costs or delivery timeframes doesn't tell you how adaptive your organisation is or where things are going wrong.

The Thrive Cycle overcomes this challenge by breaking down adaptive capability into clear stages that can be measured. By monitoring the strength of each capability within The Thrive Cycle and measuring changes, it enables your organisation to maintain focus and continuously improve. Without the Thrive Cycle most organisations have no structured basis upon which to do this.

We'll talk a lot more about continuous improvement later. In fact, there's a whole section about it in Chapter 11 where we'll explore Thrive Cycle Learning and how it will enable you to create an Adaptive Advantage Scorecard.

Applying the lessons learnt from others

How often have you heard about organisations like Apple, Amazon and Google doing something, and thought to yourself, 'Hey, we should do that'?

But when you try to apply that idea in your own organisation, it doesn't seem to have the same mind-blowing benefits.

So, why is that? In truth, it's not *what* other organisations do that matters, it's *why* they do it. What was the problem or opportunity that led to them doing what they did? When we don't understand this, we are at risk of trying to apply a fantastic solution to the wrong problem.

It's the equivalent of me looking at how Taylor Swift dresses, and believing that if I dress like her, I will become a successful performer.

So what's the alternative? Well, when you have an understanding of The Thrive Cycle (and how it works within your organisation) it helps you to analyse what others do, and learn in a far more effective way. It also means when you look to others for ideas, you do so with a clear understanding of what your organisation's areas of strength and weakness are. Thus, you can more effectively see how great ideas could actually fit and make your own organisation more successful.

Of course, without The Thrive Cycle the opposite can occur. Trying to retrofit a great solution to the wrong problem is more likely to reduce organisational capability than enhance it.

Maximising value from business improvement activities

When I first developed The Thrive Cycle Framework, I was challenged by a former colleague. 'I'm not so sure about this', she said. 'I mean… the last thing we need is yet another methodology on top of the ones we've already invested in'. It was a good point but she need not have worried.

The Thrive Cycle is not a methodology. Instead, it is an overarching framework that enables your organisation to understand what it means to be adaptive, identify the gaps it has, then address those gaps in a targeted way. The Thrive Cycle does not dictate how your organisation should address the gaps (i.e. what solutions, technology or methodology you should use) because the right solution for one organisation will be the wrong one for another. Instead, The Thrive Cycle helps you to define the required outcome then provides criteria that can be used to select the best solution for your organisational circumstances.

In this way, The Thrive Cycle ensures investment in business-improvement activities is focusing on the areas that will provide the greatest return. It also ensures that these activities are aligned with each other and are *actually* improving the adaptiveness of the organisation (not eroding it).

CHAPTER CONCLUSION

The Thrive Cycle is one of those ideas that appears obvious when someone explains it and yet it is fragmented in so many organisations. Now we have the framework however, it enables us to go far deeper with our understanding of The Adaptive Organisation. So let's put it to work.

KEY POINTS TO REMEMBER

- Being adaptive is about responding to the change-opportunities that matter because they have the potential to influence your organisation's success.
- The Adaptive Zone of Avoidance prevents organisations from understanding why they aren't adaptive and thus, prevents them from doing something about it.
- Every organisation has a Thrive Cycle. To succeed in an environment of unrelenting change your organisation requires a strong Thrive Cycle, which means it must be able to: 1) *See it*, when an opportunity appears; 2) *Understand it;* 3) *Prioritise it;* 4) *Design a response;* 5) *Plan for it;* 6) *Move to it;* and 7) *Learn from it.* Having developed these capabilities, your organisation then needs to effectively *apply* them, in the right sequence, such that each opportunity progresses, and ultimately creates value.
- The Thrive Cycle Framework unlocks The Adaptive Organisation by helping it to:
  - see the real problem, and not just the symptoms
  - overcome silo thinking
  - understand and monitor adaptive performance
  - establish a compelling reason for change
  - learn more effectively from other organisations
  - maximise value from business improvement activities

5

Surfers. Swimmers. Splashers. Sinkers.

In this chapter we'll use The Thrive Cycle Framework to develop insights into your organisation's Adaptive Profile. We'll also meet the four Adaptive Archetypes and learn how their different approaches affect their ability to thrive in the face of unrelenting change.

HAVING READ THIS FAR, YOU WILL already be starting to see how The Thrive Cycle Framework provides the basis upon which we can now begin to understand your organisation. As you can see in Figure 5-1, we've now added the labels from The Thrive Cycle to the Adaptive Profile you created in Chapter 2.

As you reflect on the scores you gave, were there particular areas that you thought, 'Ah… that's definitely a five' or 'Gee… that's got to be a one'?

Quickly jot these down while they are top of mind. They are potential strengths to build upon, and areas that may pose the greatest risk. When you do this exercise within your organisation, these 'definites' can help to bring depth to the conversation.

DEFINITE [5] – REALLY STRONG	DEFINITE [1] – REALLY WEAK

From here, we can begin to explore some of the different Adaptive Profiles you may have developed. To do this, it helps to provide a number of more extreme profiles – I call them *Adaptive Archetypes* – against which to assess your own organisation. There are four of these archetypes and all are likely to experience different outcomes when faced with relentless change.

FIGURE 5-1: The Adaptive Profile for your organisation can now include the seven core stages of The Thrive Cycle under each point.

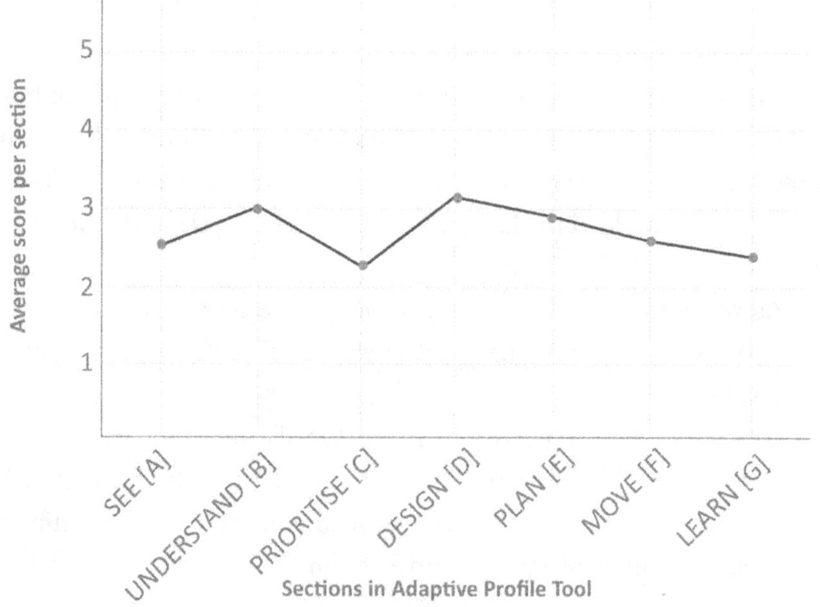

But before we get into the detail, let me share some background.

When I was growing up, every summer holiday was spent at the beach. It was always the same one – a little place called Lilli Pilli on the South Eastern Coast of Australia.

For most of the year, Lilli Pilli was a tranquil little place with a newsagency and a bait-and-tackle shop. In the summer, however, it transformed into a crowded, city-dwellers' menagerie. Many flocked to the nearby Malua Bay Beach, with its big swell and, at times, dangerous rips. The visitors to the beach shared certain qualities with the four more extreme Adaptive Archetypes.

THE SURFERS – SELECTIVE, DETERMINED AND ENERGISED BY UNCERTAINTY

Dressed in their black, full-length wetsuits *Surfers* would stand up on the dunes reading the waves. They knew what they were looking for and so could hone in on whether the swell was favourable and, if so, where the best position might be. They had insight into how the ocean worked and could use what they saw on the surface to indicate what might be happening underneath.

Surfers were selective. If the waves weren't right, or the rip was too strong, they didn't go in. Instead they would save their energy or try somewhere else.

Every Surfer had their own board. Its shape, length and weight was just right for their size, level of skill, and the kind of surfing they wanted to do. Good surfers put time into their boards, and ensured it was waxed just enough to support the right dynamics in the water.

Out in the water, the skills and experience varied considerably. Kids with their new board from Christmas, retirees and the serious surfers, all watching the water, waiting to see the first glimpse of a potential ride into shore. The sooner they saw it, the more time they had to get into position and the more likely they were to catch it.

Surfers were also discerning in their choice of wave. If they thought a wave was promising, then part way through catching it discovered it wasn't as promising or that the risks were too high, they pulled out and went back to wait for another one. They didn't waste energy on something that clearly was not going to give an appropriate return.

Every wave was different and that was what made it exciting. A Surfer never quite knew what they were going to be faced with until it was right there – bearing down on them. Then, they had to draw on their skills and experience to adapt in real-time. That's what made it fun – the thrill of taking on the waves, and winning.

Being a Surfer is not about experience or skill level. It's about attitude and a willingness to try at the risk of failure. As Taj Burrows (Australian champion surfer) describes it, 'the only difference between you and me, is time in the water'[10].

Surfers fell off. In fact, they fell off anywhere from 50 to 90 percent of attempts. That's what they expected and that's how they learned. They didn't blame the waves or their board. They just climbed back on and paddled back out to do better next time.

What does a Surfer organisation look like?

The Surfer organisation's Adaptive Profile looks something like that depicted in Figure 5-2.

The average score for a Surfer organisation falls above 3 for every stage of The Thrive Cycle. What's particularly important is the consistency the Surfer organisation has across *all seven* stages. It presents an even, almost straight line, which suggests the organisation focuses on creating and evolving its ability to navigate The Thrive Cycle. As part of this, Surfer organisations emphasise continuous improvement and learning from every change experience.

In this way, organisations A and B in Figure 5-2 are Surfers; one is just more experienced than the other.

FIGURE 5-2: Sample Adaptive Profile – Surfer organisations A and B

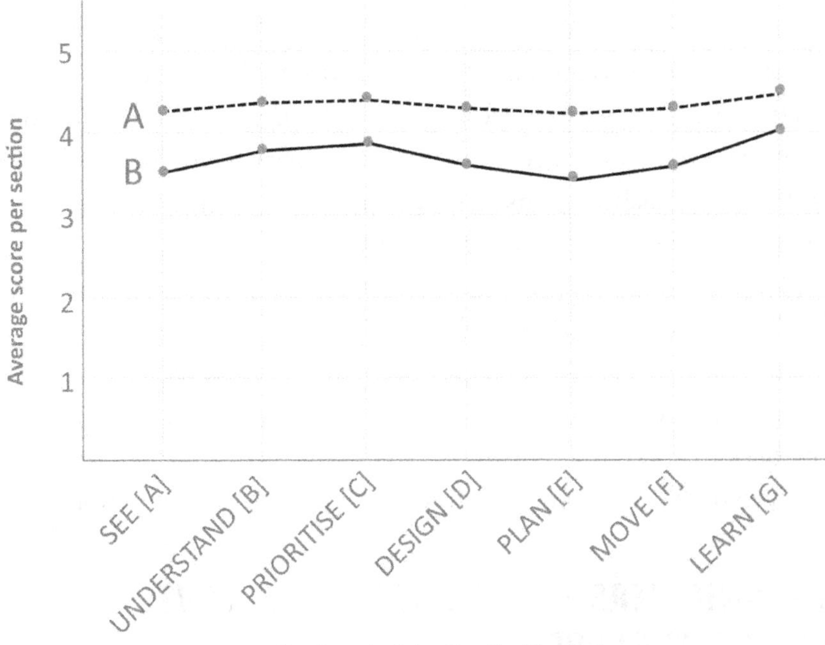

Surfer organisations are alert, selective and consistent

Surfers are consistently *looking* for opportunities, although their ability to act on those opportunities depends on their experience and level of capability.

A true Surfer organisation rarely rates itself as a 5 for anything. That's because these organisations believe that, regardless of how good they are, there is always room for improvement.

When faced with the change-dominated environment I described in Chapter 1, Surfer organisations are likely to *thrive*. That's because they will have been on the alert, looking for change well before it appeared over the horizon. When doing so, they will have a clear idea of what they are looking for and so will have been able to distil relevant change-opportunities from the broader deluge of information.

Importantly, these organisations will see opportunities before their rivals but will only embark on change for the right reasons. Their people will enjoy and embrace the challenge of change, rather than seeing it as a disruption. Surfer organisations will also be disciplined when they need to make priority choices, and be willing to stop activities when they aren't going to realise expected value. They will also be disciplined in their approach to transitioning the organisation to its new state, and ensure they effectively apply what they've learnt.

Even Surfers don't get it right all the time

These organisations are prepared to take risks, knowing sometimes even the best can be dumped by a freak wave. However, they are also the ones that venture out into the 'blue oceans'[13] and they are more likely to be there and be ready when the ultimate opportunity arrives.

THE SWIMMERS – FAST IN CALM WATER BUT SLOW IN THE SURF

The *Swimmers* on Malua Bay Beach were pretty confident in the water. On calm days, they could be seen doing laps across the bay, away from the beach crowds gathered at the shoreline. They had strong, even strokes which suggested they were regular visitors to their local pool. This enabled them to build up a good pace as they followed a straight line backwards and forwards.

Even on calm days, a rogue wave could come along unexpectedly. This caused problems for the Swimmers as they tended to have their heads in the water and didn't see the wave coming. As a result, when they turned their heads to breathe, they inhaled a mouthful of seawater, not air.

Spluttering and coughing it took some time to recover and then, slowly, the Swimmers would continue on their way. Their rhythm, however, was never quite as strong as before. Another wave, more coughing and eventually they'd come into shore.

'Surfer organisations are prepared to take risks. They venture into 'blue oceans'[13] *and are more likely to be there when the ultimate opportunity arrives, then do something about it.'*

In a large swell, it was a completely different story. Most swimmers didn't venture beyond the breakers. They stayed safe, close to shore, catching the waves as they could. While their fitness and strength were still assets, they now had to compete with everyone else.

Every now and then a swimmer might try swimming out beyond the breakers. But in the choppy seas they tended to be slow and make very little progress. Most of the time, they stayed afloat, but they certainly didn't get value from the energy they expended.

What does a Swimmer organisation look like?

A Swimmer organisation's Adaptive Profile starts off well, but its capability tends to taper off as change progresses through The Thrive Cycle (Figure 5-3).

Swimmers are, generally, successful organisations

They have historically operated in so-called stable industries (e.g. banking, insurance, automotive, airlines etc.). Traditionally, high barriers to entry have meant being highly adaptive has been seen as offering limited benefit. When everything remains the same, the real gains come from being big and efficient.

FIGURE 5-3: Sample Adaptive Profile – Swimmer organisation

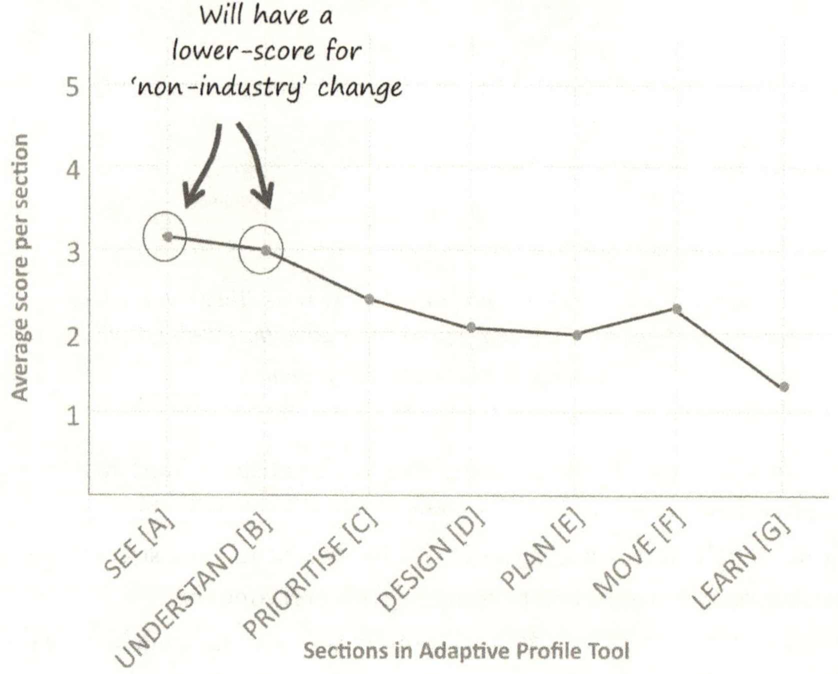

For this reason, *Swimmers* have often spent years (even decades) focusing on building scale and increasing market share. The strategies developed to do this have been built on fairly static business assumptions and a strong foundation of industry knowledge. As long as those assumptions remain true, and the industry remains fairly static, the organisation succeeds.

Priorities in these organisations are often determined by contribution to growth, and they can struggle attempting to balance short-term performance and longer-term value creation.

Over the years, there has been little reason to look too hard for change-opportunities. They've historically been fairly easy to see, or they have been industry-wide (and so, as long as a Swimmer wasn't any less adaptive than its nearest competitor, it could still be successful).

Swimmers see change-opportunities if they are relevant to immediate growth, and if they occur in their own industry. Economic downturns, regulatory reforms and product innovations in existing product categories – Swimmer organisations are 'all over it'. Beyond these, change-opportunities can be harder to see, until they make it into mainstream conversations.

Swimmers are well established and have deep pockets

One of the factors that works both for, and against, Swimmer organisations is that they are often very well established, large, and have deep pockets. When they embark on change, costs can soar into the millions, or even billions. There is an absence of constraint and the easiest solution to problems is to pay more and take more time. By way of contrast, in organisations where constraint exists (for example 'we only have $200,000 to spend on a solution') it prompts people to find a way and be creative.

Significant operational size and complexity means that individuals rarely see what happens across the organisations. A Swimmer's Thrive Cycle is fairly fragmented, if not non-existent. As such, change initiatives can leak value (i.e. cost more than they should or have their benefits diluted) without decision makers knowing that it has happened or why.

For Swimmers, it's all about perfecting what you do today and doing it faster and cheaper than yesterday. The leaders in these organisations tend to feel more comfortable *doing* than *thinking*. Swimmers tend to leap into looking for a solution rather than *understanding* the problem. They may realise they have done this halfway through implementation, and then need to retrofit the solution or drag the ship back on course. This takes time, money, and emotional energy, although no one really knows how much, because these costs become absorbed into the monthly contractor or consulting fees.

Swimmer organisations show limited commitment to learning. While they may conduct some form of post-change review, the same mistakes are often seen next time.

So, how are Swimmer organisations likely to fair when faced with the complex-change scenario I described in Chapter 1? The answer is – 'well… it depends'. It depends on where the change comes from, whom it affects, and how quickly it flips from being a change-opportunity to affecting organisational performance.

When an opportunity or threat comes from within their own industry, Swimmers will generally see it. If it doesn't, they probably won't until it appears in the papers.

Effecting change in these organisations is far harder and more costly than it needs to be. This exhausts and frustrates its most talented people, as they are the ones who need to keep the seams of the organisation from splitting apart.

However, as long as the organisation still has deep pockets, it will just end up paying increasingly more to realise the decreasing amount of value (created for customers, and thus, the organisation).

However, if a change comes from outside the industry, perhaps from a new, disruptive competitor, there may well be a very different outcome. A Swimmer may *see* it late and thus, find itself trying to rush through The Thrive Cycle to catch up.

'Swimmer organisations know their industry but will be surprised by disruptive change. Their large size and deep pockets mean that they may be slow to respond, and when they do, it takes longer and is more costly than it really needed to be.'

Finding themselves on the high seas, even the best of swimmers will struggle to stay afloat. This is especially so if the rival with whom they are competing is a Surfer.

THE SPLASHERS – GO WITH WHAT'S HOT AND DROP WHAT'S NOT

At the beach, *Splashers* were all about *looking* the part, not *playing* the part.

When they were sitting on the beach, they attempted to look like locals but… they actually didn't. They followed the latest trends with the latest swimwear, boardshorts, and perfect tans. However, they rarely went further than knee-deep in the water. They lacked commitment and didn't like to 'get their hair wet'.

The bigger the waves became, the closer to shore the Splashers would move. They complained it was too cold, there was too much seaweed and there were too many people.

With Splashers, you always had the impression they would have been happier sitting in a nice warm spa, than on a crowded Australian beach.

What does a Splasher organisation look like?

If it were honest with itself, a Splasher organisation would say it saw organisational change as a bit of an inconvenience. Something that gets in the way of the main game of achieving tangible results.

However, a Splasher organisation wouldn't say this because that's not how Splasher organisations are. They want to look good and have learned what they need to say in order to achieve this end. These organisations want to be adaptive and agile but they don't *really* want to undertake the work and commitment involved in achieving it. Some have an almost pathological fascination with winning awards, and will put more effort into *appearing to look* adaptive than building the actual capability.

Splashers are big believers in the silver-bullet. Instead of first seeking *understanding* then devising an approach that is right for them and their organisational circumstances, Splashers look at other organisations then follow the latest trend. Their philosophy tends to be 'If they can do it, we can do it'.

For example, if current thinking suggests that great organisations should have an innovation team, Splasher organisations create one. If the latest trend is to have a portfolio management system, they implement a portfolio management system.

If Google gave its employees green jelly beans to enhance creativity, the Splasher organisation would do the same. All right, I'm being a little facetious, but you can tell where I'm coming from. I am sure you've seen this type of organisation.

A Splasher's approach to being adaptive is piecemeal. They don't join the different parts together because they don't have an overarching picture of what the organisation should be trying to achieve.

FIGURE 5-4: Sample Adaptive Profile – Splasher organisation

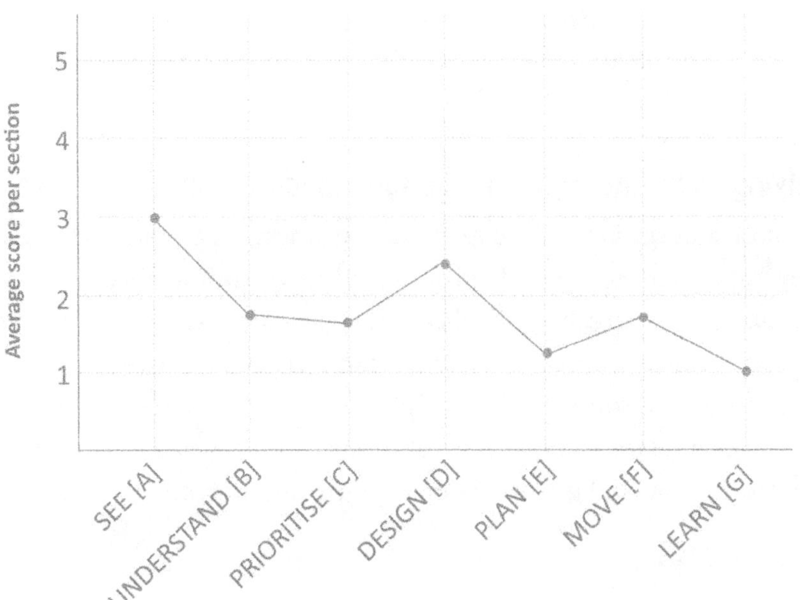

'Splashers believe in instant solutions and follow the latest trend for the wrong reasons.'

Relying on imitation, without understanding, comes at a price

Of most concern is that by copying others, these organisations believe they are *increasing* their adaptive capability, when in reality, they are *decreasing* it. That's because their focus tends to wax and wane as the trends come and go. So, rather than stopping what they used to do and starting something new, Splasher organisations leave the old initiatives in place, but lose interest in them. This creates bureaucracy and frustration, and generally slows the organisation down.

A chronically inconsistent and incongruous Thrive Cycle

There is another important point, and this is particularly relevant when understanding your own organisation. When looking at the Adaptive Profile of a Splasher, it can actually look as though things aren't in too bad a shape. That's the drawback of relying upon neat averages.

However, if you were to look at the raw scores of a Splasher organisation, they show *chronic inconsistency* across The Thrive Cycle. Looking at the Adaptive Profile in Figure 5-4, the high-level picture suggests that the organisation is scoring relatively well when it comes to *Seeing* change-opportunities, but the detail shows a different story. This Splasher organisation scored 5-out-of-5 for *'We are constantly on the alert, looking for change-opportunities inside and outside our industry'* because it introduced an innovation-hub twelve months ago. However, it didn't address the other capabilities required to *See* change-opportunities coming. This organisation therefore received a 2-out-of-5 for *'When a change-opportunity occurs we set and take action before our rivals'.* As a result, the organisation would not be seeing returns from its investment in the innovation hub and it would have created a highly frustrated group of people who had lots of great ideas that never went anywhere.

What happens to our Splasher organisation when it encounters a perfect storm of complex change?

Once again, it depends on how big the storm is. A bit like the *Swimmer*, if the organisation has deep pockets, it can probably muddle its way through (as long as there is no major shift in customer needs or how they are met). If it doesn't have deep pockets, it can find itself in deep water fairly quickly.

Splashers inflict complexity on their organisation and their people

They make change and day-to-day operations increasingly difficult. One of the biggest challenges for these organisations is their fundamental misconception that they *are* adaptive (because they perceive they do what Adaptive Organisations do). They lack the necessary self-awareness and as such, there is no catalyst (other than catastrophic failure) to prompt any kind of change. And, unfortunately, that's generally what it takes.

'Splasher organisations tend to look for "tactical quick fixes", rather than investing time and understanding then addressing the core challenges. Splashers go with the trend and copy others, but quickly lose interest.'

THE SINKERS – RECKLESS, UNDISCIPLINED AND DANGEROUS

Thankfully, over the years, the number of *Sinkers* down on Malua Bay Beach decreased. This was a good thing.

When Sinkers looked at the ocean they saw Fun! Fun! Fun! But they didn't understand the rules that governed it. They couldn't see when the sand dropped away steeply or when an undertow was likely to take them out to sea.

They were over-optimistic risk-takers and liked the idea of catching the big waves. They thought they were pretty good swimmers, but they weren't. They also thought they didn't need to swim between the life-saving flags, but they did.

These guys did everything to jeopardise their own safety and those around them. They were weak swimmers, unfit, and thought they could just walk into the two-metre swell with their boogie-boards and start surfing.

As a consequence, the Sinkers frequently got into trouble. They were dumped by the waves, driven head-first into the sand. They mowed-down young kids with their boards and placed lifeguards' lives at risk by becoming caught in rips.

Things usually ended in tears. A broken arm and an indiscrete swimwear crisis. Even so, they came back the following year for more, because they failed to make the connection between their own mindset and behaviour, and the consequences.

What does a Sinker organisation look like?

It will come as no surprise that a Sinker organisation's Adaptive Profile is not great (Figure 5-5). In its most extreme case, it 'flat-lines' along the bottom of the chart.

In the Sinker's world, every change comes as a surprise. Change is consistently responded to late and when this occurs, there is usually a mad panic. The organisation is reactive and when (or if) it does make

FIGURE 5-5: Sample Adaptive Profile – Sinker organisation

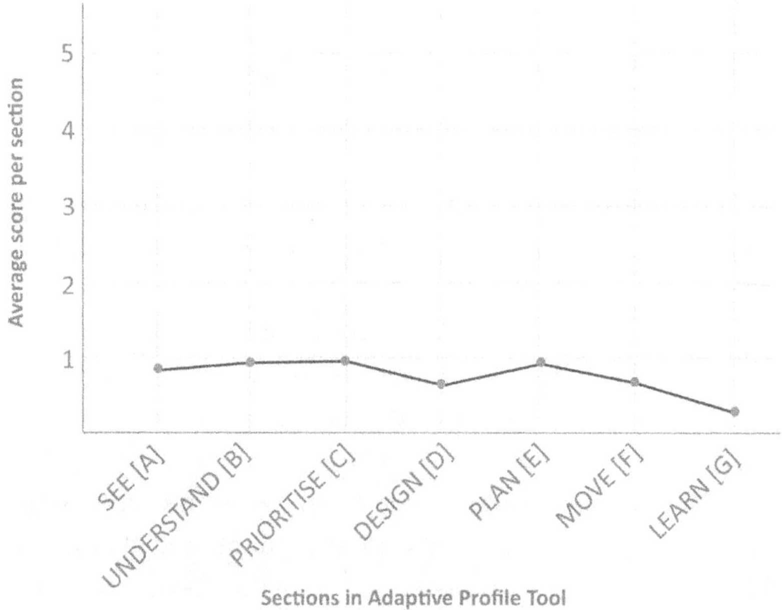

it through the stages of The Thrive Cycle, it is usually a torrid affair for everyone concerned. If these organisations added up *all* of the costs, they would find organisational change consistently erodes value, rather than enhancing it. When something is delivered, it is completely different to that which was expected and at an exponentially higher cost than was needed.

The Sinkers' approach to prioritisation is best described as 'every man for himself'. Funding and resources are determined by political influence and the ability to spin a good story.

These organisations are consistently inconsistent. There is no continuity between the different changes they undertake and the way in which they approach them. Consequently, there is constant conflict as different teams attempt to get *their* initiative through.

Sinkers jump into deep water (e.g. a major transformation), having done no preparation, and expect to be able to complete it better than anyone else. They buy companies and expect them to merge themselves. They do things like embarking on major systems upgrades or transformation programs without understanding the challenges first. They just expect things to happen 'naturally' and expect their people to cope.

When Sinkers try to *move* the organisation to a desired future-state it is chaotic. No one really knows what is going on, the implemented

'Within a Sinker organisation, any attempts to adapt involve constant fire-fighting, confusion and frustration.'

How would you describe your organisation?

IN THE ARCHETYPES just described, there may have been some aspects that resonated with you more than others. Alternatively, you may have picked one profile as being the perfect description of your organisation. So let's explore this.

If you were to give your organisation a score between 1 and 5 (1 = very similar, 5 = nothing like it) for each of the four Adaptive Archetypes, what scores would you give it? You can use a simple diagram in Figure 5-6 to plot your scores.

Now, if you drew a line between the four points, what shape does it give you? Is there more space above the 'water line' or below it?

Reflecting on this, if the tide-of-change started to rise within your environment, what is the likelihood that your organisation would 'thrive' or 'sink'?

FIGURE 5-6: How your organisation compares to the four Adaptive Archetypes.

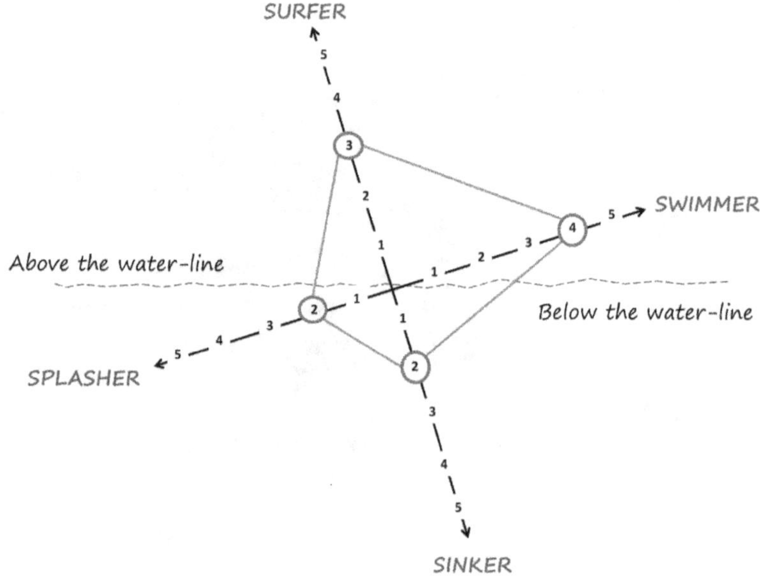

solutions rarely solve the original problem. In fact, they create bigger problems because the implemented solutions frequently break operational processes that were previously 'working just fine'.

The delivery process (and I use that term loosely) is highly dysfunctional. Almost anarchic. If a function doesn't receive the funding or solution it wants, it goes it alone. Customer service teams buy their own telephony systems and then give them to IT to implement.

As an employee, working for a Sinker organisation can be soul-destroying. It's an existence of constant fire-fighting, confusion and frustration. Poor decision-making, conflicting priorities and political agendas makes most things feel 'all too hard'. Business-as-usual and change activities rarely feel like they fit together, or make any sense.

It's probably fairly obvious what happens to a Sinker organisation during a tidal wave of change. Suffice to say, 'it ain't good'.

Taking all of the insights you've developed during this chapter, ask yourself these questions and write the answers in Figure 5-7.

- *How would you describe your organisation's ability to navigate each stage of The Thrive Cycle?*
- *How would you describe its readiness (high, medium, low) to meet future requirements?*

CHAPTER CONCLUSION

The four Adaptive Archetypes help to generate conversation and provide a shared reference point for understanding. They also demonstrate how the strength of an organisation's Thrive Cycle translates into adaptive success or failure.

It's worth remembering that they represent the 'extremes' of different approaches. The Adaptive Profile for your organisation will be unique and is likely to show some combination of all four.

FIGURE 5-7: What is your Adaptive Profile telling you?

THRIVE CYCLE STAGE	DESCRIPTION	FUTURE READINESS
SEE		
UNDERSTAND		
PRIORITISE		
DESIGN		
PLAN		
MOVE		
LEARN		

KEY THINGS TO REMEMBER

- Surfer organisations are selective, determined and energised by uncertainty. They are always on the lookout for opportunities. They see change first and are disciplined when responding. Surfers take risks and make sure they learn from their mistakes.
- Swimmer organisations are fast in calm water, but slow in the surf. They tend to operate in stable industries and have historically focused on building scale, rather than becoming adaptive. Short to medium-term growth drives priorities and they see some change-opportunities better than others.
- Splasher organisations go with 'what's hot' and drop 'what's not'. They tend to take shortcuts and copy others without really establishing what's best for their organisation. These organisations tend to implement the 'latest fad' but then quickly lose interest. They are chronically inconsistent when it comes to navigating The Thrive Cycle.
- Sinker organisations are reckless, undisciplined and dangerous. In their world, every change is a surprise. As a result, they tend to start late, panic, and then leap to the first solution that sounds plausible. In a Sinker organisation priorities tend to be determined by politics and self-interest, rather than holistically creating value.

◆◆◆

What's coming up?

This concludes Part 1. We've now defined The Adaptive Organisation and used The Thrive Cycle Framework to develop an understanding of your organisation and its Adaptive Profile. By doing so we've started to develop the core knowledge you'll need to improve the adaptive capability of your organisation. You've also met the Surfers, Swimmers, Splashers and Sinkers, and can now use these to engage others and start an adaptive conversation with your leadership colleagues.

So we've found The Thrive Cycle within your organisation, now we need to turn it into something that will deliver adaptive advantage. It's here we come to the second part of The Thrive Cycle Framework – The Six Elements of Adaptive Success.

The Six Elements of Adaptive Success

When I decided to write a book about The Thrive Cycle and unlocking The Adaptive Organisation I started by asking a question:

- *What factors, when consistently applied, make the difference between an organisation having a strong Thrive Cycle or a weak one?*

I spent almost two years researching the answer – analysing the common themes, deconstructing (then reconstructing) different scenarios and researching the experiences and ideas of other leaders, academics and practitioners. Having started with over 100 possible contenders, I eventually distilled them down to just six, and these became the Six Elements of Adaptive Success.

When you look at your Adaptive Profile and the state of The Thrive Cycle within your organisation, it is these elements that are causing it. If your Thrive Cycle is strong, it's because The Six Elements of Adaptive Success are strong. If they are weak, your Thrive Cycle will be weak (Figure 5-8).

Now we can bring the full Thrive Cycle Framework together (Figure 5-9). At the top sits the Thrive Cycle capability we explored in Part 1. In Part 2, we'll move into the next layer of detail and concentrate on the Six Elements of Adaptive Success that sit beneath your organisation's Thrive Cycle.

FIGURE 5-8: The Six Elements of Adaptive Success determine whether your organisation is a Surfer or a Sinker.

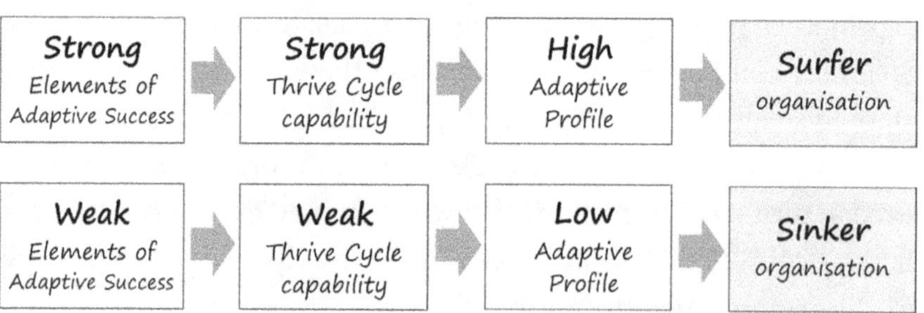

FIGURE 5-9: The full Thrive Cycle Framework including the Six Elements of Adaptive Success

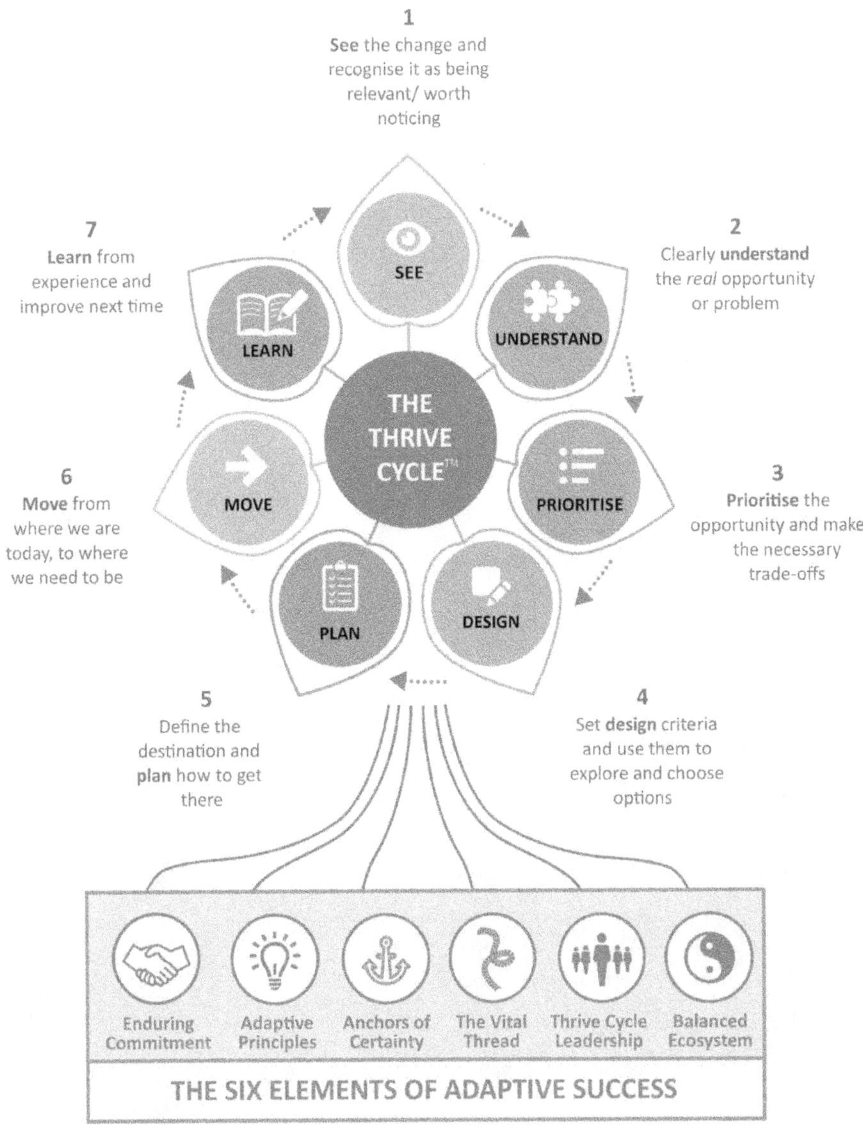
1
See the change and recognise it as being relevant/ worth noticing
2
Clearly understand the real opportunity or problem
3
Prioritise the opportunity and make the necessary trade-offs
4
Set design criteria and use them to explore and choose options
5
Define the destination and plan how to get there
6
Move from where we are today, to where we need to be
7
Learn from experience and improve next time
SEE
UNDERSTAND
PRIORITISE
DESIGN
PLAN
MOVE
LEARN
THE THRIVE CYCLE™
Enduring Commitment
Adaptive Principles
Anchors of Certainty
The Vital Thread
Thrive Cycle Leadership
Balanced Ecosystem
THE SIX ELEMENTS OF ADAPTIVE SUCCESS

PART 2

The Six Elements of Adaptive Success

The insights in Part 2 will enable you to understand what's driving your organisation's Adaptive Profile and set a clear aspiration that creates adaptive advantage. Importantly, Part 2 will enable you as a leader, to identify where you need to focus in order to drive sustained and significant organisational change.

6

The first element: Enduring Commitment

To create The Adaptive Organisation, key players have to agree what needs to be achieved and why being adaptive matters. This chapter walks through the steps that underpin Enduring Commitment. By the end, we will have set a Target Adaptive Profile for your organisation and identified the gap between today and your desired future state.

AS A GOOD YORKSHIRE FRIEND OF MINE used to say, this first element 'does exactly what it says on the tin'.

Building The Adaptive Organisation takes time and effort. What we are looking to achieve through this first element is true commitment, not rhetorical commitment. This distinction is important because while two-thirds of senior executives *say* that building organisational capability is important, there is evidence that only one-third actually focus on it[39].

In terms of change-related capability, the figures are even less encouraging. Separate research has found 88 percent of executives say that executing strategic initiatives is important, and found that the number one reason for strategic change succeeding was leadership buy-in and support. However, only half of those surveyed indicated strategy implementation received the C-suite attention it required[22].

I say all of this because it helps to explain why Enduring Commitment is the first of The Six Elements of Adaptive Success.

The good news is we've already started the journey by developing your organisation's Adaptive Profile. When we establish Enduring Commitment we follow a similar process, just on a much broader scale, and with a key focus on engagement.

In a moment I'll walk through the steps to follow. Before we do however, there's some important context to highlight.

The desired outcome

On one level, this first element is about using The Thrive Cycle Framework to set an adaptive goal for your organisation, develop a plan and communicate it. After all, without a goal, how can you achieve it?

At a deeper level however, creating Enduring Commitment is about developing organisational self-awareness and the appreciation that what has enabled your organisation to succeed in the past, is unlikely to do so in the future. This means involving the right people in conversations and working collaboratively to reach agreement, rather than just developing the answers on your own. This will take some time, but the consequential 'lightbulb moments' will create the emotional platform and commitment you'll need to create The Adaptive Organisation.

Keep this broader outcome in mind when applying the steps in this chapter within your organisation. Remember that success means achieving all of the factors I've just described, not just creating a target to aim for. So now let's explore what it takes to create Enduring Commitment.

DEFINE ADAPTIVE BOUNDARIES

We need to start by establishing some basic reference points. The first is to define the *Adaptive Boundaries* of your organisation. This makes the scope clear as well as identifying the stakeholders you'll need to bring along the journey.

To define your Adaptive Boundaries you need to explore three core areas: The Core Organisation, its Adaptive Partners, and Adaptive Influencers (Figure 6-1).

The Core Organisation

You defined this earlier when you were completing your Adaptive Profile.

The broader leadership team of this Core Organisation is the group that needs to *own* and *lead* development of The Six Elements of Adaptive Success.

The people within this Core Organisation usually need to work collaboratively to meet the expectations of the same customer groups. No one person can get the job done on their own.

When developing this first Element of Adaptive Success, and defining the Core Organisation, it is critical to have someone at the top of the hierarchy who is close enough, and committed enough, to

FIGURE 6-1: Defining Adaptive Boundaries

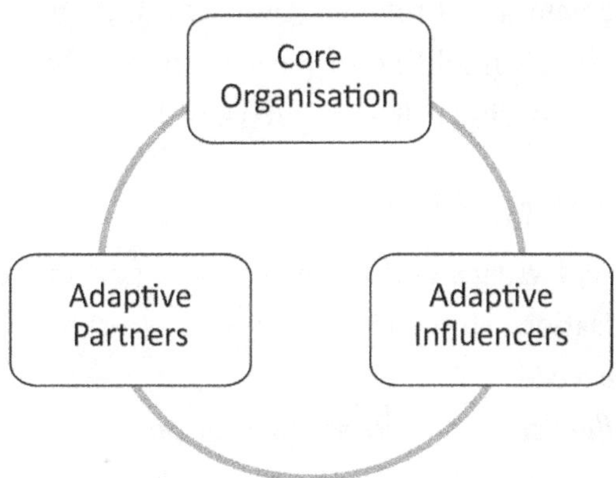

building The Adaptive Organisation. If that person happens to be you, then that makes life easier. If that person is not you, then your first job is to engage them and make them 'a believer'. We'll cover different ways to do this in Chapter 13.

Adaptive Partners

Invariably, organisations rely upon parties who are outside their boundaries of control, to deliver to their customers. These *Adaptive Partners* might be suppliers or outsourced third parties, or they may be internal shared-services providers. An Adaptive Partner could also be a government agency.

If the Core Organisation has been defined at a departmental or team level, an Adaptive Partner will be other departments, or outsourced service-providers.

If your organisation is going to improve its adaptive capability, it will need support from its Adaptive Partners. They can often provide an excellent source of independent feedback (regarding potential opportunities to improve across The Thrive Cycle). They may also need to adapt themselves in order to meet the adaptive needs of your organisation.

Identifying the Adaptive Partners early supports engagement and increases the potential contribution they may be able to make along the journey.

Early engagement also provides your organisation with an idea of how suitable partners might be to meet future needs, and whether it may be worth considering different partnerships.

Adaptive Influencers

These stakeholders will generally play no active part in creating a more adaptive organisation. However they will have a significant influence on whether it succeeds.

Adaptive Influencers have some form of power and, as such, have the ability to determine how hard or easy the journey towards The

Adaptive Organisation will be. They usually control either money, resources, voting-rights or bonuses. Typical candidates include corporate head-office stakeholders, shareholders, Board members and, potentially, large clients. As your organisation attempts to build its adaptive capabilities, it is likely to rely on its Adaptive Influencers to provide support along the way. These stakeholders need to be able to understand how the new way of doing things will enhance *their* current position. As such, they need to completely buy-in to the rationale well before anything changes and be kept informed as things unfold.

Defining your organisation's Adaptive Boundaries

THINKING ABOUT THE Core Organisation you defined earlier, who would its Adaptive Partners and Adaptive Influencers be? Are there any that would be more or less important when creating an Adaptive Organisation?

Example:

CORE ORGANISATION	**ADAPTIVE PARTNERS**	**ADAPTIVE INFLUENCERS**
Examples	*Examples*	*Examples*
Corporate	Other divisions	Global CEO
Region	Research companies	Senior finance people
Division	Technology companies	Shareholders
Business unit	Third-party supply chain	Board members
Country	Professional services	Large clients
Department	Strategic partners	
Team	Outsourced services	

INSPIRE A PASSIONATE COALITION

Once you've defined your Adaptive Boundaries, think through which individuals need to be involved, either from the Core Organisation, Adaptive Partners or Adaptive Influencers.

Changing an organisation as an individual is much harder than having a passionate coalition of people committed to achieving the outcome with you. Although big-bang engagement feels like it's faster (i.e. bring all the department heads together for a two day 'kick-off'), it is not usually the best way to start. You'll probably want to do this at some point, but it's not the first step.

What you need at the start is a relatively small group of people (i.e. a passionate coalition) you can work with to co-create the adaptive vision for the organisation. I'd generally start with your own leadership team and invite input from people who have insight into how the organisation really works. Expand the group as you start to build understanding and commitment across your broader stakeholder group.

Remember, just because someone needs to be involved at some point, doesn't mean they need to be there at the start. Be clear about why someone needs to be involved and if an important stakeholder is a non-believer, involve them early. However, do so on an individual basis to start with so you fully understand their perspective before it is raised in a group setting.

STAND ON THE SAME STARTING-LINE

Like the three-legged-race I mentioned in Part 1, in order to move an organisation forward, everyone needs to stand on the same starting line. This means working with your passionate coalition to establish a consistent view of the past as well as your organisation's current adaptive position.

Establish a consistent view of the past

When establishing a consistent view of the past, the intention is to develop a common understanding around questions like:

- *What really drives change in our organisation?*
- *How do our major changes compare in terms of the type of value they create?*
- *To what extent do we realise the value that we expect?*

While these questions may look fairly simple, in my experience they usually drive fairly robust conversation. In fact, the speed and ease with which consensus can be achieved is usually a good indicator of how adaptive an organisation is. A three hour conversation that leaves participants frustrated and no closer to agreement is symptomatic of a low level of adaptiveness.

Don't be concerned, this is all part of the process. The realisation that your organisation doesn't really know or understand its own position can be a lightbulb moment in itself.

Establish a shared view of organisational reality

One of the first requirements for improving in anything is to have a clear and consistent understanding of 'where you are' and thus, why change is necessary. This means developing a similar picture to the Adaptive Profile you developed earlier, but with much broader input and organisational engagement.

When I am working with organisations, I draw upon a number of different sources. The Adaptive Profile Assessment Tool you completed earlier provides a good starting point. However, when establishing a shared view of reality within your organisation, other data sources can also provide revealing insights. For example:

- *Reviewing strategic plans over a number of years – do they ever change? How much of what is planned is actually delivered?*
- *Reviewing project portfolio dashboards – are there any themes or patterns?*

- *Looking at changes in customers (acquisition and attrition) over a number of years – is there a correlation between spend on organisational change and having more customers?*
- *Looking at project post-implementation reviews – when viewed collectively, what picture do they create?*

IT TAKES LONGER THAN YOU EXPECT TO GET PEOPLE ON THE SAME PAGE

We've all been there. Having allocated a day to workshop an important business issue, the end of the day comes and you've only achieved half of what you were looking for. Executive diaries are booked up for the next three months, and so by the time the follow-up session can be organised the idea has completely lost momentum.

Creating a shared view of reality takes time, so be prepared to be patient. It will pay itself back in the long-run.

DEFINE ADAPTIVE ADVANTAGE

You'll recall from Chapter 2 that The Adaptive Organisation is able to identify and effect change *to a standard* and *at a pace* that *creates value* and, gives the organisation *an adaptive advantage* over its rivals.

But in practical terms what does this actually mean? What's the right pace? And, more specifically, what does adaptive advantage mean within the context of your organisation?

This is where we are going next and in the following few pages I'll share an approach you can use to answer these questions. First, we'll explore how adaptively advantaged (or disadvantaged) your organisation is today, relative to a range of comparison organisations. Then, we'll consider the future environment and explore how adaptive your organisation will need to survive and to thrive.

Three ways to deal with denial

DENIAL IS A PSYCHOLOGICAL defense mechanism that protects us from feeling bad. It shields us from emotions like guilt, regret, humiliation and sadness by convincing us that a situation is a particular way, when the evidence suggests it's not.

Denial can take many forms including discrediting the evidence or down-playing the significance of the situation. For example, smokers may downplay their actions by comparing themselves with people who smoke more than they do.

When initiating change in an organisation, it is common to come across a level of denial. People have often contributed to the way the organisation is, and therefore admitting it's imperfect can be seen as a reflection on them.

Denial can be a pretty powerful mechanism and there is no guaranteed solution. However, if you believe that denial may be contributing to a stakeholder's behaviour, I suggest trying the following:

- **Understand their point of view** – ensure that it is actually denial and not a legitimate disagreement with the process, the data or the way the conversation is heading.
- **Find the sore point** – find out whether the objection is to all of the data or if there is a particular trigger that has touched an emotional nerve. Emphasise areas of agreement.
- **Explore their evidence** – take their perspective to the next level and offer to sit down with them and work through the facts.

Compare your organisation with others

When creating your organisation's Adaptive Profile, we examined how well your organisation navigated The Thrive Cycle. However, to evaluate whether your organisation's Adaptive Profile will *actually deliver* an advantage, we need to agree what the ideal Adaptive Profile will look like.

To do this, we need to identify some other organisations with which to compare (Figure 6-2).

FIGURE 6-2: To create a meaningful definition of adaptive advantage, compare your organisation with four types of potential rivals

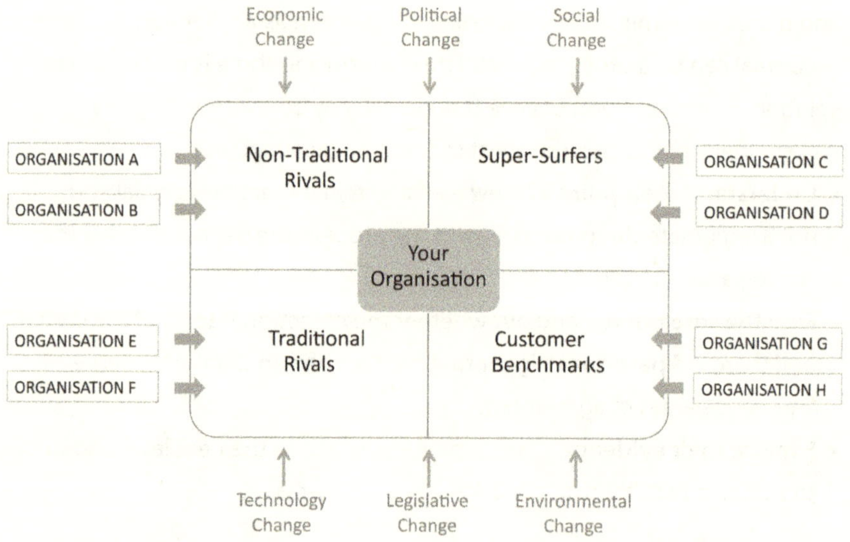

TRADITIONAL RIVALS AND NON-TRADITIONAL RIVALS

Traditional Rivals are those with whom you are competing when meeting the needs of your target customers. These contrast with the second group – the *Non-traditional Rivals.* Think of Non-traditional Rivals as the organisations or industries that could meet the same customer needs (or help overcome the same customer problems) as you do.

For example, let's say that your organisation sells pre-packaged dinners and it is in the business of 'making it easier for working parents to have healthy family meals together'. Traditional Rivals would be other businesses that also make pre-packaged dinners. Non-Traditional Rivals would be ones that 'make it easier for working parents to have healthy family meals together' some other way. These organisations might sell food or they might have services that save parents time in other areas e.g. washing up.

CUSTOMER BENCHMARKS AND SUPER-SURFERS

The third group are the *Customer Benchmarks.* These are the organisations with whom your customers interact but with whom you don't directly compete. They might fit into the same broad category as your organisation – e.g. consumer retail goods, entertainment, essential services and so on. These categories are based upon your customers' perceptions, and are used to create mental benchmarks against which your organisation will be compared.

The final group, the *Super-Surfers*, are organisations that provide an aspirational benchmark. If your organisation were to develop the ultimate 'surfer' adaptive profile, with which organisations would it share that status (regardless of their industry)?

How to create an Adaptive Leader-Board

THE ADAPTIVE LEADER-BOARD looks at your organisation's adaptive position relative to the four types of organisations you compared it with just now (Figure 6-3). As a result, it brings the environmental context into your discussions.

Take a moment to go back to the Adaptive Profile you created in Chapter 3. *Relative to the other organisations with which you'd compete, where does your organisation fit on the scale today? On what basis have you reached that conclusion?*

FIGURE 6-3 – The Adaptive Leader-Board places the adaptiveness of your organisation in context.

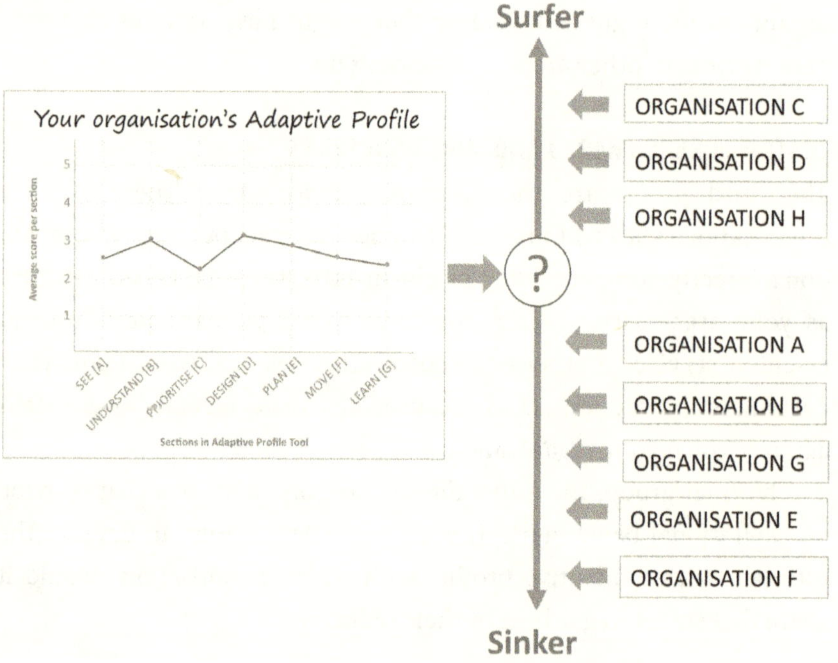

Complete a Landscape Volatility Assessment

We've developed a sense of where your organisation sits today, but what kind of Adaptive Profile should you be targeting for the future? To answer this question, we need to complete a Landscape Volatility Assessment. This is a useful way to crystallise and socialise information that is known across your organisation. It enables a constructive conversation about the way the world is and can be used to develop a shared perspective as to what might be coming your way.

So how volatile is your organisation's future environment?

This question requires your organisation to place itself in a number of potential future scenarios. However, unlike a traditional PESTLE[a] or SWOT[b] analysis (which frequently starts with the organisation's perspective), a *Landscape Volatility Assessment* starts with your customer's point of view and asks questions like:

- *How is the customer's world changing? How is this likely to impact the needs that we serve?*
- *How will these affect their expectations of the world? How will these affect their expectations of us?*
- *Which of these factors is likely to have the greatest impact on our ability to create value?*

---

a Environmental analysis that examines Political, Economic, Social, Technology, Legislative and Environmental factors.

b Analysis of Strengths, Weaknesses, Opportunities and Threats.

How to assess landscape volatility[c]

ONCE WE HAVE COLLECTED the facts, we need to start using them to create insights.

Now if I were an actuary, I might use a sophisticated risk-model to calculate the anticipated amount of future change, and the risks (upside and downside) associated with that. While that might be a useful input, there is no substitute for conversation when it comes to building a shared understanding. It's only through these conversations that your organisation can appreciate the potential triggers of relevant change (change-opportunities) and enable it to *see* them before everyone else.

So this next part is going to require some thought. However, the richness of conversation and insight it enables will make it worth the effort. It includes questions like:

- *How can you gain a sense of the magnitude-of-change that might be coming your organisation's way?*
- *Then, how can you use that to decide what action you need to take?*

The first question can be answered by using a simple framework. To support this, we need to crystallise the environmental information we have into a manageable form. I usually do this in the following way.

Have a look through the list of potential changes in Figure 6-4. Note: When you do this for real, you'll need to create a list that is relevant for your specific environment. For now, however, this one is sufficient for our purposes. Now, ask yourself:

- *How likely is it that each of these changes will affect our customers?*
- *Is that likely to significantly influence our customers' perceptions of the value our organisation creates for them?*
- *Over the next five years, what level of impact (positive or negative) would we expect these changes to have on our organisation?*

---

c This exercise provides useful background for The Vital Thread and the Change Radar that will be covered in later chapters.

You can rate each using a simple 1 to 5 scale, where 1 = very low and 5 = very high. Keep in mind that the purpose of this exercise is not to develop a detailed understanding of each type of change and accurately determine what kind of impact it will have. Instead, we are looking for big-picture insights. In the future, what kind of world will your organisation be operating within? How ready is it to do so?

Hint: If I were doing this in your organisation, I'd ask different groups to adopt alternative perspectives. For example, one group might adopt a customer perspective while another might consider the government's point of view. The more perspectives, the more rounded the conversation and the conclusions that will be reached.

INTERPRET YOUR LANDSCAPE VOLATILITY ASSESSMENT

A Landscape Volatility Assessment follows similar principles to those used in other types of risk-assessment. The bigger the number, the larger the amount of change expected to impact customers and the organisation. Figure 6-4 illustrates what this kind of assessment might look like for a car insurance company.

As the saying goes 'a picture tells a thousand words', which is why I tend to plot the numbers onto a simple *Change Volatility Map* (Figure 6-5). This snapshot indicates where the most significant changes might be coming from and encourages a customer perspective from the very beginning. It also gives an overall sense of the total amount of change on the horizon.

For the car insurer, the most significant change-drivers are expected to come from technology. In particular, the increased sophistication and adoption of autonomous vehicles (e.g. driverless cars, driverless freight transport).

So what might autonomous cars mean for its customers?

Well, fewer crashes for a start. When all cars are networked to each other, they will constantly know what each other is doing, with

FIGURE 6-4: Example of a Landscape Volatility Assessment for a car insurance company

IDENTIFIED POTENTIAL CHANGE DRIVERS	Likelihood	Level of impact	Combined
International stability	3	2	6
Climate change	2	3	6
West-East shift in economic power	4	3	12
The rise of emerging economies	4	3	12
Global population growth	4	2	8
Total Global Change			**44**
Individual empowerment	4	5	20
Co-creation	5	5	6
Social norms and values	3	3	9
Employee expectations	4	5	20
Communication trends	3	4	12
Total Social Change			**67**
Public policy	5	3	9
Political stability/security	3	3	9
Population dynamics (eg. Ageing, diversity)	3	3	9
Workforce dynamics	4	3	9
Public infrastructure (eg. Utilities, broadband access?)	4	2	6
Total Geo-Political Change			**42**
Data analytics	4	5	20
Mobile computing	4	5	20
Automation (cars, processes, robotics)	3	2	20
Customisation (3D printing?)	2	3	12
Domestic technification	3	4	6
Total Technology Change			**78**
Regulation	5	5	6
Supply and demand dynamics	2	2	4
Product innovation	4	3	20
Industry relevance	1	4	8
Competitive dynamics (new entrants? Consolidation?)	2	5	20
Total Industry change			**58**
Shareholder expectations	1	4	4
Growth trends (eg. Growth rates? Customer numbers?)	2	3	6
Customer expectations	4	4	16
Financial stability	2	3	6
Reputation (eg. Brand strength? Public trust?)	3	5	15
Total Growth Performance			**47**
Efficiency requirements	3	4	12
Talent requirements	3	5	15
Leadership requirements	5	5	25
Structural stability	2	3	6
Operational renewal (replacing legacy? Improvements?)	4	2	8
Total Operational effectiveness			**66**
TOTAL SCORE			**402**

FIGURE 6-5: Example – Change Volatility Map

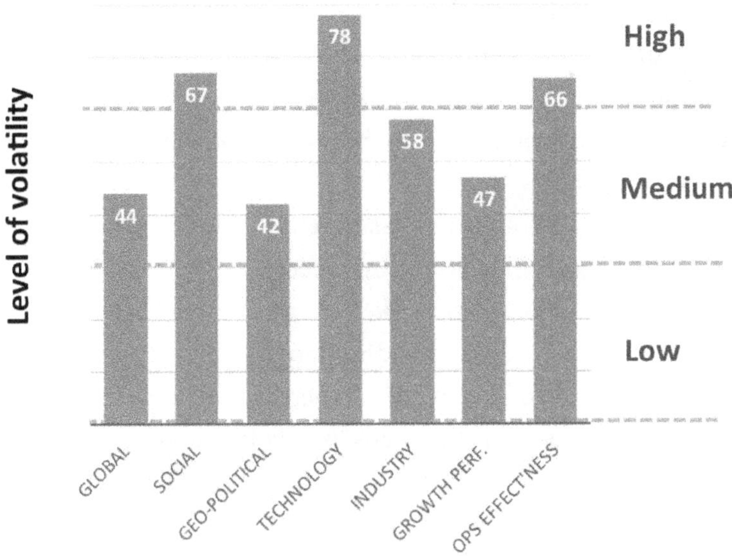

micro-second timing. Also, autonomous cars don't drink-and-drive, they don't speed to show off to their mates, and they don't get annoyed when another car cuts in front of them. These changes have the potential to open up possibilities for customers (e.g. greater peace-of-mind for parents) and close others down (e.g. reduced thrill of driving 'at speed').

While this is a very high-level example, you can see how the kinds of connections made during this kind of conversation have the potential to alter your organisation's perspective on change.

Define adaptive advantage for your organisation

This is where we start to bring everything together that we've discussed (Figure 6-6), including:

- **The Current Adaptive Profile** – how well your organisation navigates The Thrive Cycle today.
- **The Adaptive Leader Board** – how adaptive your organisation is when compared with others.
- **The Landscape Volatility Assessment** – how important the ability to adapt will be to future success.

The only reason for creating *The Adaptive Organisation* is to build a competitive advantage by providing more value for customers than your rivals . Given all of the above, we therefore need to decide what an 'adaptively advantaged' profile needs to look like in the future.

FIGURE 6-6: What adaptive advantage looks like for your organisation will be influenced by three core factors

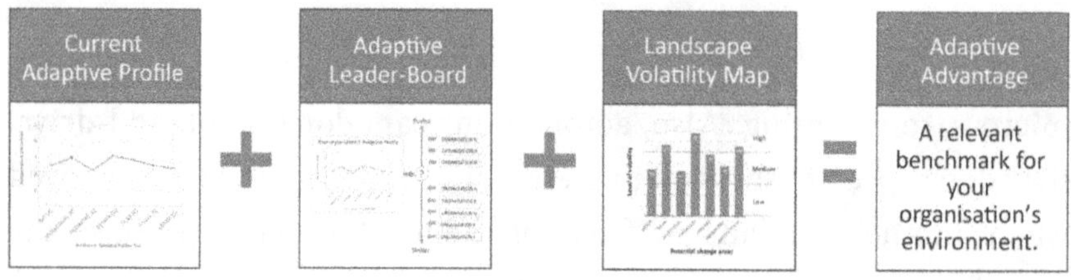

How to define adaptive advantage for your organisation

TAKE A BLANK ADAPTIVE PROFILE and segment it horizontally into three sections (Figure 6-7). Use the scoring scale on the left-hand side to decide where the graph should segment. For example, if you are predicting a volatile future, the segments might be skewed towards the top. Alternatively, they could be skewed towards the bottom if the future environment is expected to be fairly stable, with minimal change and a more predictable competitive landscape.

The top segment identifies the Adaptive Profile Range for an *adaptively advantaged* organisation (relative to the future-change world that you've just described).

The *middle segment* represents the Adaptive Profile Range for organisations that will continue to 'tick along'.

The *lower segment* identifies the Adaptive Profile Range for the organisations that are less likely to survive in the future environment.

FIGURE 6-7: Defining adaptive advantage for your organisation

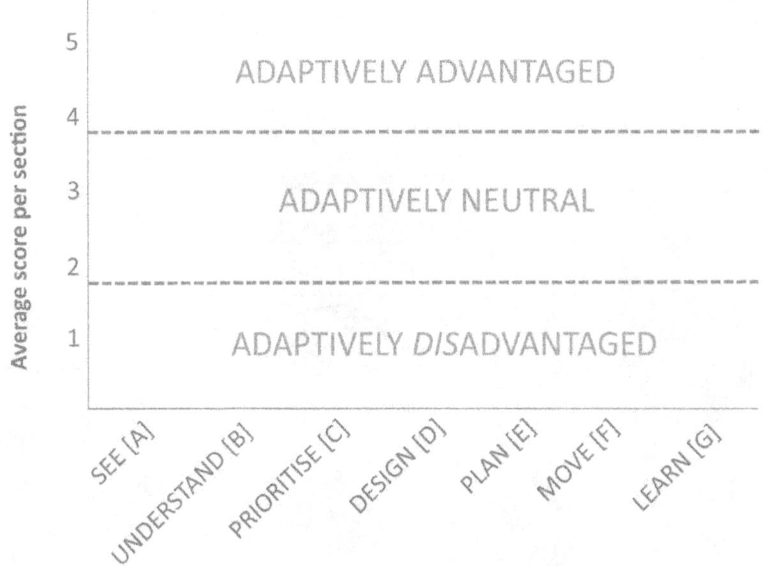

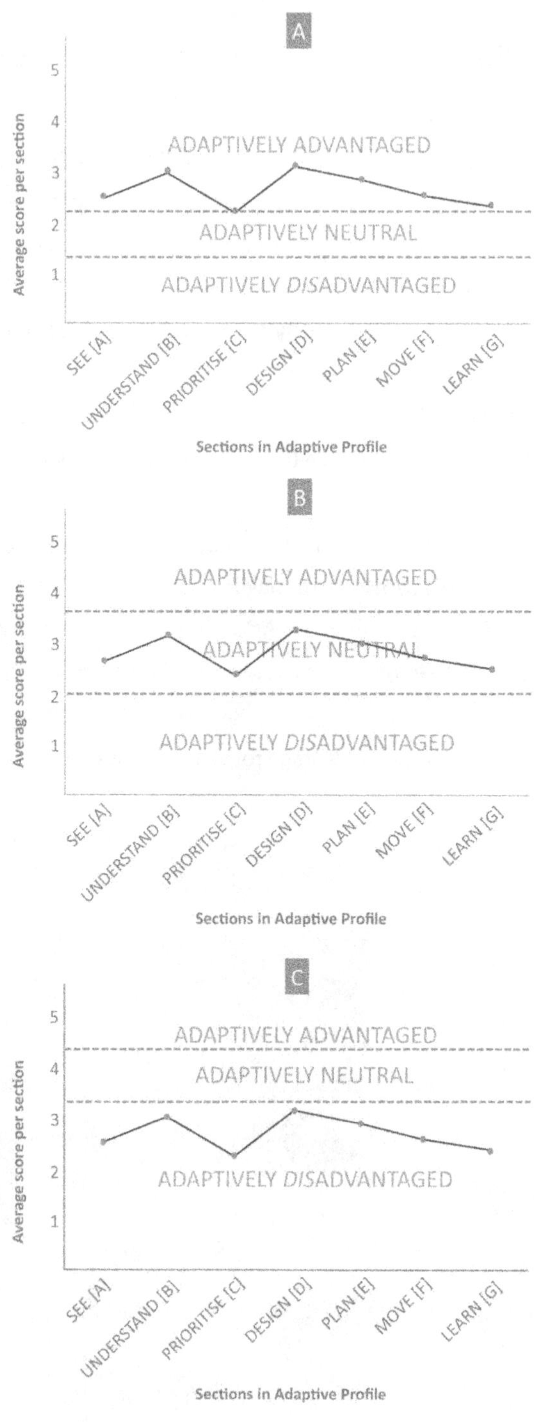
A
ADAPTIVELY ADVANTAGED
ADAPTIVELY NEUTRAL
ADAPTIVELY *DIS*ADVANTAGED
Average score per section
5
4
3
2
1
SEE [A]
UNDERSTAND [B]
PRIORITISE [C]
DESIGN [D]
PLAN [E]
MOVE [F]
LEARN [G]
Sections in Adaptive Profile
B
ADAPTIVELY ADVANTAGED
ADAPTIVELY NEUTRAL
ADAPTIVELY *DIS*ADVANTAGED
Average score per section
5
4
3
2
1
SEE [A]
UNDERSTAND [B]
PRIORITISE [C]
DESIGN [D]
PLAN [E]
MOVE [F]
LEARN [G]
Sections in Adaptive Profile
C
ADAPTIVELY ADVANTAGED
ADAPTIVELY NEUTRAL
ADAPTIVELY *DIS*ADVANTAGED
Average score per section
5
4
3
2
1
SEE [A]
UNDERSTAND [B]
PRIORITISE [C]
DESIGN [D]
PLAN [E]
MOVE [F]
LEARN [G]
Sections in Adaptive Profile

Now, overlay the Adaptive Profile you developed earlier for your own organisation. You can see in examples A, B and C, whether The Adaptive Profile from today will be sufficient to meet the challenges and opportunities of tomorrow, depends on your relative position. The same Profile is expected to be *adaptively advantaged* in one environment (A) but *adaptively neutral* in another (B). Profile (C) represents a highly volatile environment in which there is significant change and competitors are already quite adaptive. As a result the Profile is *adaptively disadvantaged.*

A friendly word of advice

When you do the above exercise within your own organisation, it may be tempting to do it in reverse order. That is, mark your organisation's position then create the three segments afterwards. I recommend against this as it unconsciously establishes your organisation as the benchmark, rather than setting a new one based upon the analysis that has been completed to date. One way to increase neutrality is to bring new people into the conversation (those who are unaware of the Adaptive Profile), give them the data from the environmental analysis, and ask them to set the segments.

SET YOUR TARGET ADAPTIVE PROFILE

Now we're ready to set the Target Adaptive Profile for your organisation. There is just one more part to complete with this step, and that is for your organisation to decide how strong its Thrive Cycle needs to be in future. This means answering questions like:

- *What Adaptive Profile should we aspire to achieve, if we are to thrive in our future environment?*
- *What are the implications of doing nothing?*
- *If we were more adaptive than we are today, what possibilities would this open up?*

This is the most critical conversation of all, and will only be successful if those who are making the decisions have the depth of understanding developed during earlier conversations. Remember, it's the 'lightbulb moments' people have along the way that drive true engagement, not the recommendations included in the Executive Summary.

Having thought the answers through, and agreed on the shared position, the *Target* Adaptive Profile can be set. As you can see in the example below, the Target Adaptive Profile was set at 4.5. This organisation, therefore, is aspiring to consistently achieve this average score, across each stage of The Thrive Cycle, for all change-opportunities it pursues.

It's worth noting that the Target Adaptive Profile for your organisation should be a relatively straight, horizontal line. Being great at *Seeing* but poor at *Moving* is not going to deliver an adaptive advantage. It's the position of the line (i.e. which of the three horizontal segments it sits in) that sets the ambition.

FIGURE 6-8: Setting your organisation's Target Adaptive Profile

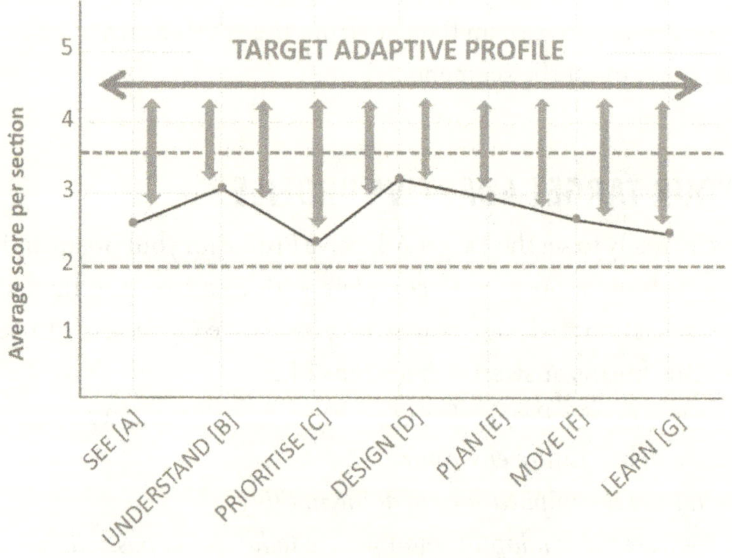

How high should you set the bar?

WHEN IT COMES TO GOAL SETTING, there are many schools of thought. Some argue that goals should be realistic and achievable. Others believe you should strive for extraordinarily high goals because it increases performance beyond that you'd have achieved had the goal been 'realistic'. I've seen both approaches result in good and poor performances.

When setting your Target Adaptive Profile (especially the first time), I'd offer the following advice. Set the target ensuring that it is:

- **high enough** to require the combined effort of the organisation to achieve it
- **low enough** for key stakeholders to buy into it
- **logical** and grounded in evidence not just opinion or assumptions

For instance, if your average Adaptive Profile score today is 2.3 across all seven of The Thrive Cycle capabilities, there is no point setting a target of 2.6. People often assume that this kind of incremental gain will happen naturally and so will not make the necessary commitment. To the second point, it's better to have Enduring Commitment to achieve a lower target (that can be revised) than flaky commitment to a higher one.

People sometimes ask me 'does the Target Adaptive Profile have to be in the Adaptively Advantaged segment?' It's a good question.

If your organisation has an average score of 1 and the Adaptively Advantaged segments starts at 4 then the goal may appear too far away to be achievable. I'd therefore suggest setting a long-term target of 4 and a lower, near-term target just to get the organisation moving.

BUILD COMMITMENT

At this point we have a Target Adaptive Profile for your organisation to strive for and hopefully there have been plenty of lightbulb moments during conversations along the way. However, to create the Enduring Commitment required for The Adaptive Organisation, there are a few more things to think about.

Agree what's been agreed

I've learnt the hard way that everyone nodding their heads at the end of a strategic workshop doesn't always mean everything's been agreed. That's why 'agreeing what's been agreed' is a vital step not to be missed. It's how you identify and clarify assumptions that could come back to bite you later on.

One way to do this is reflect on the type of organisation that has an Adaptive Profile like the target you've just described. Think about what kind of Thrive Cycle that organisation would have. When a change-opportunity entered The Thrive Cycle, what would happen to it?

Then, write this down in words, pictures, or both. Involve stakeholders in the process. This will give you a physical reminder to engage others, as well as ensuring absolute clarity regarding what you've set out to achieve. The output will be invaluable when you come to developing the *Thrive Cycle Blueprint* described in Chapter 11.

Commit to action

The great thing about creating an Enduring Commitment is that it empowers the organisation to set an adaptive standard that is right for its circumstances. Having set that standard, regardless of how high or how ambitious, the organisation – particularly its senior leaders – needs to want to 'make it so'.

As I said at the start, this first element is as much about engaging people (within the Core Organisation, the Adaptive Partners, Adaptive Influencers and your passionate coalition) as it is about 'setting a target'. If you've engaged well from the start, then gaining commitment becomes a lot easier.

However, this isn't the only aspect to be considered. I have yet to come across an organisation that has a completely empty change agenda just waiting for something like this to come along.

Building The Adaptive Organisation requires senior leaders to *be* committed, not just *say* they're committed. And I don't mean committed on a quarterly basis. Commitment needs to be agreed and built into the day-to-day fabric of your organisation.

To show you what I mean, think about *the top five priorities* of your business today and ask yourself:

- *Where does creating an adaptive advantage sit relative to those priorities?*

I would suggest that if it doesn't fall in the top three priorities of your organisation, then there is unlikely to be sufficient commitment to make it work. When you Commit to Action, these are the kinds of conversations to be had. Don't assume your organisation will just 'fit it in'. It won't.

If you've engaged effectively and people have agreed to a Target Adaptive Profile but it's still not making it into the top three priorities in your organisation, then I'd look for the *unhelpful habits of successful organisations* described in the next chapter. If they are particularly strong in your organisation, then that's a conversation that will need to be had before any sustained commitment can be achieved.

For now, however, let's assume your leadership colleagues are motivated and raring to deliver The Target Adaptive Profile and the advantage that it is promising.

Commit to a plan

At this stage, committing to a plan means committing to the desired outcome. Namely, achieving adaptive advantage as it has been defined *for* your organisation, *by* your organisation. The roadmap described in Chapter 12 will get you started.

Keep the timelines tight. The longer it takes to move into action mode the more likely personal commitment will wane. You don't want to have to go back to the beginning to build up enthusiasm.

It's easier to roll a boulder once it has built-up momentum. Getting it started, however, is where the real effort comes in. An organisation is like a massive boulder and as such, it can be hard to move if momentum is not established quickly.

USE A ONE-PAGE-WHY

So, here we are. We've made it to first base on the journey to The Adaptive Organisation. What's left now is to bring everyone else to the party. Of course, having engaged the right people along the way, this will be a lot easier than if you'd kept the process contained within the Executive Team.

I often use something I call *The One-Page-Why*. It is a very simple tool (one page, in fact) that captures the shared understanding and agreement that has been created over a period of time. It's also a bit like a hand-shake that connects the 'thinking' world with the 'doing' world.

When it comes to Enduring Commitment, a One-Page-Why can be used to synthesise what everyone has agreed, and to create a shared starting point for broader engagement. It is deliberately brief and is designed to be talked through, not read. This encourages leadership engagement and personal commitment to bringing the organisation on the journey rather than simply sending an 'FYI email'.

I've included an example of a One-Page-Why to give you an idea of what it looks like (Figure 6-9). Reading the columns from left to right provides a picture of how all of the conversations that have taken place, meaningfully come together. Keep in mind, its purpose is not just to inform people who have yet to be involved why your organisation is pursuing The Adaptive Organisation. It is also to serve as a constant day-to-day reminder for the people who were involved. When working

FIGURE 6-9: Example of the One-Page-Why

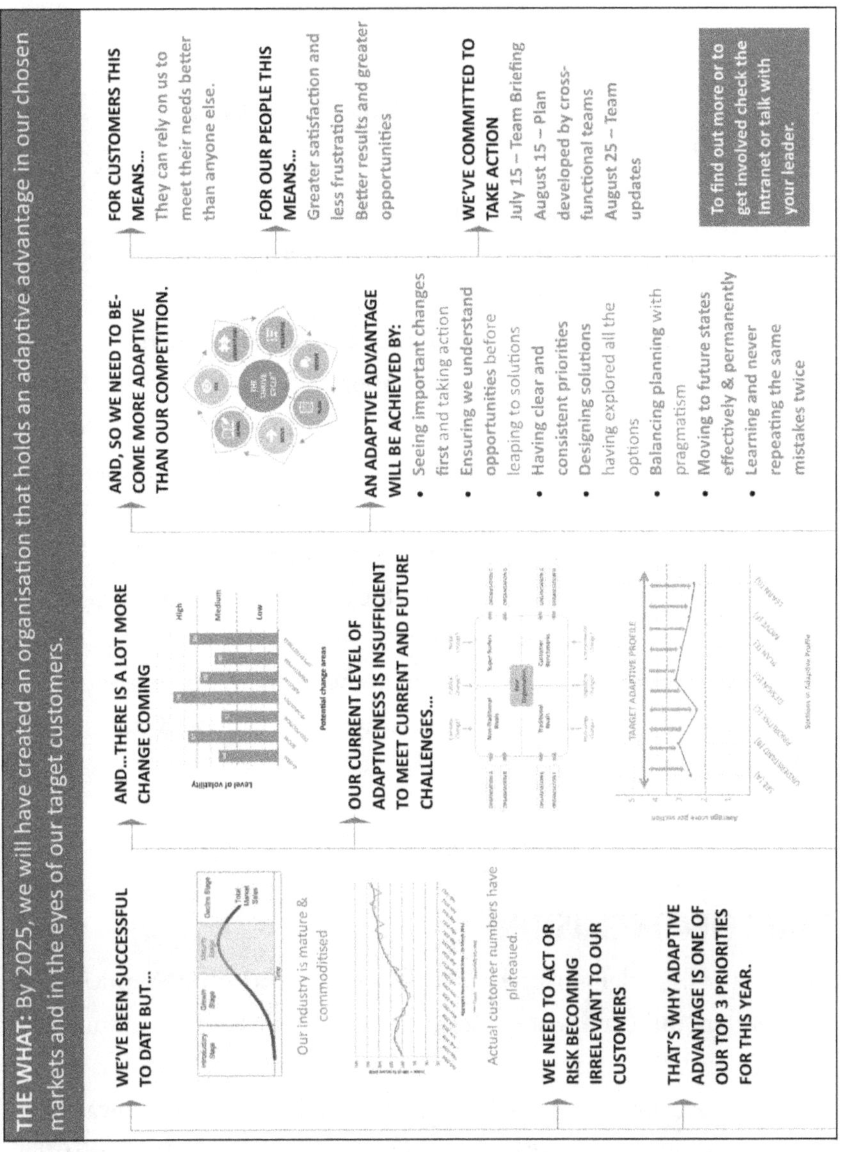
THE WHAT: By 2025, we will have created an organisation that holds an adaptive advantage in our chosen markets and in the eyes of our target customers.
WE'VE BEEN SUCCESSFUL TO DATE BUT...
Our industry is mature & commoditised
Actual customer numbers have plateaued.
WE NEED TO ACT OR RISK BECOMING IRRELEVANT TO OUR CUSTOMERS
THAT'S WHY ADAPTIVE ADVANTAGE IS ONE OF OUR TOP 3 PRIORITIES FOR THIS YEAR.
AND...THERE IS A LOT MORE CHANGE COMING
OUR CURRENT LEVEL OF ADAPTIVENESS IS INSUFFICIENT TO MEET CURRENT AND FUTURE CHALLENGES...
TARGET ADAPTIVE PROFILE
AND, SO WE NEED TO BECOME MORE ADAPTIVE THAN OUR COMPETITION.
AN ADAPTIVE ADVANTAGE WILL BE ACHIEVED BY:
• Seeing important changes first and taking action
• Ensuring we understand opportunities before leaping to solutions
• Having clear and consistent priorities
• Designing solutions having explored all the options
• Balancing planning with pragmatism
• Moving to future states effectively & permanently
• Learning and never repeating the same mistakes twice
FOR CUSTOMERS THIS MEANS...
They can rely on us to meet their needs better than anyone else.
FOR OUR PEOPLE THIS MEANS...
Greater satisfaction and less frustration
Better results and greater opportunities
WE'VE COMMITTED TO TAKE ACTION
July 15 – Team Briefing
August 15 – Plan developed by cross-functional teams
August 25 – Team updates
To find out more or to get involved check the intranet or talk with your leader.

on a potentially long-term change like this, such a consistent reminder is important (as 'the why' can easily be lost in 'the here and now').

Key features of a One-Page-Why

THE MOST SUCCESSFUL One-Page-Whys share the following criteria:

- **They fit on one page** (obviously!).
- **They accurately reflect what's been agreed** and everyone involved is literally 'on the same page'.
- **They reuse some of the imagery, photos or diagrams from the conversations that agreed the information.** There will be plenty of time to create a 'pretty version' later. For now you need leaders to be able to identify with the images and recall the conversations and conclusion that led to their decisions.
- **They can instantly be adapted to different time constraints.** For example, this One-Page-Why provides the basis for a 30-second, 30-minute or three-hour conversation.
- **They are an authentic representation of the truth.** This is not about selling the idea. This is about showing why what is proposed makes good common sense.

CHAPTER CONCLUSION

So that's the first Element of Adaptive Success – Enduring Commitment.

There are quite a few steps so the summary in Figure 6-10 provides an overview[d].

Once your organisation has commenced its journey towards its Target Adaptive Profile, this element's role is to ensure the motivation is maintained and that results are achieved, tracked and celebrated.

d A larger version of this image is available at www.thethrivecycle.com.

FIGURE 6-10: Process Summary for Creating Enduring Commitment

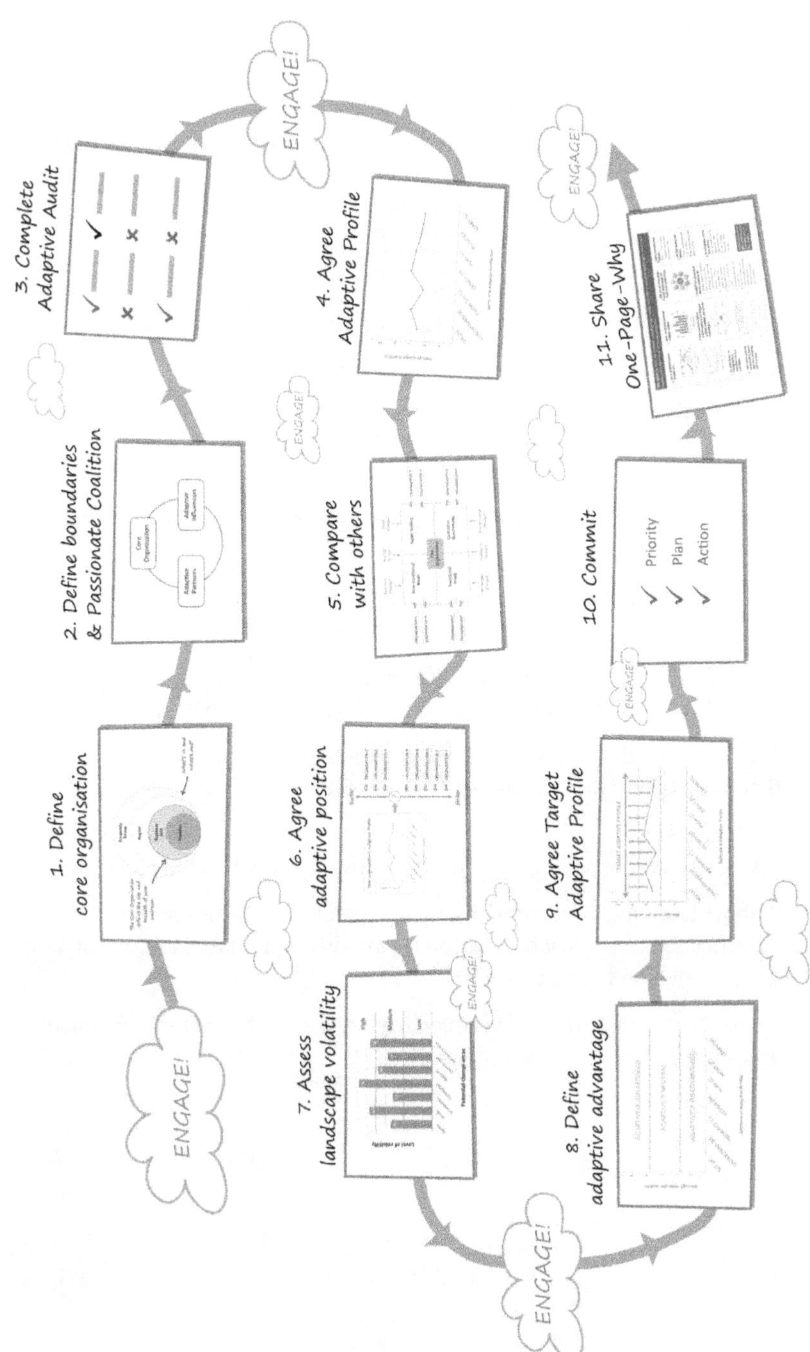

I'll talk more about how you can do this when we talk about the Sixth Element of Adaptive Success – A Balanced Ecosystem.

Remember that creating Enduring Commitment is about shifting the boulder. Therefore, don't feel disheartened if it doesn't move after the first 'shove'. We'll revisit this in Chapter 13 where we'll talk about what it takes to successfully drive this kind of change in an organisation.

KEY POINTS TO REMEMBER

- Building The Adaptive Organisation takes valuable time and energy. Your leaders therefore need to be able to see the opportunity and be emotionally committed to making it happen.
- There is no such thing as being 'half-adaptive'. Executive commitment is therefore crucial.
- The conversations that occur throughout the journey are as much about engagement as they are about setting targets.
- It always takes longer to 'get people on the same page'. However, time spent doing this in the beginning will pay off exponentially down the track.
- The key to creating Enduring Commitment is to set a Target Adaptive Profile that is relevant to the organisation and makes sense to its people.
- It is better to have a low Target Adaptive Profile than it is to not have a Target Adaptive Profile at all. The key is to get started and build from there.
- Without Enduring Commitment, an organisation is at risk of adopting a 'Splasher' approach, in which piecemeal interventions make the organisation less adaptive, and not more so.
- A One-Page-Why is a simple yet effective tool that both confirms agreement and engages the rest of the organisation.

7

The second element: Adaptive Principles

This chapter examines the fundamental mindset underpinning The Adaptive Organisation and describes the five principles an organisation needs to live by if it is to become adaptive. Along the way, we'll explore some of the unhelpful habits successful organisations can fall into and learn how following Adaptive Principles helps overcome them.

'Your beliefs become your thoughts, your thoughts become your words, your words become your actions, your actions become your habits...'

—MAHATMA GHANDI

A BOY WAS TRAVELLING IN A CAR with his sister and grandparents. It was a crystal-clear day and the occupants noticed a small plane in the air, doing sky-writing. A few letters had already been created and the family started to guess what word was actually going to appear. However, even as more letters appeared, the message became no clearer. 'What a silly pilot – he doesn't know how to spell,' said Grandpa. Most of the other passengers in the car nodded in agreement. That must have been the problem. The boy, however, had a different theory. 'No Grandpa,' he said. 'Perhaps the pilot simply doesn't know how to fly.'

As leaders, the way we think plays a significant role in the way we understand and approach organisational opportunities and challenges. For example, in the story above, the approach taken would have depended upon whether the problem was seen to be 'a spelling issue', or 'the inability to fly'.

That's why the creation of, and unwavering commitment to, *Adaptive Principles* is critical to creating The Adaptive Organisation. There are five core principles.

PRINCIPLE #1
Put customer-value first

Peter Drucker once said 'The purpose of business is to create and keep a customer'[18].

Customers are interested in your organisation when they believe it can help them to complete certain *jobs* in their lives (e.g. keeping the family healthy, maintaining friendships, or keeping their own customers happy). However, every job brings with it frustrations and opportunities for improvement, and these in turn drive customer needs.

Take the example of maintaining friendships. A customer might be frustrated by the fact that their busy lifestyle makes it difficult to maintain contact with their friends. There may also be an opportunity to increase their satisfaction by improving the quality of each interaction (e.g. enabling customers to talk with friends face-to-face rather than merely over the telephone).

Customers perceive your organisation offers them potential value when it addresses key needs that are *relevant* and *important* to them. When your organisation meets customers' needs better than anyone else – and does so at an acceptable price – customers buy its products. Further, when your organisation is able to deliver those products effectively, it drives profitability and growth and thus, it creates *Economic-Value*. This sequence describes the *Customer-Value Continuum* (Figure 7-1) and it is one of the fundamental assumptions behind any business.

So what does this have to do with The Adaptive Organisation? In short, everything. If the primary objective for an organisation is to create value for its customers, then that also needs to be the core driver behind organisational change.

The Adaptive Organisation ensures there is a customer-driven reason behind every change. It might be to enhance customer experience or protect existing customer-value from being eroded. Alternatively, the change could be about maintaining the organisation's ability to deliver customer-value or meeting new customer needs, helping with different customer *jobs* or creating value for new customer groups.

By committing to put customer-value first, The Adaptive Organisation ensures customers are the *first* consideration when a change-opportunity is being considered, and not an after-thought once the business-case has been approved and the 'train has left the station'.

FIGURE 7-1: The Customer-Value Continuum

Understand Customer Jobs
Meet Customer Needs
Deliver Customer Value
Create Economic Value
Understand customer frustrations and improvement opportunities.
Develop a proposition that addresses the most important needs.
Efficiently deliver that proposition better than anyone else, for an acceptable price...
The organisation will enjoy higher revenues, profitability and growth.

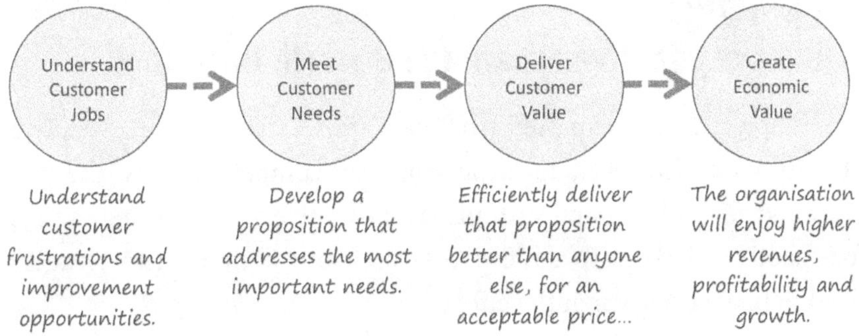

So why does this matter? Putting customer-value first is important because within established, complex organisations, if a change is not enhancing, better delivering, protecting or re-defining customer-value, the odds are, it's destroying it.

PRINCIPLE #2
Intimately understand where and how value is created

If customer-value is the primary motivation for embarking on change, The Adaptive Organisation must first understand how it creates value for customers today, and how doing so creates economic-value for the organisation and its stakeholders. Otherwise, how can it know what the effects of a change (positive or negative) will be, or the likely significance of them? Further, how can the organisation ensure the introduction of a change that creates value in one area of the business doesn't erode customer-value in another?

The Adaptive Organisation also distinguishes between its products and its ability to create value. It recognises that the products (and broader value-proposition) are only relevant to customers under specific circumstances. If those circumstances change, then the products may no longer create value. We'll explore this in Chapter 9 when we talk about The Vital Thread.

PRINCIPLE #3
Believe adaptive advantage is worth the effort

In Chapter 2 we explored the case for creating The Adaptive Organisation. However, regardless of how compelling it is, the fact remains that building and sustaining an adaptive organisation requires focus and hard work. To achieve this over a long period of time, leaders need to believe it's worth the effort.

When your organisation defines, then lives by this principle, it prevents it from succumbing to the following barriers that will otherwise stand firmly in its way.

The unhelpful habits of successful organisations

'Habits are not conscious decisions, instead they are routines. Once we start the routine, we go on autopilot...'

—CHARLES DUHIGG[19]

The key features and attributes of a living organism are determined by its genetic-code. While organisations can show many parallels with these natural phenomena, a hard-wired genetic-code is rarely one of them. This is particularly so in established organisations that have evolved over time, through a series of transformations, re-inventions and integrations.

Instead, it's up to the leaders to define the organisation's genetic-code then evolve it over time to achieve its full potential. This ability does not always come naturally, especially in an organisation that has been 'on the *growth* trail' for a while. After years of successfully managing the complexities of scale, fierce competition, commoditisation and performance expectations, organisations and their leaders can develop some unhelpful habits.

HABIT #1 – BECOMING LOCKED INTO VERTICAL THINKING

As organisations grow they need to create infrastructure to 'spread-the-load' of managing the work, while still maintaining control. Unfortunately, this process can also disrupt the Customer-Value Continuum (Figure 7-2).

Why is that? First, the connection *between* the elements can be lost. The elements are no longer stepping-stones along the same journey, and change moves from being a sequence of outcomes (where delivering customer-value drives economic-value) to being a collection of independent objectives.

FIGURE 7-2: Vertical thinking can disrupt the Customer-Value Continuum

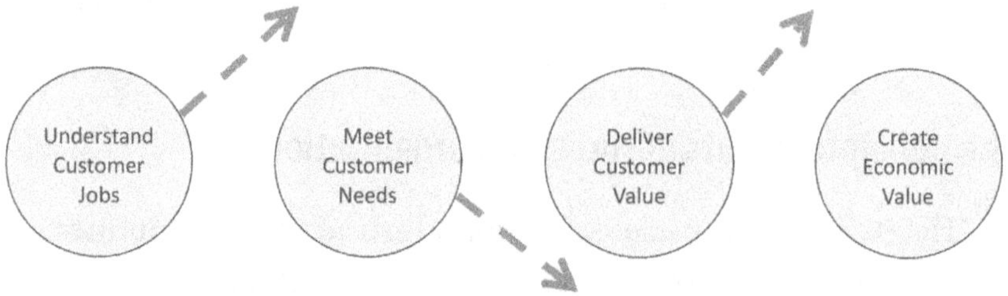

These independent objectives can inhibit organisations from creating an effective Thrive Cycle, because customer-value is no longer the driving force behind organisational change. Instead, when change is initiated, it is more likely to be driven by the individual pursuits of functional teams. This, in turn, causes priority decisions to become inconsistent. Instead of being about the collective creation of value, priorities become about politics and individuals' objectives.

One of the biggest challenges, of course, is that vertical thinking can successfully drive short-term growth and this can make it a hard habit to break. When McKinsey interviewed 1000 C-suite executives, 63 percent said that pressure for short-term performance had increased over the last five years even though 86 percent believed that focusing on the longer-term offered stronger financial returns and improved innovation[3].

HABIT #2 – TAKING THE SHORTCUT TO ECONOMIC-VALUE

Having economic-value as the primary driver for change causes irreparable misalignment across your change portfolio.

Working out ways to make money is easier than understanding the needs of customers and then adapting to those needs. Some organisations therefore choose to bypass the customer, and go straight to pursuing economic-value. As long as a change is going to make money, then it must be a *good* change.

Why is this a problem?

No change occurs in a vacuum. When you have tens, if not hundreds of change-opportunities working their way through The Thrive Cycle they need to all be moving in the same direction, otherwise they bump into each other. When organisations take the shortcut to economic-value (and put customer-value to one side) change starts pursuing not one, but many outcomes. Strategic initiatives scatter in many directions, causing changes to bump-into or run-over each other as each scrambles through The Thrive Cycle. As a consequence, huge amounts of effort are spent trying to align the changes 'retrospectively' (which, by the way, rarely works) instead of actually creating value.

If this happens in your organisation, the *whole* (i.e. the cumulative value created by your portfolio of change) can turn out to be *less than* the sum-of-the-parts (i.e. the combined individual values that each change promised).

HABIT #3 – PURSUING PSEUDO GROWTH

Sometimes when organisations reach maturity, they refuse to 'age gracefully' and accept they've reached the top of the growth curve. Instead of re-defining the way in which they create value for customers, these organisations convince themselves (and their shareholders) that short-term growth rates of the past can still be maintained, simply by doing more of what they've always done.

However, in a mature, commoditised market, pricing pressures and limited differentiation means that 'doing more of the same' tends to deliver lower, not higher, growth rates. However, shareholders still need to be satisfied[3]. The gap between actual and forecast results must somehow be closed. And so, these organisations start to pull the internal levers that contribute to the short-term profit-line. Examples include:

- cutting project budgets and impacting the quality of what's delivered
- relocating parts of the organisation to another country in order

to benefit from more favourable tax arrangements, but doing so at the expense of the customer experience
- down-sizing or relocating departments without removing or re-designing the work
- pushing through a company acquisition in order to reach annual growth targets, then worrying about integration as an afterthought.

This kind of organisational behaviour impacts almost every element of The Thrive Cycle. Change-opportunities fail to be prioritised unless they directly impact short-term growth performance. Pursuing pseudo growth leads to new ideas being rejected or being put on hold for fear of cannibalising the existing customer base. Kodak and their invention of the digital camera is a good example of this.

All of these factors weaken the foundation of the organisation. Tactical quick-fix solutions replace the real ones. Processes end up being more broken than when the change was started. If a significant change does come along, the organisation is far less likely to *See* it, *Understand* it or *Prioritise* it, and thus stands little chance of creating value from it.

HABIT #4 – SUBSCRIBING TO THE BELIEF 'IF IT AIN'T BROKE, WHY FIX IT?'

I mentioned earlier how the economic, opportunistic and human costs associated with adaptive failure are often invisible. There is no parallel-universe that shows what the consequences would have been had different choices been made or different actions taken. Therefore, organisations rarely have a clear picture of how much more quickly or effectively change-opportunities could have been responded to, because they have no basis for comparison.

Without concrete evidence to show 'what might have been', and the hard-numbers to back it up, building a case for adaptive-change, within a non-adaptive organisation, can pose a significant challenge.

HABIT #5 – WAITING FOR THE RIGHT TIME

In order to become adaptive, two factors need to align. First, the leaders of the organisation need to be enthusiastic about, and committed to, making the change happen. Second, the organisation needs to have sufficient stability and readiness to be able to effect the change (Figure 7-3).

Unfortunately, aligning these two factors is easier said than done.

Imagine that a high-cost, mission-critical change has failed. This type of event typically results in demands to understand 'how it happened' and 'how to ensure it doesn't happen again'. In this moment, senior leaders' enthusiasm for, and commitment to, becoming more adaptive are likely to be fairly high. However, because this enthusiasm is triggered by a crisis, the organisation is unlikely to have the capacity, management head-space or appetite to undertake the longer-term changes required.

As time passes, organisational memory of the failure often fades and with it, enthusiasm to do things differently. When an organisation is once again enjoying a period of stability, and the optimal conditions for effecting change, its leaders may be unmotivated to develop that capability because it is no longer critical.

Alternatively, that period of stability may never come and so attention becomes constantly drawn to what's urgent and important.

PRINCIPLE #4
Understand every change and treat it with respect

One of the exciting (and challenging) things about change is that it is multi-dimensional and so each opportunity is different to its predecessor.

Some changes are more predictable than others

Most parents expect one day their children will leave home and become independent. While it might be a first-time experience for

FIGURE 7-3: Organisational readiness and commitment to build adaptive capability are rarely aligned.

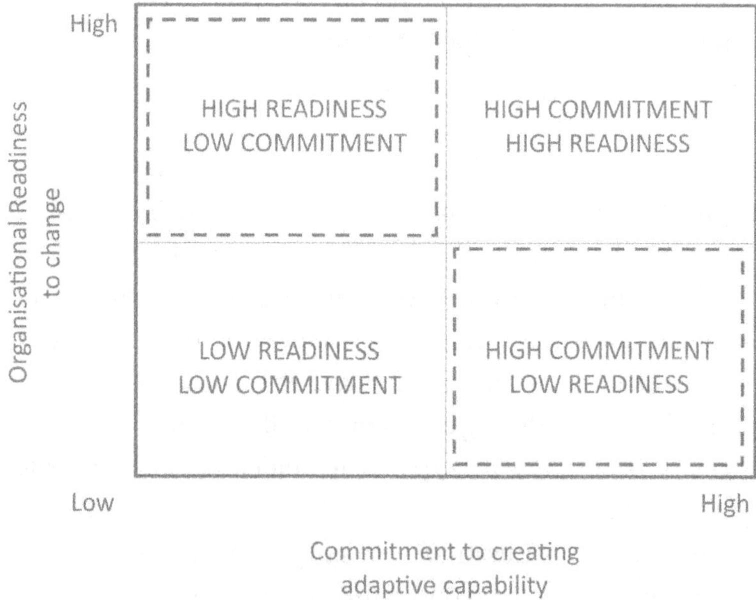

the individuals, it is a change that millions of others have experienced before. As such, we can broadly predict how the change is likely to play out when it does happen. Moving house is a bit the same. Once you've done it the first time, the second and third are much more predictable.

Contrast this with some of the macro-changes that are forecast to impact the world in the coming years. The emerging economies; the shift in economic power from the US to China; and the rise of the middle-classes. None of these have been experienced before, so when they come along, having plenty of warning doesn't always help with knowing what to do about them.

Some changes move faster than others

The speed of change or the time it takes to move from the original event (or events) that caused it, to having some noticeable effect, is another factor to be considered. This is independent of whether anyone noticed the event or not. For example, the changes that impacted Kodak weren't fast-moving changes. They happened over decades. However, to some of the people within Kodak, it's likely those changes appeared to 'come out of nowhere'.

Some changes follow different patterns to others

A change can build up to a huge crescendo over years (e.g. Y2K) or be a 'blip' that is relatively short and small (e.g. a marketing campaign). In other cases, the impacts can be significant at the start, but then rapidly reduce. Or the impacts can be significant and long term, such as an outsourcing firm losing its top three clients to a competitor.

Some changes are *sexier* than others

There's no other way to say it – some changes just aren't sexy. Unfortunately it's the boring ones that are often critical for your organisation, because they're usually the ones that enable it to stay in business. Other changes, involving creative ideas that break new ground or those that have a higher profile, will have everyone wanting to engage and be involved. Less sexy changes, like regulatory change or routine maintenance, can be seen as less interesting and even greeted with resentment. Ironically, the boring changes often require greater skill and more focus, yet in less adaptive organisations, they receive neither.

◆◆◆

For all of these reasons, The Adaptive Organisation seeks to understand change and the interplay between its various dimensions. It then uses this knowledge to define the required level of focus and capability to achieve success. The Adaptive Organisation also knows that the nature of a change is independent of its potential to create or erode value. For this reason, it maintains the same level of interest and commitment, regardless.

PRINCIPLE #5
Ensure the net-effect of change is positive

Pursuing change-opportunities comes at a cost. It requires money, resources and mental (and emotional) commitment – all of which could be channelled into other pursuits. And then there are the inevitable disruptions to the business and daily performance.

For these reasons, when The Adaptive Organisation pursues change-opportunities, it is constantly monitoring to see whether the net-effect of the change is likely to be positive. In other words, is the customer-value (and consequently, economic-value) worth the size and significance of investment that's involved in delivering it? The organisation does this on both an individual and collective basis, such that the overall value being created by all change across the business, is positive. Consequently, The Adaptive Organisation does not throw 'good money after bad' if it discovers it has made a mistake. It cuts its losses, is prepared to stop non-value-creating change initiatives and learns from the experience.

CHAPTER CONCLUSION

Any list of principles is easy to write. A flip-chart, some sticky-notes and *voila*, you can have a lovely list to put in your new employee induction packs. However, this will not create The Adaptive Organisation. To succeed, you, your organisation and its leaders need to believe in the principles and, more importantly, be willing to stand by them when other forces start to apply pressure.

KEY POINTS TO REMEMBER

- The mindset of an organisation and its leadership community is a key determinant of an organisation's adaptive success.
- The Adaptive Organisation lives by five Adaptive Principles and by doing so, overcomes many of the unhelpful habits that can develop during sustained periods of growth. These principles are:
  - Put customer-value first
  - Understand where and how value is created
  - Believe adaptive advantage is worth the effort
  - Understand every change and treat it with respect
  - Ensure the net-effect of change is positive
- When the customer is not at the heart of organisational change, it impacts alignment and places the organisation at risk of disruption.
- The Adaptive Organisation creates a distinction between the products and services it offers, and the way in which it creates value for customers.
- Just because a change is not sexy, doesn't mean it's not important.

8

The third element: Anchors of Certainty

This chapter introduces the three Anchors of Certainty, which ensure the Customer-Value Continuum remains intact and that change is initiated for the right reasons. They also empower your leaders, and their teams, to confidently 'move-as-one', in an uncertain and complex environment.

'Truly great companies understand the difference between what should never change, and what should be open for change, between what is genuinely sacred, and what is not.'

—JIM COLLINS[14]

LARGE ORGANISATIONS HAVE PLENTY OF FORCES that will pull them away from customers if they let them. To overcome these pressures (and their potential consequences on The Thrive Cycle), The Adaptive Organisation needs to have a way of ensuring that change is always driven by customer-value. The three Anchors of Certainty enable this to happen. They ensure change occurs for the right reasons, and that decisions (whether they are part of 'change' or part of BAU) are aligned with one another.

The Anchors of Certainty also play a vital role when navigating change through The Thrive Cycle. They give your people something they can rely on and that will remain constant. This builds confidence, enables decision-making and provides a safe reference point from which your people can explore the unknown.

ANCHOR #1
Create a Compelling Sense of Purpose

Purpose is a popular business topic these days. Ten years ago it was all about creating 'missions' and 'visions', but today these seem to have given way to the notion of 'purpose'. In one study, 91 percent of companies who had a strong sense of purpose were found to have a history of strong financial performance[17]. This contrasted with 66 percent for organisations that did not have a strong sense of purpose. When it comes to share price, purpose-driven, value-focused organisations also out-perform the others by a factor of twelve[36].

But why is a Compelling Sense of Purpose so important if we are to create The Adaptive Organisation (Figure 8-1)?

FIGURE 8-1: Anchor #1 – A Compelling Sense of Purpose

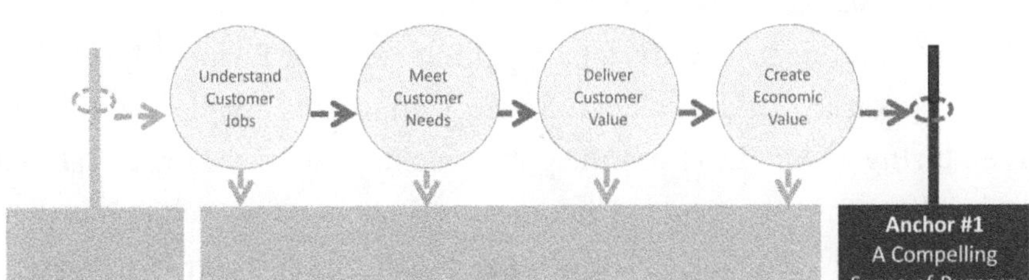

Purpose ensures that changes are pursued for the right reasons

Someone asked me the other day 'Why is Anchor #1 on the right hand-side of the Customer-Value Continuum? Shouldn't it start on the left?'

Purpose lives on the right-hand side of economic-value to create a more compelling end-game for the organisation than just 'making money'. This helps to avoid the 'unhelpful habit' described earlier in which organisations sometimes treat economic-value as the end-game and by-pass the customer to achieve it. A Compelling Sense of Purpose also helps the organisation to keep the needs of its shareholders in perspective and focused on long-term value creation, not just the arbitrary share price.

A Compelling Sense of Purpose also motivates the organisation to continue to look for different kinds of opportunities.

Unlike a goal or an objective, a purpose does not have an end date. It is enduring and so stimulates a constant desire to improve. This means The Adaptive Organisation is more likely to continue to look for opportunities and less likely to assume the status quo is 'as good as it gets'.

These strengthen The Thrive Cycle in terms of the organisation's ability to see change-opportunities and the desire to learn and improve.

Purpose makes each journey through the entirety of The Thrive Cycle easier

CREATING COLLABORATIVE ENERGY

During times of instability, a Compelling Sense of Purpose helps the organisation to build a collective energy among its people. Because it is enduring and comes from the gut, it explains 'why' the organisation is heading in a particular direction and shows how achieving the strategic goals of today will move the organisation towards a greater good. People are more willing to let go of their own, individual needs and work collaboratively towards a shared (and important) outcome.

Consider the following statements. While not all come under the explicit heading of purpose, they do describe the core reason the organisation exists.

- *'To make a contribution to the world by making tools for the mind that advance humankind.' – Apple (under Steve Jobs)*
- *'To refresh the world – in mind, body and spirit. To inspire moments of optimism – through our brands and actions. To create value and make a difference everywhere we engage.' – Coca Cola*
- *'Our goals are to provide high quality and innovative products to adult smokers, generate superior returns for shareholders, and reduce the harm caused by smoking while operating our business sustainably and with integrity.' – Phillip Morris*
- *'Wesfarmers' long standing objective is to deliver a satisfactory return to shareholders. Guided by this principle, the company has developed a unique, highly-focused and disciplined business culture.' – Wesfarmers*

As you look through these examples, or similar ones from your own organisation, do any statements engage you more than others? Assuming these organisations behaved consistently with their stated intent, for which ones would you be more willing to work through the night?

I rest my case.

BUILDING RESILIENCE, NOT RESISTANCE

Repeatedly navigating The Thrive Cycle requires an organisation and its people to be resilient. There are many unknowns at every stage, and the journey is frequently impacted by unexpected events that can knock everything off course. Purpose offers the essential stake-in-the-ground that leaders and team members can use to navigate the complexity of organisational change.

MOTIVATING PEOPLE TO TAKE RISKS

The uncertain nature of organisational change means people are often called upon to take a risk, and do something for which there is no guarantee of success. If people within the organisation are not prepared to do this, they hold back, waiting for others. This can impact speed as well as engagement. This can lead to a preference for 'sticky-tape' (superficial) solutions that don't address the real opportunity or issue, but are safer and therefore require less personal risk.

A Compelling Sense of Purpose can provide the motivation required to make taking risks an activity that's worth doing.

ENGENDERING LOYALTY AND TRUST

If an organisation's purpose resonates with its customers and people, and it is something it genuinely lives by, this will engender trust. Where there is trust and a sense of the organisation having good intentions, there is also forgiveness when things go wrong. This can be invaluable during times of change.

Conversely, behaving in a way that is contradictory to a stated purpose destroys trust – probably more so than never having created the purpose in the first place.

Consider Nike for a moment. It aims to 'Bring inspiration and innovation to every athlete* in the world (*if you have a body, you are an athlete)'.

If Nike were to introduce a new retail concept, which meant that people using a wheelchair were unable to gain access, this would be incongruous with their purpose. In addition to reducing the loyalty of this customer group, this action would also disengage its employees (who are passionate about this purpose). Alternatively, if the new retail outlets were purpose-built to ensure that people using a wheelchair had an equally fulfilling experience, it would make the change easier to implement. Not only would the customers be more satisfied, but the employees would be more willing to change the way things are done to fulfil the purpose. Likewise, if challenges came up as the organisation was transitioning from the old way to the new, its people would be more willing to work around it or find a better way.

The message here is – if you are going to weave a Compelling Sense of Purpose into your organisation, you'd better be willing to live by it.

How compelling is your organisation's purpose?

Think about your own organisation.

- *Does it have a Compelling Sense of Purpose? To what extent does it energise and motivate people?*
- *Does it provide energy and guidance to people during times of significant change?*

ANCHOR #2
A Customer-Driven Business Definition

Anchor #1 identifies a way to enable the organisation to think beyond the creation of economic-value, and make it a step-along-the-way to a more enduring purpose. It also helps to develop the energy, resilience and trust needed to transition organisational change through The Thrive Cycle. However, while A Compelling Sense of Purpose is necessary, it's not enough to create The Adaptive Organisation. What is also needed is a way to broaden the organisation's perspective and motivate it to look for opportunities that are different to those pursued in the past. To achieve this, the organisation needs Anchor #2 – A Customer-Driven Business Definition (Figure 8-2).

To illustrate why this is important, and how defining your organisation in this way makes it more adaptive, we need to come back to the fundamentals of business.

FIGURE 8-2: Anchor #2 A Customer-Driven Business Definition

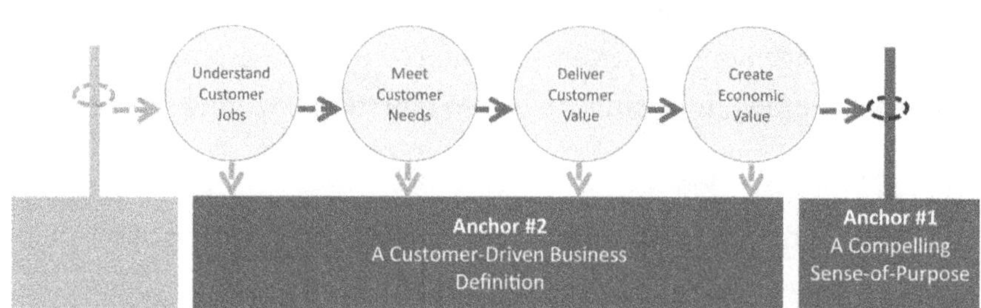

Where customer-value comes from

If all change must be driven by customer-value then in order to adapt to change effectively we must first understand what customer-value is and how it is created.

I like to do this by using a simple analogy. In our house, we have a tradition. Instead of shopping for all of our meats and vegetables at the large supermarket around the corner, we drive 12 kilometres to go to a huge farmer's market in the centre of town. The food is high quality, there's lots of variety and the prices are usually much cheaper than the supermarket. There's always lots of food to try, musicians, and great coffee.

However, the market does have some drawbacks. It's crowded at times, with both locals and tourists, which can make it a bit hard to navigate, especially with young kids. You have to walk a fair distance from the low-cost parking spots, and the aisles of the open-air vegetable section can be bitterly cold in winter.

So, why do we go to the market and not around the corner to the much closer and warmer local supermarket?

We talked earlier about customer jobs. For parents, *ensuring that the family eats well and stays healthy* is one of those customer *jobs* discussed in the previous chapter. However, while this explains why we buy food, it doesn't explain why we choose to go to the market instead of the closer, local supermarket.

I dislike any kind of shopping, but have a particular loathing for food shopping. It's boring and repetitive. So, given the food shopping has to be done, I would much prefer to enjoy the music and ambience of the market than the sterile environment of a supermarket. Also, when the kids were young the market offered a great trip out with lots of different things to see and free stuff to eat. The stall owners would make a fuss of the kids, and I could have a coffee and enjoy being out of the house. For this reason, there is an element of nostalgia associated with my visits, and the fact the food is cheaper is a bonus for me.

There is something else about the local supermarket that influences my decision. In recent times, the supermarket chain has replaced many of the familiar brands I liked with their own cheaper brand. So much so, that in many product-lines there are now only two brands on offer – the supermarket's own-brand and one other. I dislike having choice taken away from me and so I will often go somewhere else as a matter of principle.

For all these reasons, and because these factors are important to me, there is a greater *perceived value* in going to the farmer's market rather than the supermarket. It turns a frustrating, boring job into a positive, enjoyable time with the family. If these factors weren't as important, then the perceived value might drop and I might choose not to make the trip.

Now, when it comes to my husband, his motivations for choosing the market are very different.

My other half is an incessant bargain hunter. It doesn't matter what he is trying to buy or whether it is online or in a shop, he will always be driven by economic-value. He wants the highest quality for the lowest price.

That's my husband's primary reason for going to the market. And, when he goes on his own, a shopping visit rarely takes longer than half an hour because he knows exactly which stalls provide the best deals. He wants to get in and get out as quickly as possible.

My husband does not share my disgruntlement with the local supermarket's preference for own-brands. If the supermarket has something on special that is good quality, then he will still shop there.

So, why am I telling you all of this?

Even though my husband and I are both trying to get the same *job* done, and both prefer the market, the factors driving the *perceived value* (i.e. our underlying needs) are different. That's because we represent two different customer groups – the Experiential Shopper and the Economic Shopper. If we rank the factors that drive value for each of us (by giving them a rating from 1 to 5), then map how the supermarket and farmer's market measure-up against these preferences, it explains why we choose the latter.

For Experiential Shoppers like me, the market meets or exceeds my expectations on most of the factors that are important to me (Figure 8-3). I am not looking for the greatest bargain, so while this aspect creates value for other segments, it is not something the Experiential Shopper attributes high value to. In this way, the prices could go up and I would still see that the market offered high perceived value.

For the Economic Shopper however, this is not the case (Figure 8-4).

The market already performs lower than expectations from an access and an efficiency point of view. If the prices or quality were to reduce, this segment would most likely take their business elsewhere. Further investment to enhance the atmosphere of the market, or increase the range of products, would be wasted as far as this customer group is concerned. It wouldn't make them more likely to buy and, in fact, may cause them to leave due to the increased tourist crowds blocking the aisles.

So let's consider the different ways in which the farmer's market could define its business, and how each would affect its Thrive Cycle.

FIGURE 8-3: The Experiential Shopper – Value Map

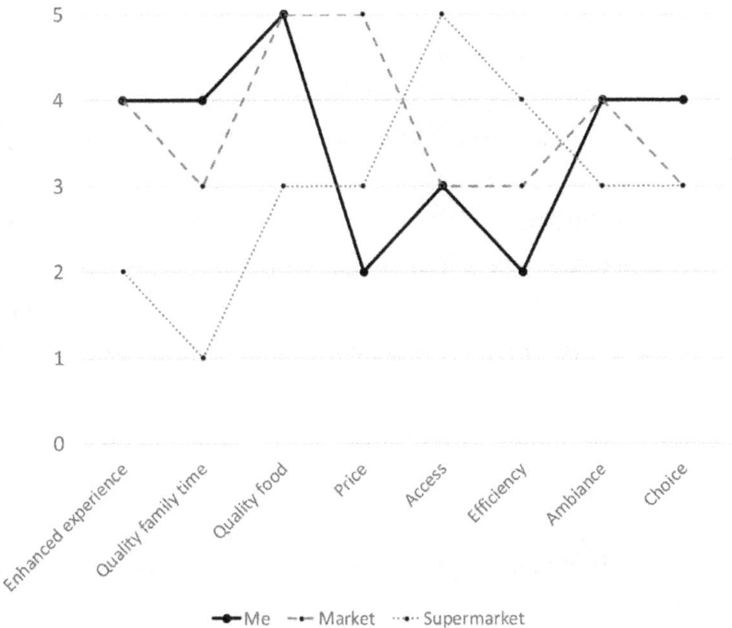

FIGURE 8-4: The Economic Shopper – Value Map

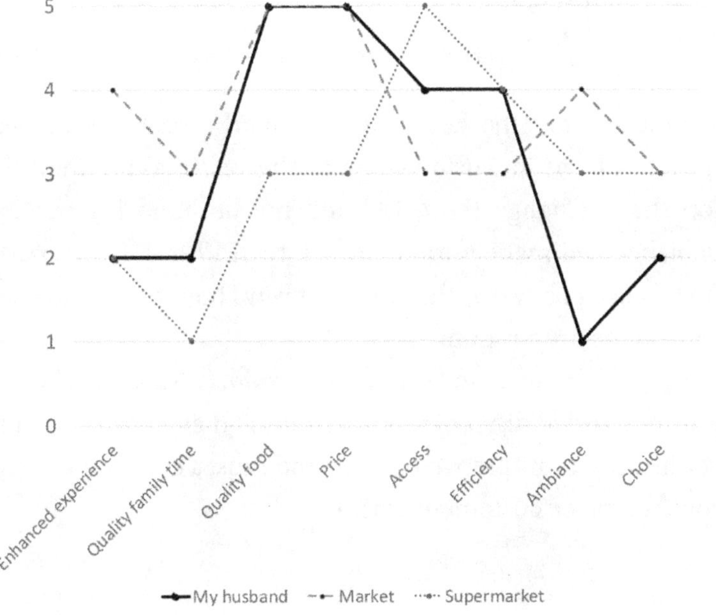

Defining the business by product or industry weakens The Thrive Cycle

Imagine that the farmer's market defined itself in the following way.

> *We are in the business of 'supplying fresh food to retail and commercial customers'. Our purpose is to 'be the biggest supplier of the freshest food in the country'.*

Defining its business in these terms would affect the way in which the market behaved, where it looked for change-opportunities and the mindset applied to its business model. It would probably see itself as competing with other fresh-food suppliers, and when doing customer research, would ask customers what kinds of fresh food they liked. It would also be more likely to focus on 'selling' as much fresh food as possible (e.g. economic-value) rather than the drivers of customer-value.

When adapting to change, this approach would weaken The Thrive Cycle in a number of ways.

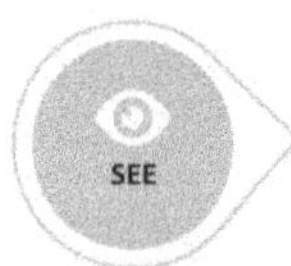

Failing to see changes in customer preferences

When products are the key focus, the market is likely to become disconnected from its customers, and the *real* reasons they choose to shop there. Change the price, and my husband leaves. Change the ambiance and make it too crowded, then I leave. If the market is focusing on *what* I buy (e.g. the food), not *why* I buy, it can unknowingly detract from its proposition.

Defining the business in terms of the product also leaves the market exposed to invisible disruption. It may miss an emerging social trend towards healthy, semi-prepared foods, and thus, a change-opportunity that could enhance customer-value.

Aligning with the industry, not the customer

When an organisation and its industry have been around for a while, they can develop an almost tribal quality. There is safety in numbers and so there are times when it can be beneficial to have others who are prepared to defend or promote shared interests. There is however, a down side. It can mean that when a change-opportunity arises, the first response is to defend the industry and investment in its business model. This mindset weakens the organisation's Thrive Cycle by limiting its ability to understand the change, and inhibiting the breadth of options it considers.

Unfortunately, these are all lessons that Kodak, Blockbuster and Blackberry learnt the hard way (Figure 8-5).

So if defining the organisation by its products weakens The Thrive Cycle, what's the alternative?

The Adaptive Organisation defines its business by the customer needs it intends to meet.

Let's consider a different way for the farmer's market to define its business. This time imagine it adopted the following approach and said:

> *'Our purpose is to ignite the taste-buds and imaginations of every visitor by making every family meal a pleasure, and creating unique culinary experiences.'*

Can you see how the second way of defining the business starts to open up possibilities in terms of how the organisation could create value for its target customers? This approach strengthens The Thrive Cycle in a number of ways.

FIGURE 8-5: Defining the business by the products prevents change-opportunities from being seen, or at least seen as being 'relevant' to the organisation

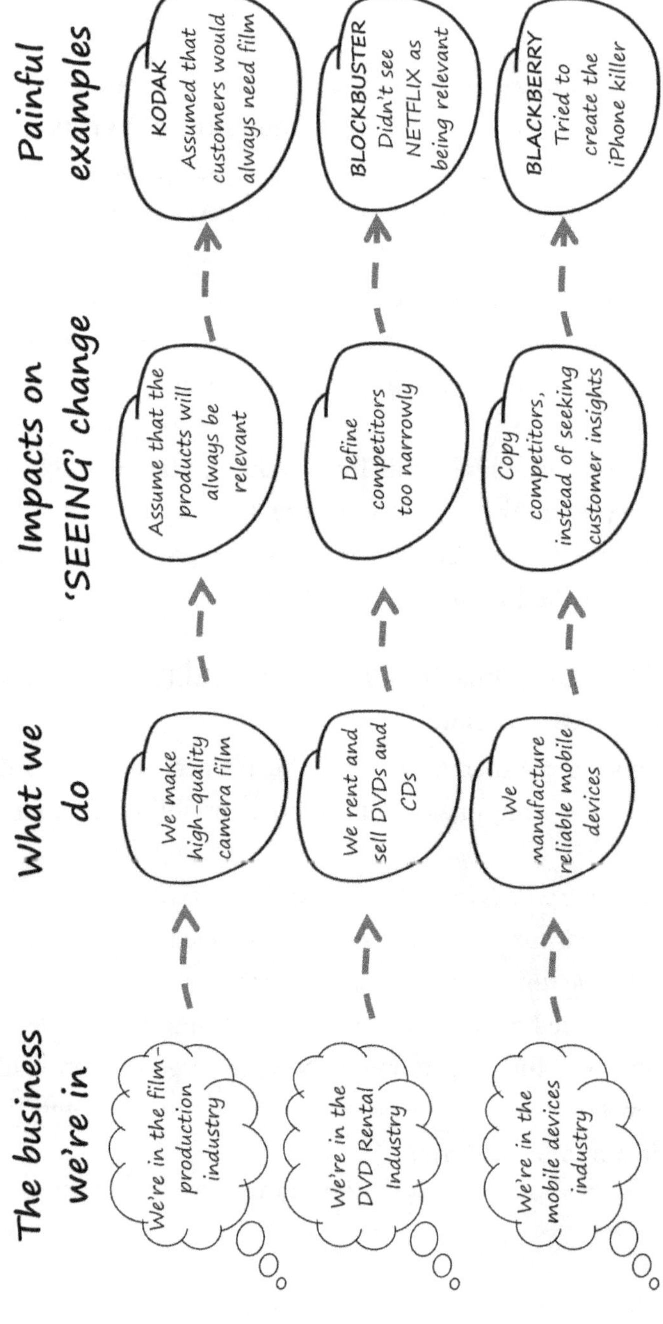
The business we're in
What we do
Impacts on 'SEEING' change
Painful examples
We're in the film-production industry
We make high-quality camera film
Assume that the products will always be relevant
KODAK Assumed that customers would always need film
We're in the DVD Rental Industry
We rent and sell DVDs and CDs
Define competitors too narrowly
BLOCKBUSTER Didn't see NETFLIX as being relevant
We're in the mobile devices industry
We manufacture reliable mobile devices
Copy competitors, instead of seeking customer insights
BLACKBERRY Tried to create the iPhone killer

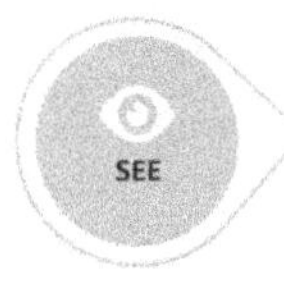

Recognising the signs of disruptive change

Defining the business according to customer needs opens up the market's thinking to future competitors. Because the market is in the business of 'making every family meal a pleasure and creating unique, culinary experiences', then its competitor is anyone who addresses, or has the potential to address frustrations, or to enhance satisfaction in any one of the jobs involved in that customer journey.

Sometimes when I say this in workshops, participants might question why the definition of competitors is so broad. Given the current business definition, a competitor could be a restaurant, a take-away food shop, a dishwasher manufacturer or a provider of an online cooking mobile app.

It's so much easier to just look at the industry and monitor the behaviour of competitors that look pretty much like your organisation. Same functions, same products and so on. However, in the world of exponential change, it is more likely that opportunities and threats will come from outside the industry. Thus, if you are only looking 'inside', the chances are, you won't *See* it coming.

Increasing focus by clarifying boundaries

Being clear about which customer needs the organisation does and does not aim to address helps with prioritisation. By defining itself by *the jobs* it wishes to help customers to complete, the organisation is also saying which jobs *it is not* setting out to help them with. From the market's perspective, it provides the first filter for any change-opportunity because it enables its leaders to ask:

Given the business that we are in, how relevant is this opportunity?

- *Does it offer customers a different way of igniting their taste-buds and imaginations? Or making meals more pleasurable? Or creating unique culinary experiences?*
- *If it does, perhaps it is an opportunity or a threat to be considered?*
- *If it doesn't, is this something we should be doing?*

Further, not only does defining the business according to customer-value enable executives to ask these questions, it also enables anyone within the business to ask it of themselves. This empowers people to make informed and aligned decisions without having to constantly seek clarification.

Recognising that today's business-model may need to change

Selling a given product suite might be the way the organisation goes about creating value today, however, The Adaptive Organisation recognises that the two may not always go hand-in-hand. This enables it to be more creative when finding new ways to create customer-value and when a change does come along, it creates many more options from which to choose.

How does your organisation define its business?

So let's apply the example from the farmer's market to your organisation[a].

- *Who are your customers? Do you define them by why they buy from you, or how or what they buy from you?*
- *Thinking about the jobs that you do, what business would you say that you are in? Given this, who are you really competing with?*

a When I do this exercise, I find that the Business Model Canvas developed by Alexander Oesterwalder and Yves Pigneur provides an excellent framework[44]. The Strategy Canvas proposed by W. Chan Kim and Renee Mauborgne in *Blue Ocean Strategy*[13] also offers a useful way of visualising how *value* is created.

- *How aligned are your priority decisions with your purpose and the business you are in?*
- *How is this potentially impacting your organisation today?*

Sometimes when I ask these questions of leaders in large or established organisations, they can be met by perplexed expressions. Years of pursuing growth can mean that the target customer becomes 'everyone' and the sense that value is created by 'offering the right products'.

First of all, accept that there are no shortcuts and recognise that answering these questions is critical to your organisation *being adaptive*. Engaging external consultants and expecting *them* to answer these questions for you will cost a lot of money and take you no closer to the answers. This is not to say that professional service firms can't add value by creating structure, expertise and offering external challenge. However, only your leaders can provide the answers.

ANCHOR #3 Value-Creating Values

Jack Welch, former CEO of GE, once said of mission and values, 'So much hot air about something so real'[53]. He couldn't have been more accurate.

A bit like purpose, the concept of *values* is something that comes up again and again in leadership books. They are particularly important within a change-dominated environment because they provide a rock-solid anchor which helps your leaders and people navigate ambiguity and uncertainty.

Why values can be hard to live up to

No matter how much we talk about them, the values of some organisations *still* aren't worth the glossy brochure they are written in. To be fair, when these organisations created their values I'm sure they intended to follow them. Unfortunately, in many cases the values are either insufficiently defined, or too easily weakened by other decision-making drivers, to do their job properly.

So why does this happen? In many instances, it's because the *creation of value*, and the *organisational values* are seen as serving two separate agendas.

The first is seen as describing 'how to grow the business', and the second defines 'how to play nicely with each other'. As long as there is no conflict between them, these two types can coexist. However, if doing one potentially inhibits the other, then growing the business can tend to win the argument.

In this way, the values become 'conditional' and as such, lose their meaning and unifying potential.

In the 1990s, Jack Welch said to a gathering of 500 employees, 'Look around you... there are five fewer officers here than there were last year. One was removed for the numbers, and four were removed because they didn't practice our values'[52].

Now that's what I call 'unconditional' values.

But how can organisational leaders have this commitment to their values, and still deliver successful performance? The answer is to make organisational values and the 'creation of value' one and the same thing.

Make values and value-creation part of the same conversation

When defined and applied effectively within an organisation, values ensure that the Customer-Value Continuum remains in its appropriate sequence, with the appropriate causes and effects. When this happens, there can be no conflict between 'growth' and 'living the corporate values' because they explicitly serve the same goals. Great performance, in this context, becomes *dependent* on living the values, not contrary to them. That's why your organisation needs Value-Creating Values (Figure 8-6).

FIGURE 8-6: Anchor #3 – Value-Creating Values

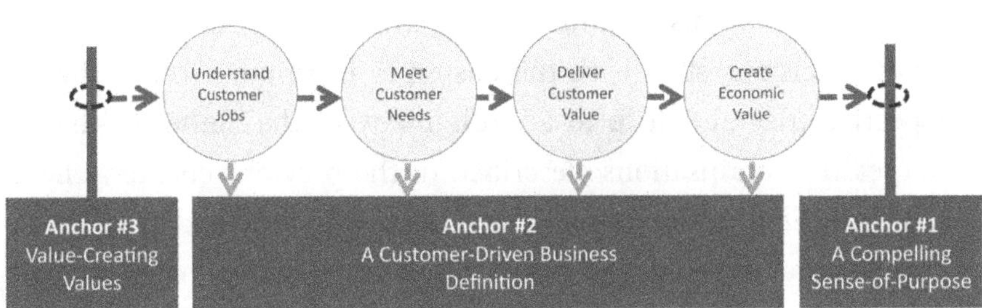

What are Value-Creating Values?

Value-Creating Values describe the behaviours and mindset a given organisation needs to have if it is to:

- perform successfully in its *defined business*, and
- fulfil its *purpose*, and
- create value for customers and the organisation.

In this way, Value-Creating Values meet the following six criteria. They:

- describe how the organisation and its employees approach value creation
- put customer-needs and customer-value creation first
- are unambiguous and enable everyone to understand what they mean
- are instructional/useful and as such guide decision-making
- are consistently demonstrated and expected by everyone in the organisation
- are reinforced though appropriate consequences.

Value-Creating Values remain consistent as long as the organisation remains in the same defined business, pursuing the same purpose. Thus, like the other two Anchors of Certainty, they make no reference to products or operational processes.

How Value-Creating Values strengthen The Thrive Cycle

The Adaptive Organisation uses Value-Creating Values to ensure key business decisions start with the customer in mind. From a change perspective they also help to address many of the 'unhelpful habits of successful organisations' described in the previous chapter. Like a Compelling Sense of Purpose, Value-Creating Values tend to make the overall journey through the Thrive Cycle, easier. They help to create energy, shared commitment and resilience. They also strengthen a number of its stages.

Removing the conflict between organisational values and making money

Value-Creating Values provide a shared starting point from which to make priority decisions. This gives a consistency that is rarely there when organisational value and creating value conflict with each other.

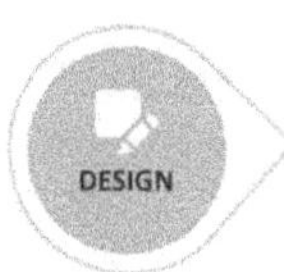

Having a pre-set filter to remove value-eroding solutions

When everyone in the organisation knows what the values are and knows that they are taken seriously, they become a useful tool. When considering a change-opportunity and developing options to address it, Value-Creating Values can act as a check-list to ensure that what is being proposed does actually create value for customers and the organisation.

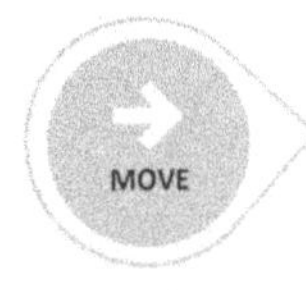

Building employee engagement when you need it most

Values are something the people within an organisation often hold dear. It can be a core reason they joined the organisation and why they stay. Therefore, when decisions are consistent with the organisation's stated values, your people are more likely to feel engaged. This is exactly what you need when you are moving the organisation to a new, future state.

When there is misalignment, people can experience a real sense of discomfort, which decreases rather than increases engagement.

Do your organisational values create value?

AS WITH MOST ASPECTS of The Adaptive Organisation, simply copying someone else's values (because they sound good) will not deliver the desired outcome.

Value-Creating Values reflect not only what an organisation is trying to achieve, but its overall 'outlook on life'. Your organisation needs to create the set of values that aligns with its purpose and chosen business. These values can also bring clarity to some of the more controversial topics, like:

- What will the relationship be between long and short-term decisions?
- What is the organisation's approach to creating shareholder value?

Start by reflecting on your organisation's values and compare them against the six criteria from the previous page. Ask yourself:

- *To what extent do our values, create value?*
- *Do they describe the behaviours that create value or do they adopt a more generic approach of 'how we do things around here'?*
- *Do our values make decisions easier or harder?*

EMBEDDING THE ANCHORS OF CERTAINTY – AN EXAMPLE

With this second Element of Adaptive Success, the key is to define Anchors of Certainty that work within the context of your organisation. That said, sometimes it can help to have an example to get you started.

Procter & Gamble (P&G) is a disciplined organisation, and its approach to the Anchors of Certainty reflects this. It is very specific in terms of its purpose (Figure 8-7), the business it is in, and the values and principles that underpin its behaviours. The company's purpose encapsulates not only how it creates value for customers but also how this leads on to broader creation of economic-value.

The values and principles that support Procter & Gamble's purpose are very detailed. This once again reflects the disciplined style of the organisation[b].

They are too numerous to repeat in full here, but as you can see in Figure 8-8, the values and principles make it clear what is expected when pursuing the purpose, and what is 'valued'.

So, how did Procter & Gamble fare in this context when they were facing difficulties finding a profitable market for an innovative new water purification powder[43]? There was pressure to stop the unprofitable initiative because it was damaging growth objectives. However, instead of stopping it, the company created a partnership with government and other non-profit organisations and kept the initiative going, while addressing profitability issues.

The true test of an organisation's values lies in what its employees say about it. Glassdoor.com is a website where employees can rate their organisation on a number of factors, including its culture and values. Of the 2,600 online reviews, Procter & Gamble scores an average 4 out of 5 for its culture and values. 82 percent of reviewees would

---

b Source: Procter & Gamble website – June 2015

FIGURE 8-7: Procter & Gamble's purpose

FIGURE 8-8: Example of Procter & Gamble's Values and Principles

Values	Principles
• PASSION FOR WINNING - We are determined to be the best at doing what matters most	• INNOVATION IS THE CORNERSTONE OF OUR SUCCESS - We place great value on big, new consumer innovations
• LEADERSHIP - We develop the capability to deliver our strategies and eliminate organizational barriers.	• WE SEEK TO BE THE BEST - We learn from both our successes and our failures.
• OWNERSHIP - We all act like owners, treating the Company's assets as our own and behaving with the Company's long-term success in mind.	• WE ARE EXTERNALLY FOCUSED - We develop close, mutually productive relationships with our customers and our suppliers.

recommend working at P&G to a friend. One employee, commenting on the website sums up her experience like this:

> **Pros:** Great Culture; Friendly people, Very people focused, Great Systems, Great Learning, One of the best.
>
> **Cons:** None really.
>
> **Advice to management:** Keep up the great work.

CHAPTER CONCLUSION

Concepts like customer-value, purpose and values are not new and have been part of everyday business language for years. Thinking of them as Anchors of Certainty gives them the required focus and context to create The Adaptive Organisation.

When the Anchors of Certainty are strong, your people have the critical reference points to guide them when the path is unclear. When the Anchors of Certainty are weak or inconsistent, your organisation becomes like a boat that has broken its moorings in a storm. Consequently, you can never be quite sure where it's going to end up.

KEY THINGS TO REMEMBER

- The three Anchors of Certainty ensure that organisational change is consistently customer-driven. They also provide the necessary guidance to enable empowered decision-making in an uncertain and complex environment.
- Anchor #1 – A Compelling Sense of Purpose extends the organisation's focus beyond economic-value and overcomes many of the unhelpful habits described in Chapter 7.
  A Compelling Sense of Purpose also creates the positive energy and resilience that people need to overcome the challenges and frustrations that accompany intense, organisational change.
- Anchor #2 – A Customer-Driven Business Definition enables the organisation to differentiate between the creation of value, and the machine that delivers that value (i.e. the operating model).
  When organisations define themselves in terms of their industry, they can focus on defending their operating model, when in reality, it is no longer relevant.
- Anchor #3 – Create Value-Creating Values. When an organisation's values conflict with the way in which the organisation creates value, they lose their potential power and become superfluous.
- Value-Creating Values are customer-driven, unambiguous and are reinforced by appropriate rewards and consequences.

9

The fourth element: The Vital Thread

This chapter describes one of the most powerful Elements of Adaptive Success. You'll be introduced to Orion Healthcare, a Surfer organisation, and see first-hand how The Vital Thread enables alignment across the hearts, minds and priorities of the organisation.

A FRIEND SHARED THE FOLLOWING STORY with me the other day, and I was struck by its relevance to this particular Element of Adaptive Success.

> *A stranger was travelling through town and came across three carpenters working on a construction. 'What are you doing?' the stranger asked the first man.*
>
> *'I'm hammering in nails,' said the man.*
>
> *When the stranger asked the second man, he said, 'I'm building a school.'*

> *And when the stranger asked the third man he said, 'I'm giving our children the education that they deserve so that they can have happy and prosperous lives.'*

The Vital Thread means that when responding to change-opportunities, the people in your organisation are consistently thinking about *giving children the education that they deserve*, not *hammering in nails.*

WHAT IS THE VITAL THREAD?

The Vital Thread is a 'tool' that helps organisations, their leaders and their people to remain aligned and continue to deliver maximum value, while moving change-opportunities through The Thrive Cycle. In technical terms, The Vital Thread is:

> *an* ***evolving*** *and* ***unambiguous*** *statement of how your organisation could* ***create maximum value*** *for its customers, compared with how it does it today.*

In more practical terms, it is a single piece of paper that answers three core questions about your customers, your organisation and its priorities (Figure 9-1).

What makes the Vital Thread so vital?

When I first created The Vital Thread, I thought it best to describe it using terms that were already quite familiar to a business audience. Words like strategy; innovation; business delivery; value-proposition and so on. However, this proved to be problematic.

Over time, these words have come to mean so many different things that they've lost some of the clarity they were meant to achieve.

As we explore The Vital Thread some aspects may be familiar to you. However, it is the way in which those aspects are brought together, and the way in which The Vital Thread is consistently understood, developed and applied, that enables The Adaptive Organisation to be created.

FIGURE 9-1: The Vital Thread answers three core questions

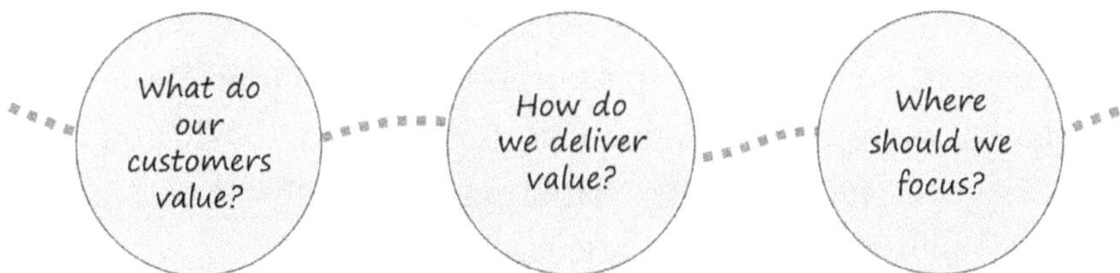
What do our customers value?
How do we deliver value?
Where should we focus?

- Who are our customers?
- What jobs do we help them complete?
- What problems do we help them to solve?
- How important are those problems?

- Why do our customers come to us?
- What do we promise them?
- How do we deliver that promise? What enables us to do so sustainably?
- How does reality compare with aspiration?

Given where we are today, where should we focus to ensure that:

- we take every opportunity to re-think value creation?
- we continue to enhance and protect customer value?
- we deliver more sustainably?

More specifically The Vital Thread:

- **reduces the impact of volatility** by providing a consistent way to understand 'patterns of change'. This understanding enables your organisation to distil the information that is relevant, from the plethora of data that bombards it every day.
- **makes uncertainty less threatening**, by helping your people to understand where they are going (even if the route and mode of transport keep changing).
- **enables your organisation to embrace complexity**, by understanding, then focusing on, the things that really matter.
- **reduces the potentially disruptive effects of ambiguity** because your organisation becomes less reliant on things being known and able to 'flex' while still moving as a single entity.

ORION HEALTHCARE – A WORKED EXAMPLE

The best way to illustrate The Vital Thread is via a worked example. The organisation created for this purpose is called Orion Healthcare. While the company itself is fictitious, the scenarios in which it finds itself are real, and have been based on research conducted across multiple industries and organisations.

Orion is an international healthcare company operating mainly in the South Pacific and South-East Asian regions. It is based in Singapore and operates in five countries, offering services in health provision, diagnostic services, dental care, primary care (e.g. general practitioners) and on-site occupational health.

Orion has the Adaptive Profile of a Surfer organisation. It navigates The Thrive Cycle consistently well as a result of its ongoing focus on The Six Elements of Adaptive Success.

Orion has a *Compelling Sense of Purpose* (Figure 9-2), which energises its people and builds resilience. It also has Value-Creating Values, which drive business decisions and behaviour.

Orion has developed a Vital Thread for one of its emerging South-East Asian markets (Figure 9-3).

HOW THE VITAL THREAD WORKS

The Vital Thread has a very specific structure and as we progress through the next few pages, it will become increasingly clear why this is important. It works something like this.

THE TOP ROW IS ALL ABOUT CUSTOMERS AND WHAT'S IMPORTANT IN THEIR WORLD

It makes it clear who the target customers are and what 'opportunities' and 'frustrations' they come across in their everyday lives. Of particular relevance are the opportunities and frustrations your organisation is potentially able to help them with.

FIGURE 9-2: Orion Healthcare's Compelling Sense of Purpose and Value-Creating Values

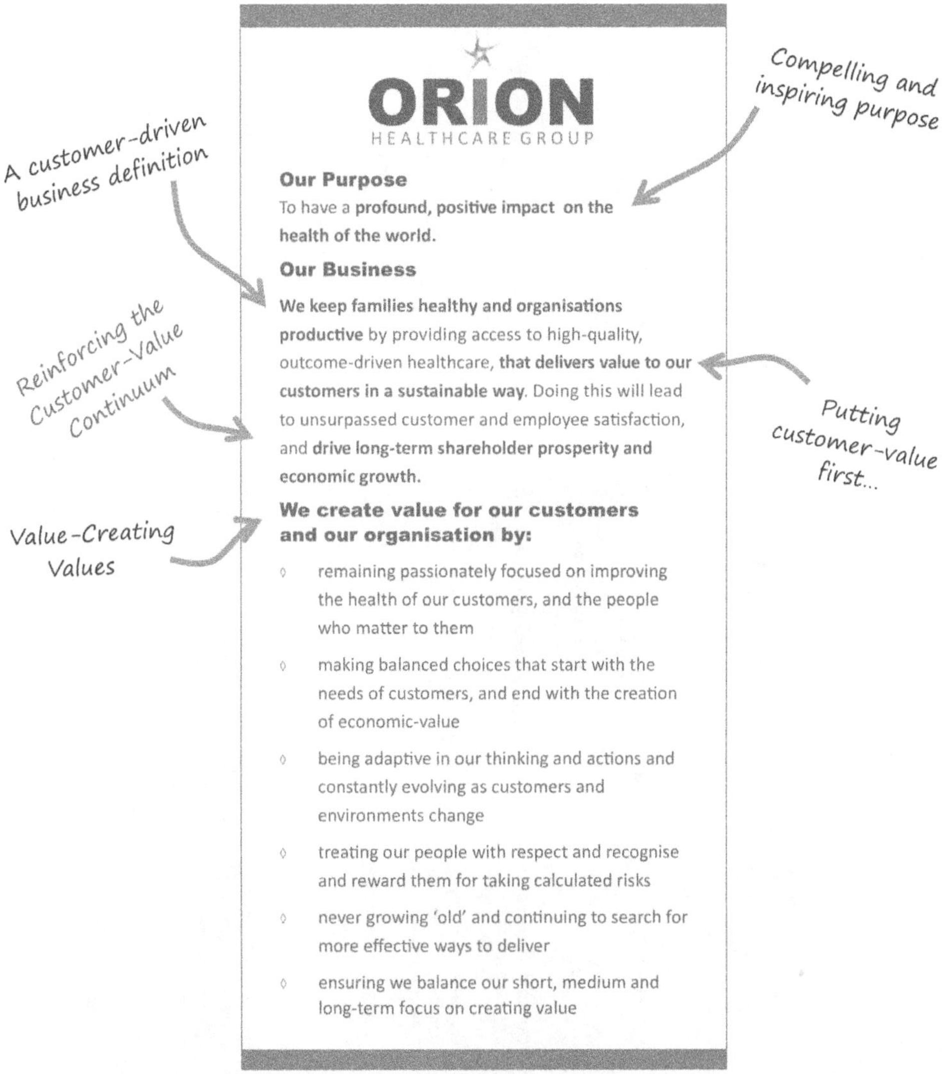

ORION
HEALTHCARE GROUP

Our Purpose

To have a **profound, positive impact on the health of the world.**

Our Business

We keep families healthy and organisations productive by providing access to high-quality, outcome-driven healthcare, **that delivers value to our customers in a sustainable way**. Doing this will lead to unsurpassed customer and employee satisfaction, and **drive long-term shareholder prosperity and economic growth.**

We create value for our customers and our organisation by:

- remaining passionately focused on improving the health of our customers, and the people who matter to them
- making balanced choices that start with the needs of customers, and end with the creation of economic-value
- being adaptive in our thinking and actions and constantly evolving as customers and environments change
- treating our people with respect and recognise and reward them for taking calculated risks
- never growing 'old' and continuing to search for more effective ways to deliver
- ensuring we balance our short, medium and long-term focus on creating value

A customer-driven business definition

Reinforcing the Customer-Value Continuum

Value-Creating Values

Compelling and inspiring purpose

Putting customer-value first...

To the right of the top row, The Vital Thread describes the key factors that are driving customers to prioritise the needs immediately to the left. If those factors change, customer needs – or at least their priorities – are also likely to change.

FIGURE 9-3: Example of Orion's Vital Thread

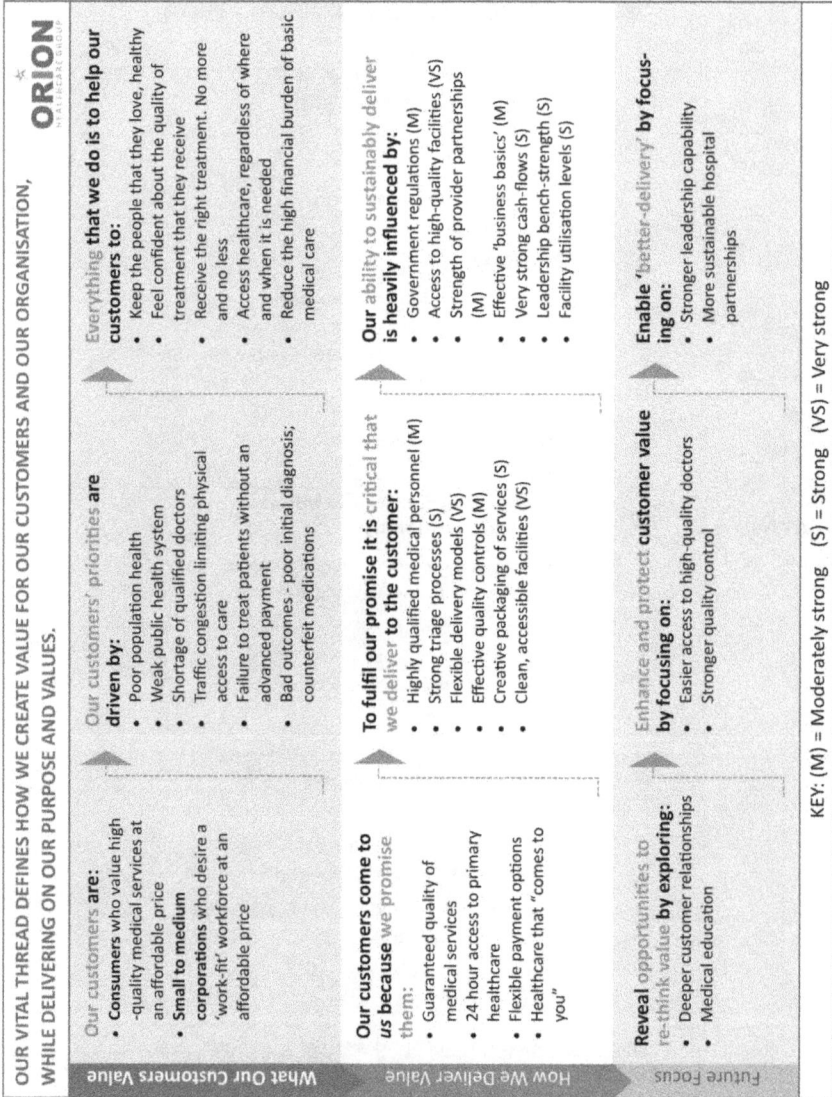

OUR VITAL THREAD DEFINES HOW WE CREATE VALUE FOR OUR CUSTOMERS AND OUR ORGANISATION, WHILE DELIVERING ON OUR PURPOSE AND VALUES.

ORION HEALTHCARE GROUP

What Our Customers Value

Our customers **are:**
- **Consumers** who value high-quality medical services at an affordable price
- **Small to medium corporations** who desire a 'work-fit' workforce at an affordable price

Our customers' priorities **are driven by:**
- Poor population health
- Weak public health system
- Shortage of qualified doctors
- Traffic congestion limiting physical access to care
- Failure to treat patients without an advanced payment
- Bad outcomes - poor initial diagnosis; counterfeit medications

Everything **that we do is to help our customers to:**
- Keep the people that they love, healthy
- Feel confident about the quality of treatment that they receive
- Receive the right treatment. No more and no less
- Access healthcare, regardless of where and when it is needed
- Reduce the high financial burden of basic medical care

How We Deliver Value

Our customers come to *us* because we promise them:
- Guaranteed quality of medical services
- 24 hour access to primary healthcare
- Flexible payment options
- Healthcare that "comes to you"

To fulfil our promise it is critical that we deliver **to the customer:**
- Highly qualified medical personnel (M)
- Strong triage processes (S)
- Flexible delivery models (VS)
- Effective quality controls (M)
- Creative packaging of services (S)
- Clean, accessible facilities (VS)

Our ability to sustainably deliver **is heavily influenced by:**
- Government regulations (M)
- Access to high-quality facilities (VS)
- Strength of provider partnerships (M)
- Effective 'business basics' (M)
- Very strong cash-flows (S)
- Leadership bench-strength (S)
- Facility utilisation levels (S)

Future Focus

Reveal opportunities to re-think value **by exploring:**
- Deeper customer relationships
- Medical education

Enhance and protect **customer value by focusing on:**
- Easier access to high-quality doctors
- Stronger quality control

Enable 'better-delivery' **by focusing on:**
- Stronger leadership capability
- More sustainable hospital partnerships

KEY: (M) = Moderately strong (S) = Strong (VS) = Very strong

THE SECOND ROW IS ALL ABOUT THE ORGANISATION

There's a clear focus in this row on how the organisation creates value for customers. At the left is what might sometimes be described as the customer-value proposition or customer promise. Importantly, the logic behind this proposition flows clearly from the customer needs in the row above. In this way, The Vital Thread follows in the philosophies put forward by W. Chan Kim and R. Mauborgne's *Blue Ocean Strategies*[13]. As such, it sees competitiveness coming from the ability to meet the changing needs of customers, not the ability to have better products or lower prices than traditional competitors.

Next, the 'how we fulfil our promise' section, describes the critical elements that will determine whether or not the organisation lives up to customers' expectations. While these six dot-points look pretty simple, they have been distilled from dozens of possible capabilities the organisation needs to have. This part of The Vital Thread needs to answer the question: 'Above all else, which operational elements of our business do we need to execute perfectly, if we are going to maximise customer-value, and therefore, maximise our returns?'

You will notice in this section, letters such as (M), (S) and (VS) appear at the end of each element. These indicate the perceived strength of those elements (Moderate, Strong, Very Strong) as measured by customer feedback.

Moving to the far right-hand side, the 'ability to sustainably deliver' section looks at the organisation's internal environment. It considers the factors that will most heavily influence whether or not the organisation is able to deliver the operational capabilities in the centre. I tend to think of this section as saying 'what keeps us healthy on the inside', whereas the section to the left describes 'what keeps us healthy on the outside'.

Once again, you can see the letters (M), (S) and (VS) to indicate the perceived relative strength. This time, however, they are internally assessed by specialists and other relevant stakeholders.

THE FINAL ROW TAKES THE INFORMATION FROM THE PRECEDING ROWS AND INDICATES THE AREAS THAT REQUIRE THE MOST FOCUS TO CREATE THE GREATEST LEVEL OF VALUE

This row talks about the organisation's big-picture priorities as they stand today. Note: these are entirely driven by the information in the first two rows. Consequently, a well-developed Vital Thread shows a clear link between the customers' world, how the organisation meets expectations and the areas in which improvements need to be made.

Eight success criteria for The Vital Thread

In order to be effective, The Vital Thread needs to fulfil the following eight success criteria. It must:

- **be dynamic (not static)** and as such, *evolve* to reflect changing circumstances that surround the organisation and its customers. The Adaptive Organisation therefore has a means of ensuring that The Vital Thread does evolve, and doesn't become set in stone.
- **be underpinned by The Anchors of Certainty.** In this way, whenever questions are answered, they always start with 'Given our purpose and given that we are in the business of [x]...'
- **receive consistent focus** if it is to be strong enough to hold the organisation together (particularly during times of significant change). Conversely, if it is not maintained by the organisation, and change rocks its foundations, then The Vital Thread soon unravels.
- **be unambiguous,** which enables The Vital Thread to be easily communicated and understood across the organisation. This makes it a practical source of guidance when the unexpected happens and ambiguity makes decision-making difficult.
- **adopt an organisational, not functional, perspective.** As such, its delivery cannot be 'carved-up' and 'owned' by individual functions within the organisation. It discourages silo-thinking and provides a shared focus. It also makes it possible for anyone to contribute to any part, which drives creativity and encourages continuous improvement.

- **focus on creating maximum value for customers first**, and as a consequence, delivering maximum value for the organisation, and its shareholders.
- **define which operational capabilities are critical** to creating maximum customer-value. It looks beyond the basic hygiene factors and asks, 'Which capabilities make the difference between creating maximum value, and failing to do so?'
- **make it clear where the organisation is today**, with regard to its ability to realise that customer-value. Because of this, it provides a reference point against which change-opportunities can be identified and managed.

◆◆◆

So, we have our Vital Thread, but how does it help to create The Adaptive Organisation? More specifically, how does it enable your organisation to more effectively navigate The Thrive Cycle and ensure that change-opportunities create maximum customer and economic-value?

HOW THE VITAL THREAD STRENGTHENS THE THRIVE CYCLE

One of the great things about The Vital Thread is its simplicity. Once it has been created, it enables people to align with what the organisation is wanting to achieve. Here are just a few of the many ways in which The Vital Thread strengthens The Thrive Cycle.

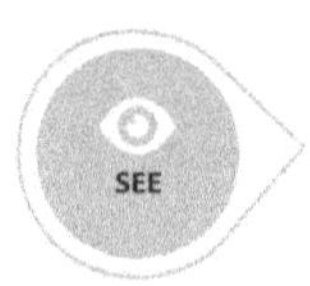

The Vital Thread makes it easier to sort the relevant change from the irrelevant

Today's organisations and their leaders are constantly being bombarded with information. Further, in a change-dominated environment, the relationship between cause-and-effect can easily be lost. The Vital Thread makes it easier to distil the relevant change-opportunities from the rest of the 'noise'. The secret to doing this lies in the structure of The Vital Thread and the information it contains. In this way, when an organisation understands the factors that drive the priorities of their customers, it can be more targeted when it is looking for opportunities (Figure 9-4).

In Orion's Vital Thread, the 'weak public health system' is a core driver underpinning the customers' desire for a private alternative. Therefore, if the Government significantly upgraded the public health facilities, this would potentially reduce the attractiveness of the private offering.

Similarly, customers place a high priority on keeping the people they love, healthy. When attempting to do this, they are frustrated by the high prices being charged by poor-quality doctors. If, let's say, the Government changes also introduced tighter requirements for doctor accreditation and higher penalties for non-compliance, then it may become easier for consumers to keep their families healthy.

Both of these scenarios could potentially reduce the perceived-value of the 'customer promise' and take the organisation one step closer to commoditisation.

If an organisation has developed its Vital Thread effectively, not only will external drivers of value be understood, but the internal ones will be understood as well. For example, what if Orion Healthcare experiences a failure in the contracting system that manages the accreditation and training of all doctors?

FIGURE 9-4: The Vital Thread helps Orion Healthcare to distil the relevant changes from the 'noise'.

1

Changes that impact here can change customer priorities or perceptions of value...

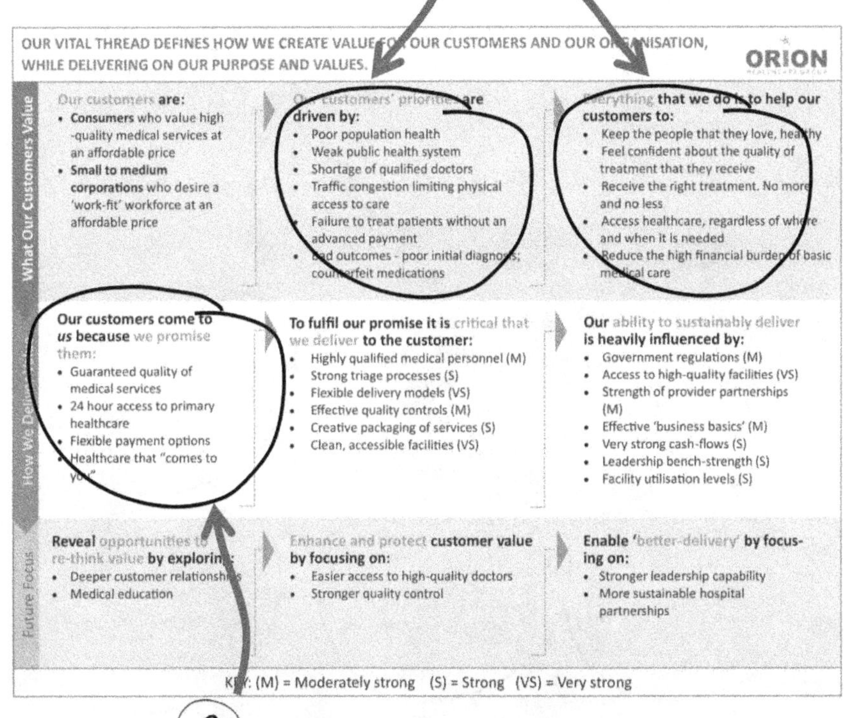
OUR VITAL THREAD DEFINES HOW WE CREATE VALUE FOR OUR CUSTOMERS AND OUR ORGANISATION, WHILE DELIVERING ON OUR PURPOSE AND VALUES.
ORION
What Our Customers Value
How We Deliver
Future Focus
Our customers are:
Consumers who value high-quality medical services at an affordable price
Small to medium corporations who desire a 'work-fit' workforce at an affordable price
Our customers' priorities are driven by:
Poor population health
Weak public health system
Shortage of qualified doctors
Traffic congestion limiting physical access to care
Failure to treat patients without an advanced payment
Bad outcomes - poor initial diagnosis; counterfeit medications
Everything that we do is to help our customers to:
Keep the people that they love, healthy
Feel confident about the quality of treatment that they receive
Receive the right treatment. No more and no less
Access healthcare, regardless of where and when it is needed
Reduce the high financial burden of basic medical care
Our customers come to us because we promise them:
Guaranteed quality of medical services
24 hour access to primary healthcare
Flexible payment options
Healthcare that "comes to you"
To fulfil our promise it is critical that we deliver to the customer:
Highly qualified medical personnel (M)
Strong triage processes (S)
Flexible delivery models (VS)
Effective quality controls (M)
Creative packaging of services (S)
Clean, accessible facilities (VS)
Our ability to sustainably deliver is heavily influenced by:
Government regulations (M)
Access to high-quality facilities (VS)
Strength of provider partnerships (M)
Effective 'business basics' (M)
Very strong cash-flows (S)
Leadership bench-strength (S)
Facility utilisation levels (S)
Reveal opportunities to re-think value by exploring:
Deeper customer relationships
Medical education
Enhance and protect customer value by focusing on:
Easier access to high-quality doctors
Stronger quality control
Enable 'better-delivery' by focusing on:
Stronger leadership capability
More sustainable hospital partnerships
KEY: (M) = Moderately strong (S) = Strong (VS) = Very strong

2

...and make the customer-promise more, or less, relevant here.

Having *highly qualified medical personnel* is a critical capability that underpins 'the promise' being made to customers. Therefore, the failure of a system that underpins this capability will have a potentially high impact on the organisation's ability to create value (Figure 9-5).

FIGURE 9-5: The Vital Thread enables Orion to identify the internal and external drivers of change

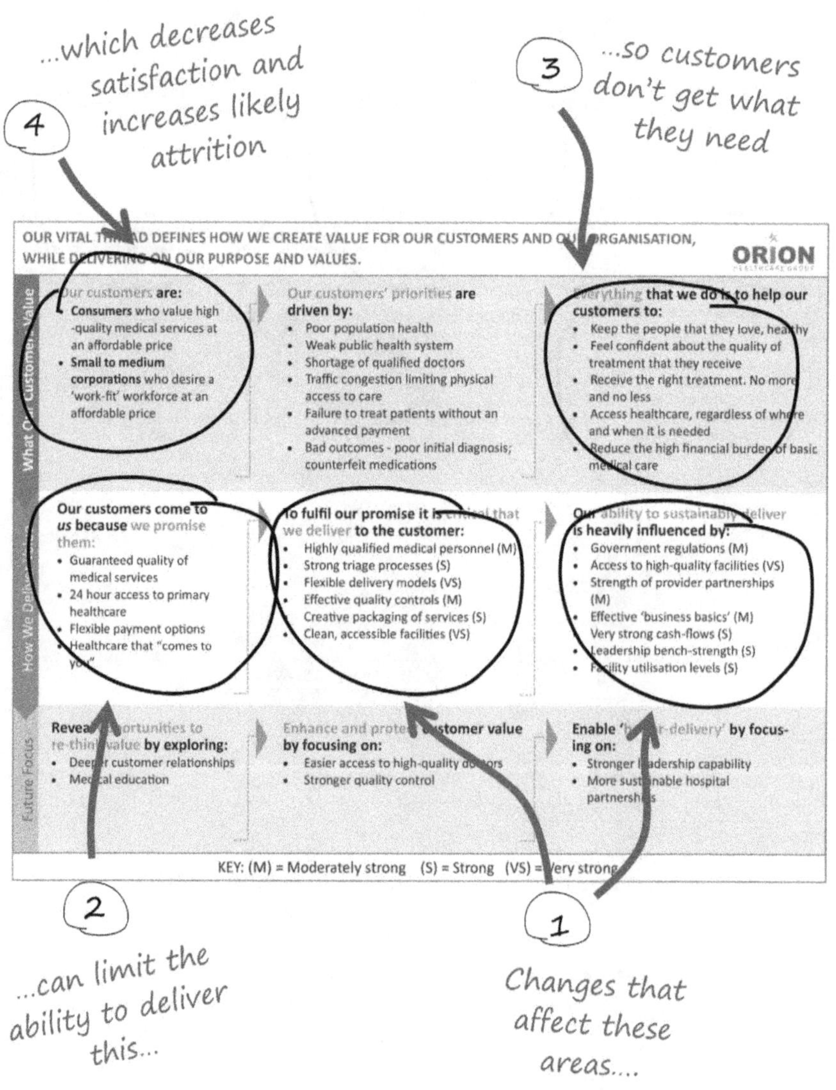

...which decreases satisfaction and increases likely attrition
4
3
...so customers don't get what they need
OUR VITAL THREAD DEFINES HOW WE CREATE VALUE FOR OUR CUSTOMERS AND OUR ORGANISATION, WHILE DELIVERING ON OUR PURPOSE AND VALUES.
ORION
What Our Customers Value
Our customers are:
Consumers who value high -quality medical services at an affordable price
Small to medium corporations who desire a 'work-fit' workforce at an affordable price
Our customers' priorities are driven by:
Poor population health
Weak public health system
Shortage of qualified doctors
Traffic congestion limiting physical access to care
Failure to treat patients without an advanced payment
Bad outcomes - poor initial diagnosis; counterfeit medications
Everything that we do is to help our customers to:
Keep the people that they love, healthy
Feel confident about the quality of treatment that they receive
Receive the right treatment. No more and no less
Access healthcare, regardless of where and when it is needed
Reduce the high financial burden of basic medical care
How We Deliver
Our customers come to us because we promise them:
Guaranteed quality of medical services
24 hour access to primary healthcare
Flexible payment options
Healthcare that "comes to you"
To fulfil our promise it is critical that we deliver to the customer:
Highly qualified medical personnel (M)
Strong triage processes (S)
Flexible delivery models (VS)
Effective quality controls (M)
Creative packaging of services (S)
Clean, accessible facilities (VS)
Our ability to sustainably deliver is heavily influenced by:
Government regulations (M)
Access to high-quality facilities (VS)
Strength of provider partnerships (M)
Effective 'business basics' (M)
Very strong cash-flows (S)
Leadership bench-strength (S)
Facility utilisation levels (S)
Future Focus
Reveal opportunities to re-think value by exploring:
Deeper customer relationships
Medical education
Enhance and protect customer value by focusing on:
Easier access to high-quality doctors
Stronger quality control
Enable 'better delivery' by focusing on:
Stronger leadership capability
More sustainable hospital partnerships
KEY: (M) = Moderately strong (S) = Strong (VS) = Very strong
2
1
...can limit the ability to deliver this...
Changes that affect these areas....

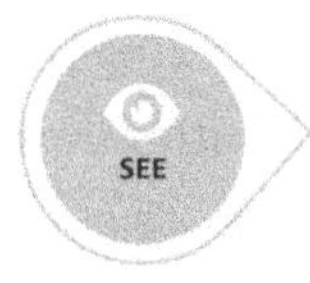

The Vital Thread enables the organisation to see beyond the complexity and brings the important connections to the surface

One of the most crippling aspects about a change-dominated environment is the complexity. Not only is the outside world complex, but the inside world is too.

By its very nature, complexity is not something that can be managed. 'Managing' suggests a certain degree of control, which is frequently absent in a change-dominated environment. It is in this area that organisations can fall into a number of traps.

TRAP #1 – Over-simplification

When organisations over-simplify (because it feels more comfortable and easier to deal with) they miss key opportunities and are more likely to be hit by apparently random changes coming from left field. This type of thinking can also lead to organisations denying that there is a problem, simply because they can't see how what has gone wrong affects the experience of the customer, or the sustainability of the organisation.

TRAP #2 – Becoming bogged in the detail

If an organisation tries to understand all of the detail about everything, it can quickly find itself spending lots of money and spinning around in circles.

Having too much information, without a way of easily structuring it and making it meaningful, leads to information-overload and inertia.

TRAP #3 – Focusing on the wrong things

Sometimes organisations want to feel in control and therefore focus on the things they are either most familiar with, or most interested in. In the short term, this can provide a sense of comfort and optimism that 'everything is going to be OK'. However, this approach frequently leads to significant gaps in understanding. It can also distract attention from more important factors. And, given that this is the first stage of The Thrive Cycle, the effects of these gaps intensify as the journey continues through subsequent stages.

OVERCOMING THE COMPLEXITY TRAPS

To embrace complexity, your organisation needs to be able to attend to the elements that matter, and block out the rest. A strong Vital Thread enables your organisation to do this and therefore avoids the traps I've just described. It does so by enabling a 'network-of-understanding' in which the underlying factors that influence each value-driver are understood and recognised by a broad group of people. This is not to say that everyone in your organisation understands every 'link', although this should be the case across the core leadership community.

And, as a result of this understanding, when people in your organisation notice a change, they have something to compare it with and determine whether it matters or not.

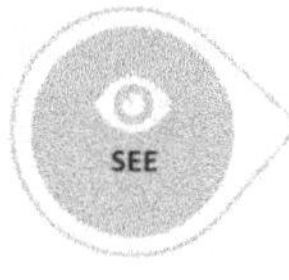

The Vital Thread provides a practical way to make customer-value the key driver of change

It's all very well to say 'make customer-value the driver of all change', but until your organisation knows *how* to do this, little progress is likely to be made.

The Vital Thread defines Four Key Drivers of Change (Figure 9-6). Two focus on customers (Customer Priorities and Customer Needs) and the other two (Delivery Drivers and Delivery Enablers) on your organisational delivery.

If something changes any of these drivers, then there is a potential change-opportunity in the wind for your organisation. Further, all

Figure 9-6: The Four Drivers of Change identified in The Vital Thread

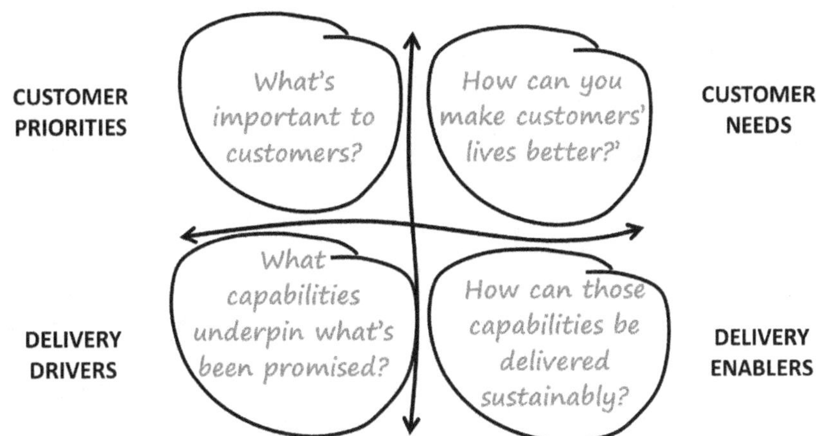

are directly linked to your organisation's ability to deliver value to customers in a sustainable way. Thus, by focusing on The Vital Thread your organisation maintains its focus on 'the customer' (Figure 9-7).

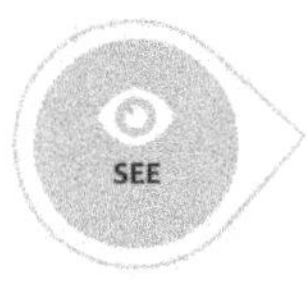

The Vital Thread enables better communication between those who 'see it', and those who can 'do something about it'

There is little point *Seeing* the biggest opportunity of the decade if it's too complex or requires a level of detail that decision-makers don't understand. Conversely, if the people who have the insight are unable to communicate it in a way that can be understood, then they aren't much help either.

In this way, The Vital Thread empowers the people who understand the detail and the decision-makers. It provides a meeting of minds by giving the detail-people some meaningful 'hooks' upon which to hang their insights. It also gives the decision-makers a starting point from which they can go into the detail (and still have a clear sense of where they are in the big picture).

FIGURE 9-7: The Four Key Drivers of Change within The Vital Thread identify the factors that are most likely to trigger significant change

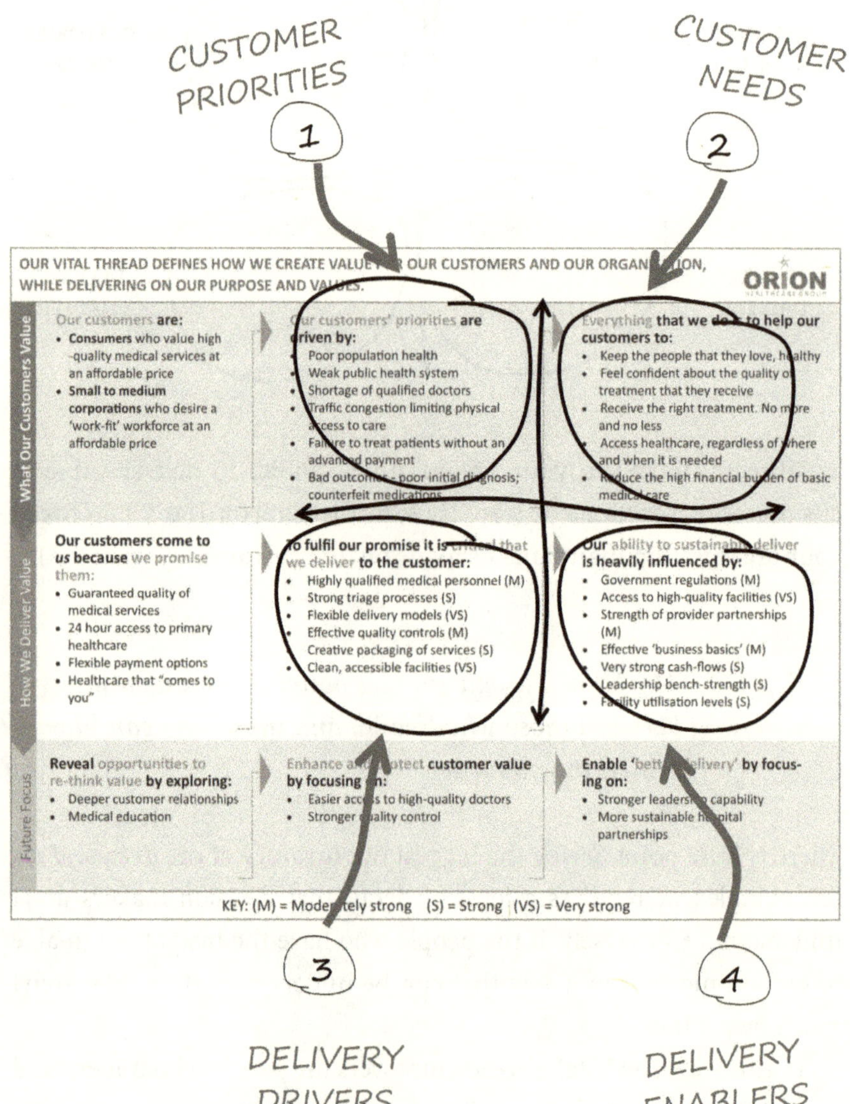
CUSTOMER PRIORITIES
1
CUSTOMER NEEDS
2
OUR VITAL THREAD DEFINES HOW WE CREATE VALUE FOR OUR CUSTOMERS AND OUR ORGANISATION, WHILE DELIVERING ON OUR PURPOSE AND VALUES.
ORION
What Our Customers Value
Our customers are:
• Consumers who value high-quality medical services at an affordable price
• Small to medium corporations who desire a 'work-fit' workforce at an affordable price
Our customers' priorities are driven by:
• Poor population health
• Weak public health system
• Shortage of qualified doctors
• Traffic congestion limiting physical access to care
• Failure to treat patients without an advanced payment
• Bad outcomes - poor initial diagnosis; counterfeit medications
Everything that we do to help our customers to:
• Keep the people that they love, healthy
• Feel confident about the quality of treatment that they receive
• Receive the right treatment. No more and no less
• Access healthcare, regardless of where and when it is needed
• Reduce the high financial burden of basic medical care
How We Deliver Value
Our customers come to us because we promise them:
• Guaranteed quality of medical services
• 24 hour access to primary healthcare
• Flexible payment options
• Healthcare that "comes to you"
To fulfil our promise it is critical that we deliver to the customer:
• Highly qualified medical personnel (M)
• Strong triage processes (S)
• Flexible delivery models (VS)
• Effective quality controls (M)
• Creative packaging of services (S)
• Clean, accessible facilities (VS)
Our ability to sustainably deliver is heavily influenced by:
• Government regulations (M)
• Access to high-quality facilities (VS)
• Strength of provider partnerships (M)
• Effective 'business basics' (M)
• Very strong cash-flows (S)
• Leadership bench-strength (S)
• Facility utilisation levels (S)
Future Focus
Reveal opportunities to re-think value by exploring:
• Deeper customer relationships
• Medical education
Enhance and protect customer value by focusing on:
• Easier access to high-quality doctors
• Stronger quality control
Enable 'better delivery' by focusing on:
• Stronger leadership capability
• More sustainable hospital partnerships
KEY: (M) = Moderately strong (S) = Strong (VS) = Very strong
3
4
DELIVERY DRIVERS
DELIVERY ENABLERS

The Vital Thread makes it easier to 'start conversations' on the same page

How often have you witnessed a discussion in a meeting when the participants suddenly realise they weren't in disagreement, just talking about two different topics?

A change-dominated environment, with many unknowns, makes this kind of misunderstanding a common occurrence. Therefore, when a change-opportunity comes along it can save considerable time, and emotional-energy, if people have a common starting position from which to *understand* the opportunity.

The Vital Thread is something that is shared, and widely understood across your leadership community. When *Understanding* a change-opportunity, the conversation starts with The Vital Thread and asks:

'How does this change-opportunity potentially impact the Four Key Drivers of Value for our organisation?'

When doing this kind of analysis, using the Change-Drivers Framework can be useful (Figure 9-8).

When a potential change is identified, your organisation can work through each of the four quadrants and assess what's changed and what it means. To show how this works in practice, let's come back to our friends at Orion Healthcare who have just learnt that the Government intends to restrict the number of work visas being granted to international doctors.

How does the Change-Drivers Framework help Orion adapt to this new development?

Looking at the top row of The Vital Thread, Customer Needs would appear to be relatively unaffected. However, the Customer Priorities (in terms of their level of importance) may increase (because, at least in the short term, good doctors will be even harder to come by). This is good news for Orion because it is likely to make its 'customer promise' more attractive. However, further analysis of the change-opportunity

FIGURE 9-8: The Change-Drivers Framework helps to make sense of change, starting with a customer's perspective.

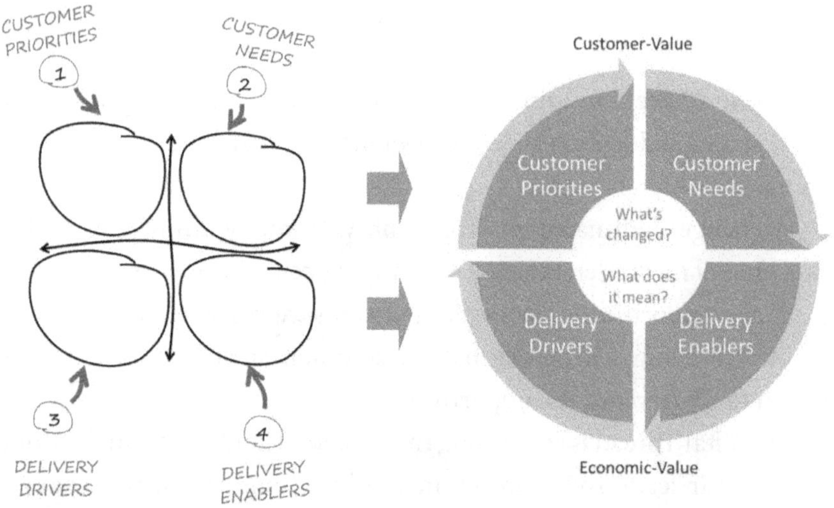

reveals significant downside in terms of the Delivery Drivers and Delivery Enablers.

The organisation is heavily reliant on having highly-qualified doctors in order to fulfil its 'unique customer promise'. Further, this critical value driver only rates as being 'moderately strong' today. And so, even before this change came along, doctor quality was already an issue.

There is also another potential impact.

Appropriately-qualified, local doctors are scarce. Without the competition from overseas-trained practitioners, demand for these local doctors is likely to increase, and with it, their fees.

Thus, the change also has implications for a number of delivery enablers including 'business-basics' like cost-management, strength of cash-flows and facility utilisation.

◆◆◆

Using the Change-Drivers Framework enables the change-opportunity to be understood holistically in a relatively short space of time. When you have a strong Vital Thread and the right experts in the room, the above high-level analysis can be done in half an hour.

Second, the Change-Drivers Framework ensures that the early thinking remains open, looking for different types of value-opportunities. If the organisation tries to lock-in understanding too soon, it can fall into traps such as assuming that it is just *protecting value*, when there may be an opportunity to *create more* or *re-think* it as well.

The Vital Thread ensures the 'heavy thinking' has been done before the platform catches alight

The Vital Thread requires thinking time, collaborative conversations and patience, in order to get it right. However, as you will be starting to realise, when it comes to navigating The Thrive Cycle, such early investment will pay off considerably.

Consider once again the example of Orion and the changes regarding overseas doctors. What would have happened if the organisation had not invested time creating The Vital Thread in advance?

In truth, it would have been what happens in many less-adaptive organisations today. When attempting to understand what the change 'meant', different parts of the organisation would have had nothing to bring them together. As a result, it is likely that the different 'functions' would have tried to *Understand it* on their own. Instead of having a cohesive organisational position on the change, Orion would have had several functional positions. These are likely to have been accompanied by some fairly strong views as to what Orion Healthcare should be doing, driven by a primarily functional perspective.

Different starting points, different end points, and every perspective in between. You can see how the gaps develop when there is no

Vital Thread to keep the various parts of the organisation together. Further, these gaps become even wider, and deeper, when the change-opportunity is accompanied by a time constraint or worse, the threat of an 'ugly' outcome.

So, having a single organisational view is important before a wave of change comes your way. However, The Vital Thread also makes the process of *understanding* change-opportunities more efficient. It provides a shared starting point, which effectively gives the process of understanding a head-start.

This benefit is realised not just once, but *every time* a new change-opportunity comes along (Figure 9-9). Further, it means there is a level of consistency in the way in which opportunities are understood. This, in turn, enables an alignment to be developed across the entire change portfolio, which is a necessary prerequisite if the organisation is going to holistically create value from organisational change.

FIGURE 9-9: Investing in The Vital Thread achieves multiple benefits

INVESTING IN
THE VITAL THREAD
Time &
Effort
The
Vital
Thread
VS
NOT INVESTING IN
THE VITAL THREAD
Time &
Effort
It takes LESS time and effort to understand opportunities and makes future alignment EASIER
It takes MORE time and effort to understand opportunities and makes future alignment HARDER

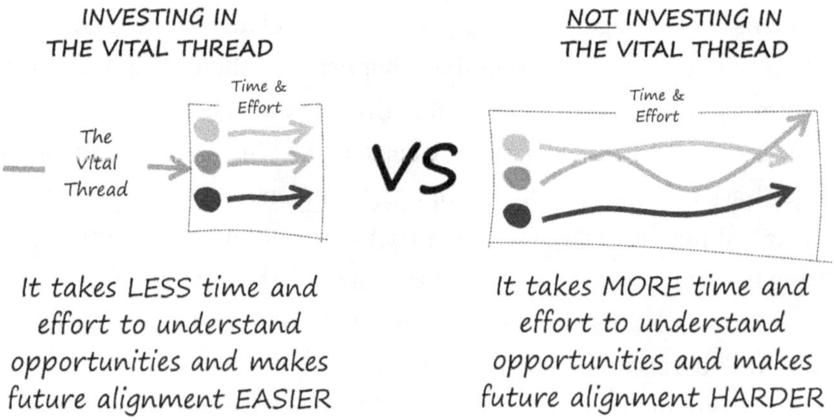

The Vital Thread puts short, medium and long-term value-creation back on the same continuum

When I'm working with leaders, one dilemma is always guaranteed to come up. It's the short versus long-term paradox. However, for many reasons (including some of the *unhelpful habits* discussed earlier) there seems to be a disconnect between these two concepts.

Orion's Vital Thread has identified 'easier access to quality doctors' as an opportunity to improve its ability to create value (Figure 9-10). It has subsequently used this to develop a high-level view of how 'easier access to quality doctors' can be achieved through short, medium, and long-term initiatives. These three points along the timeline indicate not only the amount of time taken to deliver, but usually the level of investment required to deliver to associated activities. They also indicate the relative value that each is expected to deliver. In this way, a longer-term opportunity generally means that the initiative is more costly, going to take longer to deliver but is expected to provide cumulatively high value.

Orion has thought through this opportunity across a single continuum, where the short-term initiatives are delivering early benefits, while also moving the organisation towards the longer-term outcome.

In some other organisations, this is not how short and long-term thinking seems to work. It's almost as though when a fork develops in the road, the short-term becomes disconnected from the long-term. When this occurs, the organisation can subconsciously start to work towards a new driver, namely short-term growth performance (Figure 9-11).

The issue here is not that there is a focus on short-term performance. That's necessary and important. The real issue is the belief that the combined outcome of the short-term, economically-driven initiatives

FIGURE 9-10: How Orion's short-term activities generate long-term value

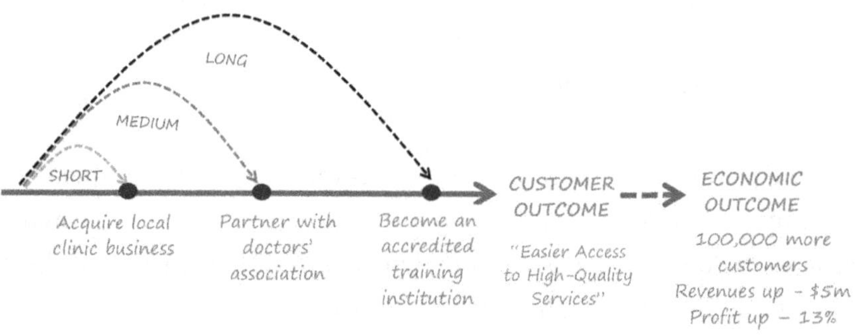

FIGURE 9-11: Focusing on short-term economic value creation delivers a different long-term outcome

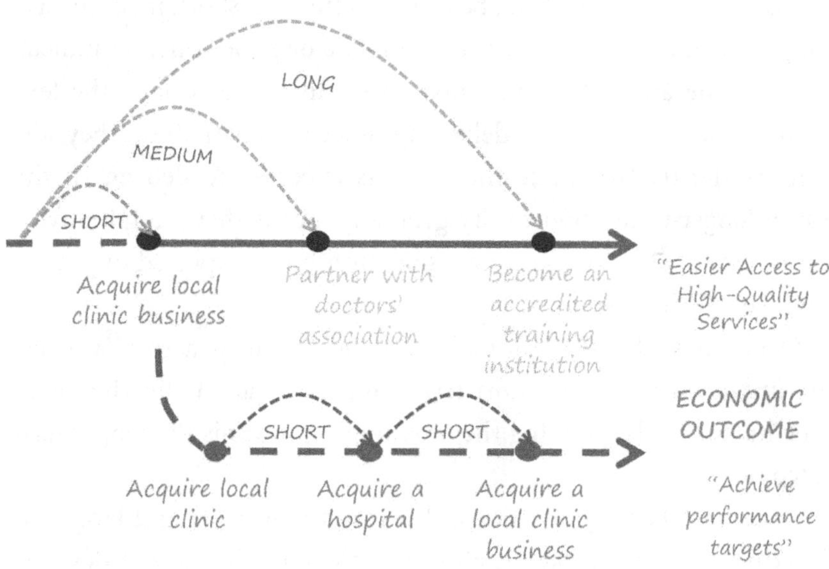

is equivalent to delivering the longer-term customer-driven outcome. And that is rarely the case. *What if this happened at Orion Healthcare? How would it affect its ability to adapt to meet future customer needs?*

These illustrations show how having short-term economic-value as *the* core driver of change, takes the organisation down a different path to that identified in The Vital Thread. Further, because the initiatives *look* like they are somehow related to 'providing easier access to quality doctors' they receive priority. That's because they are seen as providing the perfect combination of large, short-term returns and large, long-term returns. However, they don't really change the organisation to make it better at meeting the needs of customers. In fact, the more likely consequence is they make the organisation less adaptive because the planned acquisitions are unlikely to fit within The Vital Thread. Complexity goes up. Value goes down.

The Vital Thread highlights and addresses customer blind-spots

Within The Vital Thread, the customer promise is the organisation's *interpretation* of what creates value for target customers, taken at a given moment in time. It is often built upon a set of insights and assumptions about the priorities customers assign to given jobs, and the associated frustration and satisfaction. As long as these insights remain consistent, the organisation can still be highly successful, focusing on delivering its core proposition. This follows from our earlier discussion regarding the perils of defining your business in terms of the products it sells.

Over time, organisations can develop customer blind-spots (Figure 9-12). It can be as though they take a static photo of the customers' perspective of the world, and then stick the picture on all the windows. There is little requirement to look outside because the fundamental customer needs are the same as they've always been. The Vital Thread overcomes this by highlighting these blind-spots and encouraging the organisation to be constantly looking for signs of change.

FIGURE 9-12: The Vital Thread ensures your organisation doesn't develop customer blind-spots

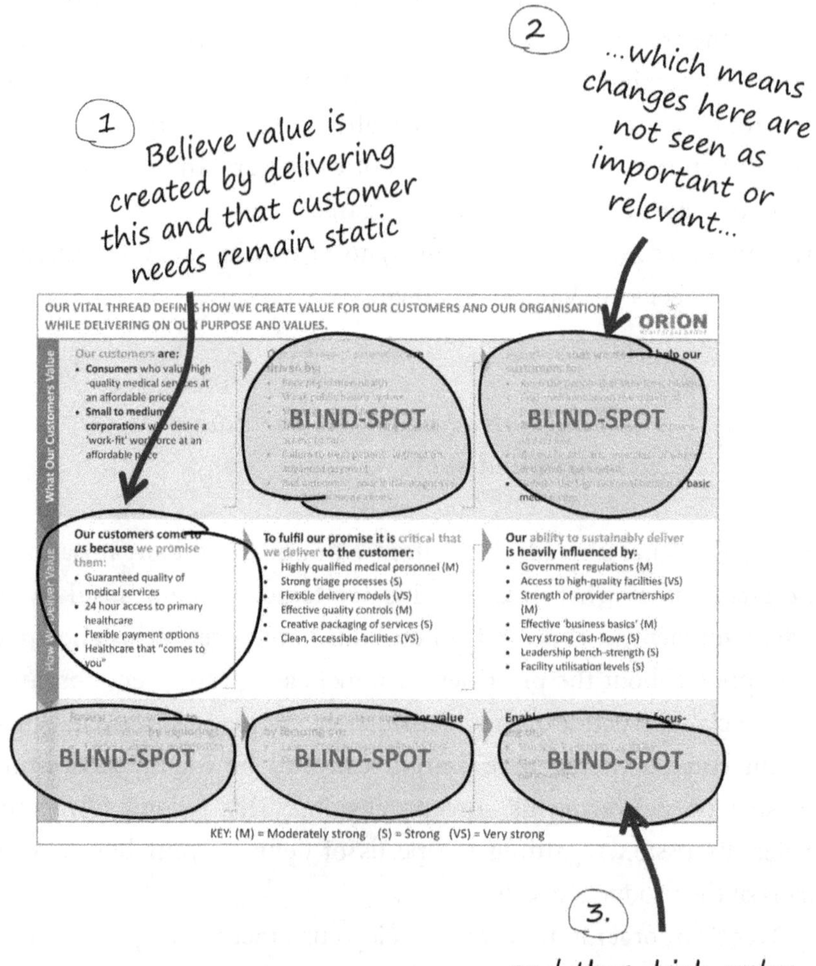
1
Believe value is created by delivering this and that customer needs remain static
2
...which means changes here are not seen as important or relevant...
ORION
BLIND-SPOT
BLIND-SPOT
What Our Customers Value
How We Deliver Value
To fulfil our promise it is critical that we deliver to the customer:
Highly qualified medical personnel (M)
Strong triage processes (S)
Flexible delivery models (VS)
Effective quality controls (M)
Creative packaging of services (S)
Clean, accessible facilities (VS)
Our ability to sustainably deliver is heavily influenced by:
Government regulations (M)
Access to high-quality facilities (VS)
Strength of provider partnerships (M)
Effective 'business basics' (M)
Very strong cash-flows (S)
Leadership bench-strength (S)
Facility utilisation levels (S)
BLIND-SPOT
BLIND-SPOT
BLIND-SPOT
KEY: (M) = Moderately strong (S) = Strong (VS) = Very strong
3.
..and thus, high-value opportunities don't receive the priority that they need

The Vital Thread enables early priority decisions without depending on false certainty

Return-on-investment (ROI) is commonly used by organisations to answer the question, 'If we invest this much, what are we likely to get back?' In a fairly static, predictable environment, this kind of assessment makes logical sense. That's because a reasonable ROI calculation requires significant detail to be understood. This works for some repetitive changes. For example, if I were building a shopping mall (having built fifty of them before), then I should have a pretty good idea as to the overall cost and what I should be expecting regarding the returns.

However, when it comes to 'big strategic' change, this level of certainty is rarely available. So what is an organisation to do? Moving change-opportunities through The Thrive Cycle requires investment (funding, people, management focus and so on). But how can an organisation make the right priority choices when there is insufficient information available to reach any definitive conclusion?

The Vital Thread enables early prioritisation to occur without this information. It removes the pressure and prevents your organisation from committing to 'fictitious' numbers and timeframes too early. In fact, it means that when it comes to making the big investments (i.e. during the latter stages of The Thrive Cycle), your organisation can invest more confidently, knowing the change-opportunity is aligned with what your organisation is collectively trying to achieve.

I can appreciate that for some leaders, waiting until much later in the process to create some 'hard ROI numbers' may feel a little uncomfortable at first. It means investing in something when you don't really know if it is going to pay-off.

To be clear, I'm not saying that financial metrics have no place in prioritisation. I am saying it's important to achieve a balance. In this way, if an organisation attempts to apply ROI calculations to an opportunity at an early stage (i.e. beyond the kind that you scribble on the back of an envelope), the certainty it is creating is *false certainty.* It might make the accountants feel better but the returns are no more guaranteed.

This has a number of implications for change initiatives and their likely success during The Thrive Cycle.

First, relying on false certainty creates a completely fictitious benchmark against which the organisation will assess the initiative going forward. It doesn't matter how much people say, 'I know that it's early days but can you just give me a ball-park figure?' When you give out numbers that have a dollar sign in front of them, they become etched into people's brains. This means that the fictitious benchmark starts to drive the conversation and it becomes about 'finances' not 'value'. It places the organisation at risk of placing economic-value ahead of customer-value.

This approach has another consequence. When an organisation has a weak Vital Thread, and ROI *is* the key driver for early priorities, it plays into the hands of pet projects and politics. It promotes a mindset of 'Just promise big-numbers and your project will win the funding'. In these types of organisations this kind of speculative-ROI works because frequently, no one goes back to see whether the benefits were realised anyway. Once the annual budget 'ticks over' into a new year, all is forgotten.

The Vital Thread brings consistency and transparency to priority decisions

When The Vital Thread is used as the basis for prioritisation, the decisions become more consistent. This builds your organisation's ability to adapt in a number of ways.

First of all, it makes it much clearer to everyone in your organisation where the focus is, and where it is not. This provides a sense of certainty and as we explored before, any certainty you can create in a change-dominated environment, is like gold when it comes to engagement.

Secondly, when the same criteria are used to make priority decisions (whether they are formally made by a committee, or made by individuals during the day-to-day) people get better at making them. Where priority decisions fail is when they are either unclear or the implications have not been thought through. Further, because The Vital Thread is consistent, people start to develop rules-of-thumb regarding what kinds of things have a higher priority than others. Decision-making is not only better but also faster and clearer.

The Vital Thread enables decision-makers to confidently challenge low-value opportunities

Sometimes it is just easier in the short term to approve too much and then deliver too little.

We've previously explored how the *Anchors of Certainty* provide a first value-focused layer for prioritisation. This asks the question 'is this change (and the proposed solution) in line with our purpose, the business that we're in and our values?'

The Vital Thread provides the second value-focused layer of prioritisation. It does this by referring to the Four Key Drivers of Change. If a change-opportunity is in line with those priorities, then it is promoting the overall improvement of the organisation and its ability to deliver customer-value.

If however, a change-opportunity is not contributing to those areas, then it prompts a further conversation about why the change-opportunity is being put forward in the first place. It leads to the question:

- *Have our priorities changed or is this something that should be done later (or not at all)?*

The Vital Thread enables the organisation to move beyond functional silos and creates a platform for collaboration

Once again, when a response needs to be developed, a strong Vital Thread provides a consistent starting point from which to collaboratively develop an answer – whether this is done for a single change-opportunity or as part of a much broader strategic review process. In either case, the benefits are equally significant.

The Vital Thread is functionally agnostic. Therefore, it enables the change-opportunity to be articulated in organisational terms. This means the only way to design a solution that meets the requirements is to adopt an organisational mindset (not a functional one). This helps in a number of ways.

Functional silos are frustrating for leaders and people who are just trying to 'get stuff done'. Therefore, any situation that offers people the opportunity to work together and collaborate is often positively received.

Also, when people have an opportunity to contribute to designing the response (because a strong Vital Thread enables them to do so), they are more likely to feel engaged and excited about the delivery.

How planning 'horizontally' delivers value

MORE THAN TEN YEARS ago I was responsible for the strategic planning of a financial services business. For years it had produced yearly plans that amounted to a wish-list of things that the different functions wanted to do. When I came into the role, I discovered that the business only delivered 30 percent of the changes on its list. Each year, the same ones that had long-term importance would slide to the bottom of the list and never even start.

A new approach was required.

The Executive Team developed the top five outcomes the organisation needed to achieve, and then each Executive became the champion for one of those outcomes. Then, instead of sending the functions away to come up with their list under each outcome, the Executive Champions led self-selected, cross-functional teams who worked collaboratively to *understand* problems or opportunities that needed to be solved, and *design* an appropriate response.

The strategic priority list for that year went down from over 80 initiatives to 45. Of which, 90 percent were delivered. Also the level of engagement for the participating leaders went through the roof. Of those who were part of the new approach 86 percent said they were confident that this year the organisation would deliver its strategy, and 91 percent said they were feeling more confident than in previous years.

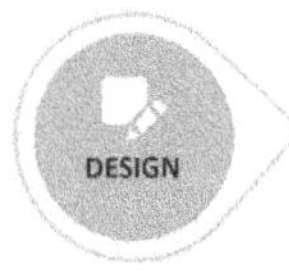

The Vital Thread makes it easier to holistically choose the highest value solution

One of the most difficult aspects of responding to change-opportunities is that *uncertainty* can make choosing the best option difficult. That's because all the answers are rarely available when a decision needs to be made.

However, when your organisation has The Vital Thread it makes this task much easier. Further, the ability to combine the 'customer view' and the 'economic view' means the right choices are made for the right, value-creating reasons.

You'll recall at the start of this chapter, I introduced the Change-Drivers Framework as a way of understanding opportunities. This same framework can be used as a means of evaluating proposed options, and whether, when they are considered from an overall perspective, they are likely to create value (Figure 9-13).

FIGURE 9-13: How the Change Drivers Framework can be used to evaluate options

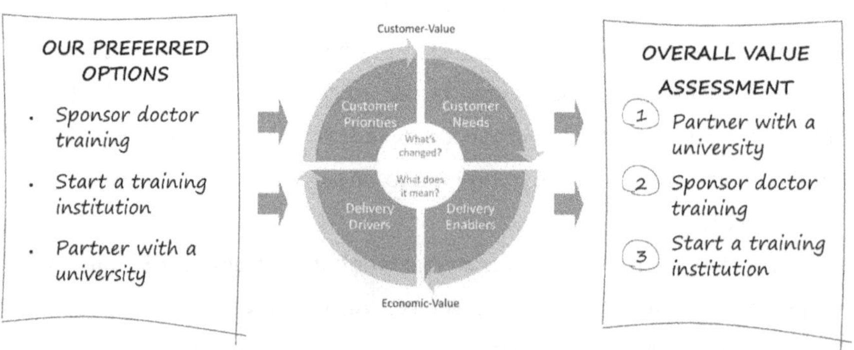

This approach provides a useful check and can avoid the trap of one part of your organisation responding to a change in one way, then another part of the organisation destroying that value somewhere else.

The Vital Thread ensures that the plan protects the things that matter

Once a major organisational change starts to gain momentum, it can feel like a runaway train. This can be fun, scary and frustrating all at the same time. There are so many moving parts it is impossible to keep track of everything because one aspect blends into another.

When planning, The Vital Thread enables the most important elements to be identified and protected. These are the things that matter, and if all else fails these are the outcomes that need to be preserved. When these are clearly articulated and understood, your leaders and their teams can see beyond the plan and the complexity, and just worry about what really matters.

The Vital Thread creates a life-line for people so when the unexpected occurs, they stay on course

Within a change-dominated environment, 'the unexpected' is to be 'expected'. Assumptions turn out to be wrong, people make mistakes and solutions are found to be different from that 'described in the brochure'.

When this occurs, your people need a way to quickly understand the situation they are now facing and assess their options so that they can pull 'the train' back on track. It is during these moments major organisational change is at risk of either grinding to a halt or taking a costly and painful detour.

However, because The Adaptive Organisation constantly applies The Vital Thread during The Thrive Cycle, the 'unexpected' becomes much easier to address (both logistically and emotionally). It means regardless of where they are, or what their involvement, people can come back to the core principles. Namely:

- *What was the value we set out to create?*
- *What was driving that value?*
- *How have the current circumstances changed?*
- *Is it still possible to create that value?*
- *What options do we have?*

You can appreciate how much easier these questions are to answer having embedded The Vital Thread into conversations from the very start. You can also appreciate how difficult it is to return a major organisational change to the correct course when The Vital Thread is weak. It essentially leaves people 'flapping-around' making knee-jerk reactions and frequently searching for someone to blame.

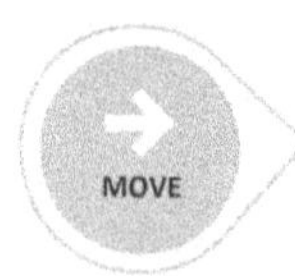

The Vital Thread builds engagement through an ability to say 'why' and 'why not'

People resist either what they don't understand, or what doesn't make sense. During times of significant change, the most useful tool an organisation can have is the ability to authentically and consistently answer questions like:

- *Why* have we decided to take this approach, not that one?
- *Why* did we need to close down the factory?
- *Why* are we entering this new market, not that one?
- *Why* did we buy that company?
- *Why* is that project more important than the other one?

Coming back to Orion Healthcare and its challenge with changing government legislation, it used The Vital Thread to explain its chosen priorities to its people (Figure 9-14).

WHAT HAPPENS WHEN THE REASONS FOR CHANGE ARE UNCLEAR?

A utility company had traditionally served its customers via a number of retail shopfronts. Five days a week the customers could walk in, pay their bills, connect new services and ask for advice. While the Internet had reduced some of the foot-traffic, a large section of the customer base still preferred branches. And so, they remained open.

Quite separately, another part of the organisation had been developing a new product line – selling electrical and gas appliances. These were sold via both retail and online channels.

Now, both of these product lines had a retail presence in the same shopping centre. It also so happened that the lease of the appliances business expired at the same time as a shopfront becoming available next door to the utility services branch. So, a new lease was signed and the move commenced.

Two shopfronts with two entrances. Same brand. Right next to each other. The organisation had not decided a combined retail presence

FIGURE 9-14: How Orion Healthcare uses The Vital Thread to explain its choices

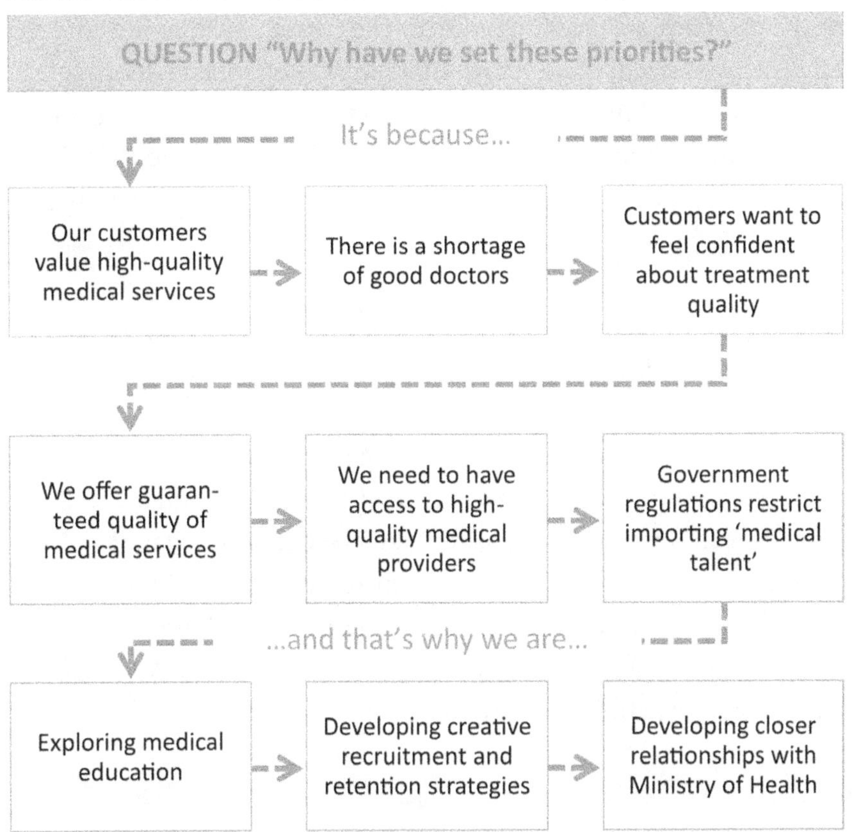
QUESTION "Why have we set these priorities?"
It's because...
Our customers value high-quality medical services
There is a shortage of good doctors
Customers want to feel confident about treatment quality
We offer guaranteed quality of medical services
We need to have access to high-quality medical providers
Government regulations restrict importing 'medical talent'
...and that's why we are...
Exploring medical education
Developing creative recruitment and retention strategies
Developing closer relationships with Ministry of Health

would create the best value for its customers. It was just something that 'seemed like a good idea at the time'.

As a result, what should have been a simple relocation process became exponentially complex. Even simple questions became difficult because it was unclear why the two shops had been put together in the first place. For instance, should they knock down the wall between the two shopfronts?

An initial response might be, 'Well of course they should, they're the same company'. But, it wasn't that simple.

Each shop had different opening hours, different uniforms and even different logo styles. The people doing similar jobs in each branch were on different pay scales. The two stores were on two separate leases, and so the company was paying more for the two stores than it would for an equivalent sized, single store. There were two separate doors.

It took several months and many meetings with very senior people to work through questions that would have been easy had there been a shared view of *why*, that started with creating value for customers.

The Vital Thread provides a consistent starting point from which to improve

The Vital Thread takes time to create and have people understanding it. However, this effort will be wasted if the world changes, and The Vital Thread doesn't change with it. At the end of the day, The Vital Thread is an organisation's perception of how the world works and what will create value for customers and the organisation. Thus, an Adaptive Organisation is always willing to challenge The Vital Thread and question whether perceptions still match reality.

How strong is your organisation's Vital Thread?

HAVING LEARNT ABOUT The Vital Thread and explored how it can be used to strengthen The Thrive Cycle, let's bring the conversation back to your organisation.

Having a Vital Thread that is sufficiently robust to keep your organisation together during The Thrive Cycle journey requires more than just a piece of paper with points written on it. The strength comes from the understanding and alignment of thought that sits beneath it. Further, its value comes from the fact that the leadership community 'get it' and understand what the organisation is trying to achieve. In this way, it should be the first thing that new leaders learn when they join the organisation.

Given all of the above, when deciding what needs to change within your organisation, it makes sense to start with a realistic view of what you already have. Reflecting on your own organisation and looking at the examples contained within this chapter, ask yourself:

- *How easily could we create one of these within our own organisation?*
- *How aligned would our leaders be in their understanding of it?*
- *How well-aligned are the priorities we set?*
- *How clearly do our leaders understand how we holistically create value?*

If the answers to these questions were either 'I don't know' or 'Not very' then The Vital Thread within your organisation is probably not as strong as it needs to be. This will be affecting adaptive performance and will be driving what appears in your Adaptive Profile.

How to create your first Vital Thread?

THE VITAL THREAD is structured in a way that makes it easy to create.

The following template will help with structuring the conversation. Start in the top left-hand corner, and just work your way, row by row, down to the bottom right. Do so in a way that is inclusive, not exclusive, and draws on the experience, insights, knowledge and passion of the people within your organisation. Note: The same questions apply whether your Core Organisation is a corporate group, a business unit or a functional team. However, who your customers are, their jobs, and how your Core Organisation creates value will most likely be different.

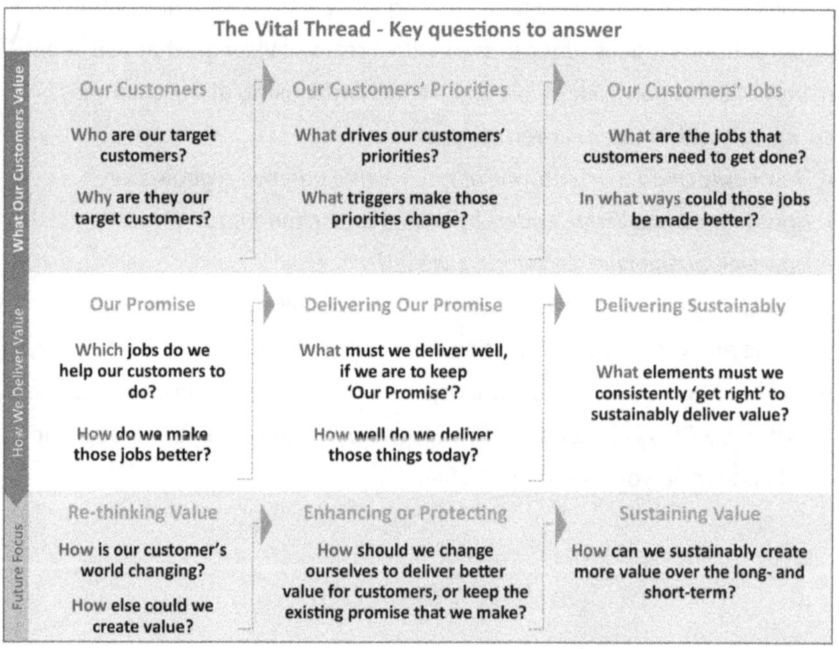

The Vital Thread - Key questions to answer
What Our Customers Value
Our Customers
Who are our target customers?
Why are they our target customers?
Our Customers' Priorities
What drives our customers' priorities?
What triggers make those priorities change?
Our Customers' Jobs
What are the jobs that customers need to get done?
In what ways could those jobs be made better?
How We Deliver Value
Our Promise
Which jobs do we help our customers to do?
How do we make those jobs better?
Delivering Our Promise
What must we deliver well, if we are to keep 'Our Promise'?
How well do we deliver those things today?
Delivering Sustainably
What elements must we consistently 'get right' to sustainably deliver value?
Future Focus
Re-thinking Value
How is our customer's world changing?
How else could we create value?
Enhancing or Protecting
How should we change ourselves to deliver better value for customers, or keep the existing promise that we make?
Sustaining Value
How can we sustainably create more value over the long- and short-term?

CHAPTER CONCLUSION

So that's The Vital Thread. It's an incredibly powerful tool when developed and used appropriately. The secret to getting it right is to focus on why you are creating The Vital Thread in the first place. Use the examples and eight success criteria (described at the start of the chapter) to develop one and then test it out. It's so much easier to start with something then refine it, than it is to be staring at a blank sheet of paper, trying to get it perfect.

It's also worth remembering that The Vital Thread is never 'complete' because it needs to constantly evolve with changing circumstances. We'll go into this further when we talk about the Balanced Ecosystem in Chapter 11.

KEY POINTS TO REMEMBER

- The Vital Thread helps The Adaptive Organisation, its leaders and its people to remain aligned and deliver maximum value, while moving through The Thrive Cycle.
- The Vital Thread makes it easier to identify relevant changes and to see beyond the complexity of the organisation. It ensures that organisational change is customer-driven; that important opportunities make it onto the organisational radar; and that value-creation remains the ultimate focus.
- By having a strong Vital Thread, The Adaptive Organisation ensures the heavy thinking has been done before the big opportunities materialise. This enables the organisation to focus on realising the potential of the opportunity, rather than 'getting on the same page'.
- The Vital Thread enables priority decisions to be made without creating false certainty and brings an underlying consistency to the organisation's change agenda. Importantly, it puts short, medium and long-term value back on the same value-continuum.
- When pursuing a change-opportunity The Vital Thread offers a lifeline to hold onto, maintaining focus when assumptions and plans turn out to be wrong.
- The Vital Thread enables the organisation to authentically and consistently answer the question 'Why?' and overcome many of the underlying causes of resistance.

10

The fifth element: Thrive Cycle Leadership

Leading change through The Thrive Cycle requires the ability to apply specific behaviours at specific times. To achieve this and create The Adaptive Organisation requires all leaders to develop three core capabilities.

IT WAS MAY 2014 AND THE AFRICAN Development Bank was hosting a conference in Kagali[1]. Its theme was 'Leadership for the Africa we want'.

On Day 1 of the conference there was a plenary session where a panel of experts was posed the following question. The host asked:

'When you look at the challenges facing the youth of Africa today, and the challenges of emerging economies, education and healthcare and so on, where on Earth should we begin?'

One of the panel speakers was the former President of the Republic of Nigeria, H.E. Olusegun Obasanjo.

'Well,' he said, 'we need to start by asking "What kind of Africa do we want?" I mean, shouldn't we be able to work that out for ourselves?'

He continued.

'Africa where nobody feels oppressed,

'Africa where everybody will have opportunity,

'Africa where there will be democracy with full participation,

'Africa, where everybody will be able to develop their full potential.'

Obasanjo paused and then proceeded to tell a story.

'About six months ago, I was very uncomfortable because a girl wrote me a letter. In it, she said, "I am worried and I am concerned. I am in a situation where we have a past that I do not understand, we have a present that is confusing and we have a future that I have no confidence in".

'I wrote back to her and said, "We need to talk". So, she came with fifteen of her peers... and we spent the whole night talking about the past, the present and the future.

'I mean, they weren't asking for anything extraordinary. We've talked about different kinds of leadership.

'Any leadership that has no vision is no leadership.

'Any leadership that cannot transform is no leadership...

'... a leader must be a leader and the job of a leader, is to lead. Lead in all aspects of the form.

'... we need a critical mass of performing leaders... when we have that, we will get where we want to get to.'

That second last phrase is my favourite.

'A leader must be a leader and the job of a leader is to lead'. There are few who would disagree. However, in the complex world in which many leaders now find themselves, the understandable response is 'Sure... but how?'

THE ILLUSIVE CAPABILITY

Companies whose leaders are adaptive, are three times more likely to rank in the top 20 percent of financially performing organisations than those whose leaders are not[26]. However, when an IBM study interviewed 1500 CEOs, eight out of ten said that they expected their future environment to significantly increase in complexity but less than half felt able to deal with it successfully[32].

Adaptive leadership and what makes the difference between *good* and *great* leaders has been the subject of research for many years. Enter the phrase *adaptive leadership* into any Internet search engine and it will return millions of results.

John Kotter talked about *change leadership*, describing it in terms of a leader's ability to facilitate an eight-step process[34]. The ability to create a sense of urgency, build a guiding coalition and the ability to communicate with and empower employees were among the leadership skills Kotter identified as being most important.

Ron Heifetz, one of the most prolific academic writers on adaptive leadership, adopts a more situational approach. Sometimes leaders are required to make decisions when both the issue and potential solutions are clear. Heifetz describes this as *technical* leadership. Most of the information is available and so it's a matter of the leader making a timely choice between *known* alternatives.

Adaptive leadership, Heifetz says, is different. It requires decisions to be made when neither the issue nor the solution can be determined without significant learning[30]. The challenge, of course, comes when there is a mismatch between when the decision is required and the time available to learn.

Building on their work with emotional intelligence, Travis Bradbury and Jean Graves in *Leadership 2.0* used their research to identify both core and adaptive leadership skills[8]. The latter include such qualities as self-awareness, the ability to face and tell the truth, focusing on learning and developing others and concern with achieving the right outcome.

Applying the right behaviours at the right time

Being an adaptive leader is not like switching on a light. You don't mentally flick-over into 'adaptive mode', generically apply a list of skills and everything works. Success comes from applying the right mindset and behaviour for the given circumstance and usually, when you've never been in that kind of situation before.

For example, being creative is often listed as part of an adaptive leader's toolkit. Indeed, creativity is an adaptive-leadership behaviour when generating and exploring options and solutions. However, when you are in the final stages of *Moving* an organisation, other skills such as decisiveness become more important. In fact, being overly creative and revisiting options in this situation can actually be *non-adaptive.*

So leaders need to be able to work out when it's more important to be creative (or apply any other adaptive trait) and when it's not. But how can they do this?

When I think back to the most adaptive leaders I've worked with, most were either incredibly experienced (i.e. have learnt the contextual patterns to look for and applied their skills to great effect) or, they were naturally intuitive and sensed when a certain approach was required.

So here's the challenge.

For your organisation to effectively and consistently navigate The Thrive Cycle it requires a 'critical mass of performing leaders'. However, waiting for twenty years and hoping leaders will develop the capability or only recruiting those who are naturally intuitive, is not going to achieve this outcome.

What's needed instead is a way for your organisation to understand, teach and develop these kinds of leadership skills in such a way that any one of your leaders, regardless of their experience or personal style, can learn how to use them.

That is why your organisation needs Thrive Cycle Leadership.

THRIVE CYCLE LEADERSHIP

Imagine you've entered a car in the *Monte Carlo Formula 1 Grand Prix*. You've spent years and billions of dollars creating one of the fastest, most aerodynamically-manoeuvrable cars on the planet.

It's the morning of the race, your phone rings and it's your driver. He's had a cycling accident and won't be able to drive. It's at this point you become acutely aware of a simple truth – no matter how much you've invested or how fast your car is, if no one knows how to *start* or *drive* it, you're still not going to win the race.

The same truth applies when investing in Thrive Cycle capability. The benefits from your investment will only be realised when your organisation's leaders are consistently able to mobilise then navigate changes through it.

In other words, your leaders need to put *the cycle* into The Thrive Cycle.

What is Thrive Cycle Leadership?

Every time a change-opportunity comes along, it touches The Thrive Cycle within your organisation. Sometimes it enters, other times, it just passes by.

When a change-opportunity enters The Thrive Cycle it's called *a rotation*. This refers to the unique path the change-opportunity follows, regardless of whether it progresses through all seven stages or not.

A rotation can apply to a macro-change (e.g. an overall change that might affect the entire organisational strategy) or a micro-change (e.g. a new product or a response to a regulatory change that affects only part of the organisation). Regardless of the size of the change, the objective of every rotation is to create maximum value for customers and thus, the organisation.

Within this context, the purpose of Thrive Cycle Leadership is to ensure that:

- only change-opportunities that create value enter The Thrive Cycle

- each stage achieves the required outcome and focuses on value
- the change is given every chance to succeed
- the change-opportunity proceeds at the appropriate pace
- there is decision-making continuity between the stages
- the organisation's Thrive Cycle capability improves with each change-cycle.

The Thrive Cycle Leader

The Thrive Cycle Leader is a situational role that can be played by any person who holds a leadership position within your organisation. A leader mentally moves into the Thrive Cycle Leader role whenever they find themselves leading, facilitating, or supporting a rotation through The Thrive Cycle.

Note that Thrive Cycle Leadership is different to project sponsorship and to the professional disciplines of change management or project management. Thrive Cycle Leadership capability needs to be practiced by *every* leader when they find themselves involved in a change, regardless of whether they are driving the change or not. In this way Thrive Cycle Leadership places accountability for creating value on all leaders that are involved in the change, not just the leader who is officially 'driving' it[a].

Thrive Cycle Leadership operates outside the organisational hierarchy. It makes no difference whether you are an Executive Team member, a finance manager or a team leader in the service centre, the same skills apply. What's more important, is where you are in The Thrive Cycle.

In this way, if a Corporate Sales Manager needed to change some of the processes within the sales team, he or she would need to invoke their Thrive Cycle Leadership capabilities. Similarly, if a member of your team came to you requesting approval for a new system, it would

---

a It's important to note that the Driver of a change is still accountable for success. However, their accountabilities and required skills are different and in addition to those required for Thrive Cycle Leadership. We'll come back to this in Chapter 13 when we talk about your role as the Driver behind The Adaptive Organisation.

be you who needed to invoke the same Thrive Cycle Leadership skills. If however, the team member was asking for approval as part of a business-as-usual process, the role of Thrive Cycle leader would be less relevant and could stay in the background.

Thrive Cycle Leadership starts with you

As an experienced leader, you already know that *leadership* is not one of those things where you can say to your team 'from now on *you* need to apply Thrive Cycle Leadership' without modelling the behaviour yourself. We'll explore this in more detail in Chapter 11 where we'll look at how leadership capability across the hierarchy affects adaptive capability.

For now, however, the message is simple. To create the required critical mass of highly-capable Thrive Cycle Leaders, it needs to start with you, your Executive Team and most senior leaders within your organisation.

So let's move into the next layer of detail and explore what it takes to be a great Thrive Cycle Leader.

THREE LEADERSHIP CAPABILITIES

Every rotation through The Thrive Cycle needs to achieve certain outcomes if it is going to create value. The job of a Thrive Cycle Leader is to ensure the outcomes for every stage are achieved. To do this, a Thrive Cycle Leader must *match* the right leadership mindset and behaviours with the relevant stage of The Thrive Cycle.

Being a great Thrive Cycle Leader requires three leadership capabilities. From your perspective, this means being able to:

- Recognise when you've entered a Thrive Cycle rotation.
- Pinpoint which stage of The Thrive Cycle you're in.
- Apply the right mindset and behaviours for that stage.

In the remainder of this chapter we'll look at each of these capabilities and examine how they enable The Thrive Cycle to *go 'round.*

CAPABILITY #1 – Recognise when you've entered a Thrive Cycle rotation

The ability to recognise when you've entered a Thrive Cycle rotation will enable you to know when to 'switch-on' your Thrive Cycle Leadership skills.

You may recall in Part 1 we defined a change-opportunity as *any event (or events) in which the potential consequences could alter the rhythm, or balance, of our world and thus, our future chances of success.*

One of the most obvious ways to recognise a 'rotation conversation' is when someone brings one of these types of events to your attention. Another give-away is when someone actually says they want to change something within the organisation or respond to a change outside the organisation. Involvement in strategic planning of any kind usually brings with it a need to apply Thrive Cycle Leadership.

Unfortunately, identifying a rotation conversation is not always this easy, especially when the change-opportunity starts in a less familiar part of the organisation. Some phrases that may indicate you're part of a change-cycle conversation include:

- *'I think it's time we updated our...'*
- *'We really need to take a closer look at...'*
- *'I've got a great opportunity that I'd like to share with you.'*
- *'We need a new...'*
- *'I need some money and it's not in the budget.'*
- *'We need to deliver this by...'*
- *'Our competitors have just...'*
- *'Our customer research is telling us that...'*

How to identify Thrive Cycle conversations

NEXT TIME YOU ARE in your workplace listen to the conversations going on around you.

- *How many of them are talking about maintaining the business in its current state, and how many are part of a Thrive Cycle rotation?*

You may be surprised how many change-related conversations are going on at any one time.

Doing this simple exercise on a regular basis will refine your 'change antennae' and make it easier to know when to engage your Thrive Cycle Leadership skills.

CAPABILITY #2 – Pinpoint where you are in The Thrive Cycle

If you're going to reach a specific destination, it helps to know where you are on the map. Being an effective Thrive Cycle Leader means being able to identify the point at which you've entered a rotation conversation (i.e. determine which stage you're at).

Once again, remember that Thrive Cycle Leadership is not about whether certain stages in a project methodology have been 'ticked-off' or whether 'approval gates' have been passed. That's a change-management professional's job. Your role is to ensure the change is well positioned to create value. The way to do this is to look at each stage of The Thrive Cycle and evaluate whether the desired outcomes have been achieved within that specific rotation. The checklist in Figure 10-1 will provide a useful guide.

Work through each item from the top. Every time you are satisfied the outcome has been achieved, move onto the next one. Continue to do this until you reach a criterion that has not yet been addressed. This is the stage that you've entered the Thrive Cycle rotation and thus, you will need to apply the Thrive Cycle Leadership capabilities that support the outcomes for that stage.

FIGURE 10-1: Use this checklist of Thrive Cycle outcomes to pinpoint where you are in The Thrive Cycle.

SEE	• The opportunity to create value has been openly and objectively assessed • It's clear why now is the right time to act • The opportunity is driven by customer-value
UNDERSTAND	• Stakeholders have a clear and consistent view of the problem or opportunity that this change creates • Stakeholders have a clear and consistent view how taking action will create value for customers and the organisation
PRIORITISE	• It is clear where this change sits within organisational priorities • The assigned priority reflects the potential value of the opportunity • Resource allocation reflects its assigned priority
DESIGN	• It is clear what value-criteria the solution needs to meet • Broad options have been developed by the right people • A direct link can be drawn between the proposed solution and the creation of value
PLAN	• The key drivers of value have been articulated within the plan • The plan describes how value will be protected, as well as created, throughout delivery
MOVE	• Key stakeholders clearly understand the nature and size of the value the change needs to deliver • Key stakeholders are motivated and empowered to deliver in an adaptive way
LEARN	• The value created by the change has been openly and objectively assessed • The created value is sustainable into the foreseeable future • Improvements have been identified and embedded into The Thrive Cycle

Watch out for this Thrive Cycle Leadership trap

THE APPROACH I'VE JUST DESCRIBED sounds pretty methodical. Use the checklist, tick-off the outcomes and there you have it – you've located where you are in The Thrive Cycle.

However, sometimes when you do, you may find a number of stakeholders believe their progress is more advanced than your assessment suggests.

This can happen when there has been an over-emphasis on process and an under-emphasis on value. It's also driven by human nature. People usually want to reach the 'Move' stage of a Thrive Cycle rotation as quickly as possible. That's when you start to see the most tangible evidence of a change. This feels good!

However, if when doing your assessment, you are unconvinced that critical outcomes have not been achieved during earlier stages, then subsequent activities are unlikely to be maximising value. In fact, in my experience this can mean that change is running full speed toward the wrong finish-line.

This is one of those times when you need to be brave and remain focused on value-creation, rather than being swept along by the prevailing opinion. Doing so will pay exponential dividends down the track.

CAPABILITY #3 – Apply the right mindset and behaviours for that stage

It was 1985 when Edward de Bono introduced the world to his *Six Thinking Hats* and demonstrated how different types of thinking were needed to achieve a given outcome[16]. This concept of wearing different hats provides a useful analogy when developing Thrive Cycle Leadership.

The outcomes for each Thrive Cycle stage are different. As a result, each stage requires a different way of thinking and behaving to achieve them. As the leader, you need to understand then wear the right Thrive Cycle Leadership *hat* for the stage in which you find yourself. Further, as the change-opportunity rotates through the different stages, you'll need to change 'hats' if you are to ensure that value is being created throughout.

So looking at the outcomes for each Thrive Cycle stage[b], what are the different Thrive Cycle Leadership mindsets and behaviours that will drive success?

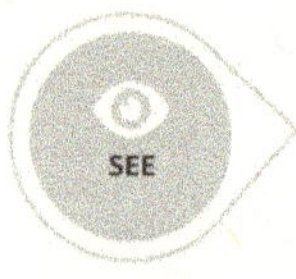

Only value-creating opportunities enter The Thrive Cycle, they do so at the right time and clearly strengthen the Customer-Value Continuum

The *See* stage of The Thrive Cycle requires a delicate balance of ensuring the right opportunities enter the organisation while not overwhelming it with changes of low value. If too many change-opportunities enter your organisation it can create a log-jam, such that none of them progress. Alternatively, if high-value opportunities pass your organisation by, or they enter late, other challenges arise at later stages of The Thrive Cycle.

So how do you get the balance 'just right'?

Be curious, open-minded and constantly seek new insights

The *See* stage of The Thrive Cycle is the gateway to your organisation. Thrive Cycle Leadership ensures that the gate is always open to considering new opportunities. However, it does so using The Vital Thread to ensure shared focus.

This stage requires a passion for learning. Not just your own but that of the people around you. This is the case regardless of who they are, what position they hold and whether they are part of your team

b These outcomes are a summary of those listed in Figure 10-1.

or not. When potential opportunities are raised, make comments that open up the conversation. For example:

- *Tell me more about your idea.*
- *What do you think our biggest opportunity is here?*
- *How could we make it even better?*
- *What are we missing?*
- *How does the customer fit into this story?*

Remember that as a Thrive Cycle Leader, your role is also to understand The Vital Thread as it exists today and evolve it when necessary. Therefore, if new information suggests The Vital Thread no longer represents the real world (e.g. customer-needs have changed or internal Delivery-Drivers are weaker than The Vital Thread suggests), it needs to be considered, rather than dismissed.

This is not to say that a Thrive Cycle Leader is willing to throw out The Vital Thread at the first signs of change. Rather, it means being prepared to consider the possibility, as opposed to defending the status quo at all costs.

Make it easy to 'speak-up'

A Thrive Cycle Leader listens to opportunities, even if they suggest a mistake may have been made in the past. This type of leadership is essential if your people are going to feel safe raising potential change-opportunities.

The following wouldn't happen in The Adaptive Organisation.

> *A services company had found a growing opportunity providing local banking services to migrants who were about to enter the country on a working visa. This service was required as part of the migrants' visa application process.*
>
> *About 18 months earlier a young woman started work in the mailroom. One day she was making a cup of coffee in the kitchen when a leader from another part of the business happened to walk in. The woman approached the leader.*

'I'm sorry to bother you but I wanted to ask something. I think we have a problem and I've tried to raise it four times within my own department but I've been told that I shouldn't mention it any more. In fact, I'd be in big trouble if my boss knew that I was talking to you.'

The leader looked a bit confused at this point, and the young woman continued.

'You see, I've been looking at this returned mail coming back from these overseas customers.' The woman held up a small white envelope. 'I think I've identified why so many keep coming back. Look here! What do you notice?'

The leader looked and then saw what the team member was referring to. The country had not been included in the address.

The point in this example is not that the system had neglected to include the full address. The bigger concern was that this team member was afraid to raise something that created no value for herself, and significant value for the affected customers.

Making it easy to speak up doesn't have to involve major process re-engineering. Lou Gerstner, former IBM CEO who brought the company back from the brink of bankruptcy, instigated something called 'The IBM Jam'. It was a dedicated conference phone line open for several days that any employee could call in and discuss important topics or share insights[38].

Be analytical and use the available data from which to make decisions

It sounds rudimentary doesn't it? Of course you'd use the data available, even if it's a small amount. However, for many different reasons this is not always the case. In fact, when asked, only 29 percent of over a thousand CEOs said that they used the data available when making their most recent big decision[23].

Being analytical, in this context, is not to be confused with insisting upon having all of the information before making a decision. The latter is *not* adaptive.

Give ideas time to brew

It's not always obvious from the first conversation how much value an opportunity offers. Let's face it, we've all got busy agendas and sometimes it can be tempting to dismiss an apparently silly or low-value idea (so we can get on with important stuff).

When it comes to ideas, I'm a big believer in *brewing-time.* If you dunk a tea-bag for 5 seconds, you're not going to enjoy the best cup of tea. However, if you give it time to brew, the results will be far more satisfying.

Often the first idea put forward is not the best one. It needs time to brew i.e. be explored and enhanced through conversations. It's through this process that the real 'gems' emerge. If the idea is shut-down in the first instance, this never happens.

Invoking 'brewing-time' means saying something like:

- *'How about getting a few people together around a whiteboard and see where this idea takes us?'*
- *'How about sharing this idea with (names) and see if there are other possibilities we've yet to consider?'*

Allowing ideas time to brew during the *See* stage delivers another invaluable benefit. It means the people who are putting forward the ideas feel heard. While you haven't given 'the green light' and approval to invest in it, you've left open the future possibilities. To an employee excited by an idea, that is really empowering and means they are likely to put more ideas forward in the future.

I should mention that like a tea-bag, it's important not to leave an idea brewing for too long. If it has been explored, its potential value is understood and it's not worth pursuing at this time, then make a decision and put it on-hold. When doing so be clear about why you've made that decision and under what circumstances you would consider the idea again. Then, personally communicate it to the person who put it forward.

Relevant stakeholders have a clear and consistent understanding of the opportunity, or problem, to be addressed. They also agree how addressing it will create value for customers and the organisation

The *Understand* stage of The Thrive Cycle is where the direction (and often, the fate) of an organisational change is usually determined. This is way before the approach has been developed or a business-case has even been discussed.

If this stage is not well led and the outcome above is not achieved, then it can spell disaster later on.

Be patient and seek understanding first, before seeking the answer

When a change-opportunity comes along, a Thrive Cycle Leader steps-back before leaping in to find a solution. They do this regardless of the amount of time available within which to achieve the desired outcome.

Now you might be thinking to yourself, 'Hey... hang-on... when it's urgent you can't spend all day naval-gazing. You've got to get on with it'. If you are thinking this, you wouldn't be alone.

All I can say is, if I had a magic-wand that could change just one thing and make organisations significantly more adaptive overnight, it would be this one. Failing to understand the *real* problem frequently triggers a chain-reaction of mistakes, misunderstandings, wrong-turns, heightened stress and costs. Further, as with so many aspects of The Thrive Cycle, these issues often only surface once you've financially and emotionally committed to delivering what is probably the *wrong* solution.

Just stop, take a deep breath and ask 'what problem are we really aiming to solve here?' Then, see what people say. If they start huffing and puffing and talking about how obvious it is, but can't articulate it, the chances are they don't know the answer.

Apply systems-thinking

Systems-thinking is a principle-based approach to solving problems. First popularised by Peter Senge in *The Fifth Discipline*, systems-thinking is underpinned by three characteristics[50].

- The desire to continuously seek out new information and learn.
- Self-awareness and the recognition that our own perspective on what's going on is always limited.
- The realisation that in order to see the whole picture and thus, understand the whole problem, we need to collaborate with others.

Senge used the term collective-intelligence. In his own words '*It's not about [being] "the smartest guys in the room" it's about what we can do collectively.*'

To be a great Thrive Cycle Leader you don't have to be most intellectually-accomplished person in the group and you don't need to have an MBA. You do, however, need to be aware of your own perspective and how it affects your ability to solve problems on your own.

A great Thrive Cycle Leader also recognises the organisation as a series of interdependent systems. They look for patterns in the environment and focus on the core triggers that change those patterns. In a practical sense, this means worrying less about what 'the dots' look like (because they'll be different tomorrow), and more about how they are connected to one another.

The priority of the opportunity is clear, relative to others. Its importance and resource allocation reflects the value it's expected to create

I spent several years leading the strategic change portfolio within a large corporation. In addition to overseeing delivery, the role included allocating funding and resources for around 100 strategic initiatives every year. So when I say that prioritisation is one of the most challenging jobs of a leader, I'm speaking from experience. In fact the word I'd use is *thankless*, because no matter how much you try to get priority decisions right, there will always be someone who believes you got it wrong.

When finding themselves in the *Prioritise* stage of The Thrive Cycle, other leaders may choose to back-away and either leave the difficult choices to others, or simply leave them un-made. A Thrive Cycle Leader however, never does.

Be consistent and let customer-value be your guide

It's doesn't matter whether the decision involves billions of dollars or next year's Christmas party, the same principles apply. Thrive Cycle Leaders consistently see customer-value as the basis of economic-value and business performance.

Be decisive

Recognise that poor prioritisation is one of the biggest causes of organisational inertia. Step-up to the task, make the necessary trade-offs, give clear direction and build momentum.

Decisiveness really comes down to three things – timing, clarity, and follow-through. This applies not only to priority decisions but other choices as well.

- **Timing** – A Thrive Cycle Leader makes decisions when they need to be made. Not before, and definitely not after.

So why not before? Surely, the sooner a decision is made, the sooner it can be translated into action. While this may be true in an operational situation, a change-dominated environment is uncertain and ambiguous. Therefore, if a leader makes a decision today, it is possible the factors that led to that decision may no longer hold true in a week's time (when the decision actually is required). Thus, in order to maximise the chances the decision is the best one, it needs to be made at the right time.

Of course, there are times when the right time to make a decision feels far too early. Having to make a decision when very little information is available is scary, especially if there are significant consequences. That's why a Thrive Cycle Leader is not only decisive, he or she is clear about which part of a decision needs to be made when.

What do I mean by this?

Well, usually a 'big decision' isn't a big decision at all. It actually comprises several smaller ones. By chunking the decision down, it is sometimes possible to maintain momentum while making some decisions later, when more information is known.

- **Clarity** – The clearer priority decisions are, the easier they are to apply. A Thrive Cycle Leader is also willing to say 'no' to a great idea or stop an initiative part way because something else represents greater value.
- **Follow-through** – A decision is only a decision when someone acts on it. A Thrive Cycle Leader knows this and follows through to ensure the decision has been consistently translated into action.

BE TRANSPARENT

When priority decisions are transparent it is clear why and how a given decision was reached. This offers two benefits. First, it helps your people to make lower-level decisions that are in keeping with the original intent. Second, it fosters perceived 'fairness' and this creates trust.

Now you might be thinking to yourself 'Hey… this is business, not some game in a school playground'. So here's the logic.

When your people believe a priority decision has been made fairly and in the interests of customers, they are more likely to feel positively about it. Conversely, when it is believed that politics or some back-door decision-making process has been followed, they are more likely to question its value.

Note here that making priority decisions transparently doesn't guarantee everyone will like them. It does however make engagement easier down the track.

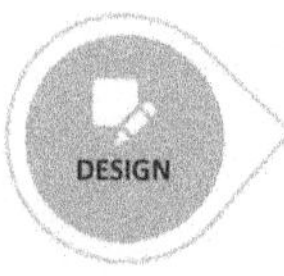

The chosen solution has been selected from a broad range of options and is the one that will deliver the greatest value

The *Design* stage of The Thrive Cycle is the pivot-point between *thinking* and *doing*. While you need both orientations in all stages, this is where the ratio starts to change in favour of *doing*. The role of The Thrive Cycle Leader is to maintain the delicate balance and ensure nothing becomes lost is translation.

Use The Vital Thread to guide the solution

One of the fundamental requirements of a Thrive Cycle Leader is to know how the organisation creates value. This means understanding the levers that determine whether value is created or not. It is here that The Vital Thread becomes one of your most important leadership tools.

Dr Ralf Speth, CEO of Jaguar once said 'If you think that good design is expensive, you should look at the cost of bad design'. Never truer words were spoken when it comes to turning a change-opportunity into something that creates value.

Design and knowing what a solution needs to achieve is paramount. That's why there is a *Golden Rule* that a Thrive Cycle Leader must reinforce for every change.

Always set design principles before looking for the right response

Think for a moment about the difference between designing something, and developing it.

Design starts with the success criteria then works out how to meet them. In the context of change, the first success criterion should be that the final solution must create value. When we produce 'a design' we are focused on ensuring what we are designing delivers what it sets out to do.

Development is really the next stage after design, looking at different possibilities (or options) that meet the requirements set by the design.

Unfortunately the *Design* stage is yet another one of the Thrive Cycle stages that is easy to miss. People just want 'the answer'. That's why as a Thrive Cycle Leader it's your role to encourage, I'd even say insist on, developing Design Principles for every change-opportunity. Doing so will deliver the following benefits.

- **Avoid nasty (and expensive) surprises** – When you've built half your rocket ship, it's a bit late to realise it needed to take six passengers, not two.
- **Reduce the risk of people falling in love with their own ideas** – When this happens, it can make it harder to see alternatives. Avoiding this means the solution is more likely to achieve the desired outcome, rather than being someone's 'pet project'.
- **Make it easier for stakeholders to engage early** – Design Principles enable stakeholders to picture the outcome sooner and more fully engage without becoming bogged in the details.

Facilitate emotional and intellectual alignment

The degree of emotional and intellectual alignment of stakeholders achieved *before* a change-opportunity moves into the *Plan* stage is commensurate with its likely success. Therefore, as a Thrive Cycle Leader it's important to maximise alignment. This is true *regardless* of whether you are the person driving the change or supporting it.

I've sometimes had people challenge me on this point and say 'but isn't it the *Driver's* job to ensure there is alignment?' As you'll see in Chapter 13, the technical answer is 'yes… one of the Driver's roles is to facilitate alignment'. However, the belief that creating alignment is *entirely* up to the Driver can result in poor leadership behaviours. I have seen this happen many times. Leaders *waiting* for the Driver to engage them rather than stepping forward to start the conversation.

Once again I come back to the words of Africa's H.E. Olusegun Obasanjo. '*…a leader must be a leader and the job of a leader, is to lead. Lead in all aspects of the form*'. As a Thrive Cycle Leader it is your job to do whatever it takes to foster alignment. This doesn't mean agreeing with everything the Driver says, but it does mean proactively working towards understanding and the best outcome.

So when you find yourself in the *Design* stage how do you foster alignment?

It's not always easy and so it can be helpful to be prepared for the different scenarios you may encounter (Figure 10-2).

As a Thrive Cycle Leader, you are aiming to build *Strong Consensus* between key stakeholders. This means there is a common understanding and a common commitment to delivering the desired outcome. This promotes the kind of adaptive behaviour that navigating The Thrive Cycle through a complex and changing environment requires.

Any other combination will reduce the amount of value being delivered.

For instance, if stakeholders are highly committed to the outcome, but don't really understand it, the result is *Blind Devotion*. This means stakeholders will do what you tell them to, but won't really be able to think for themselves. This scenario is unhelpful in a change-dominated environment in which you cannot possibly know all the answers.

Conversely, if there is shared understanding but commitment is lacking, then you will be faced with *Informed Skepticism.* While people will 'get' what you're saying they are unlikely to share your enthusiasm and they definitely won't instil enthusiasm in their teams.

Then of course, there is *Weak Consensus,* which is characterised by low commitment and low consensus. Needless to say if you find that by this stage of The Thrive Cycle you are caught in this kind of 'alignment vacuum', you've got a long road ahead of you. That said, it is far better to be aware of this at this stage in the Thrive Cycle than to discover it further down the track.

We'll talk more about alignment in Chapter 13 and explore ways to engage the non-believers.

FIGURE 10-2: Four scenarios of stakeholder alignment[a]

COMMITMENT		UNDERSTANDING: Low	UNDERSTANDING: High
	High	**Blind Devotion** People do what you tell them but become lost in a changing environment	**Strong Consensus** People are committed and understand what they are doing and why
	Low	**Weak Consensus** No one 'gets it' and no one is interested in doing anything about it	**Informed Skepticism** People understand the outcome but are unmotivated to act

a This matrix and terminology has been adapted from work by B. Wooldridge and S. Floyd[55].

Use a One-Page-Why to bridge the gap between the opportunity, solution-design and delivery

Effective communication is a must at every stage of The Thrive Cycle. However, in this transitional stage, it is particularly important. Once again, our friend the One-Page-Why is able to assist. It does so for a given change-opportunity by summarising the conversations and decisions from earlier stages of The Thrive Cycle.

To illustrate, let's once again come back to the scenario being faced by our friends at Orion Healthcare. You will recall in Chapter 9 this organisation was facing the Government's change of policy regarding overseas doctors.

Orion has now reached the point where they need to design their response. To do this, they use a One-Page-Why to engage the people who are best positioned to help address the problem (Figure 10-3). There are a number of features worth highlighting.

Notice how, from the very beginning, the driver behind the change is made patently clear. Also, because the people within the organisation already understand The Vital Thread, they can quickly orient themselves. Without it, hours would have been spent developing PowerPoint presentations (which few participants would have read) and having meetings, just to understand why the opportunity *is* an opportunity.

The Design Principles on the right give the people involved in designing the solution guidance as to what a proposed solution needs to achieve. Also, because the One-Page-Why only contains information that has *already* been agreed, there is considerable alignment regarding the messages being communicated.

FIGURE 10-3: One-Page-Why used by Orion to engage its people during the 'Design' stage of The Thrive Cycle.

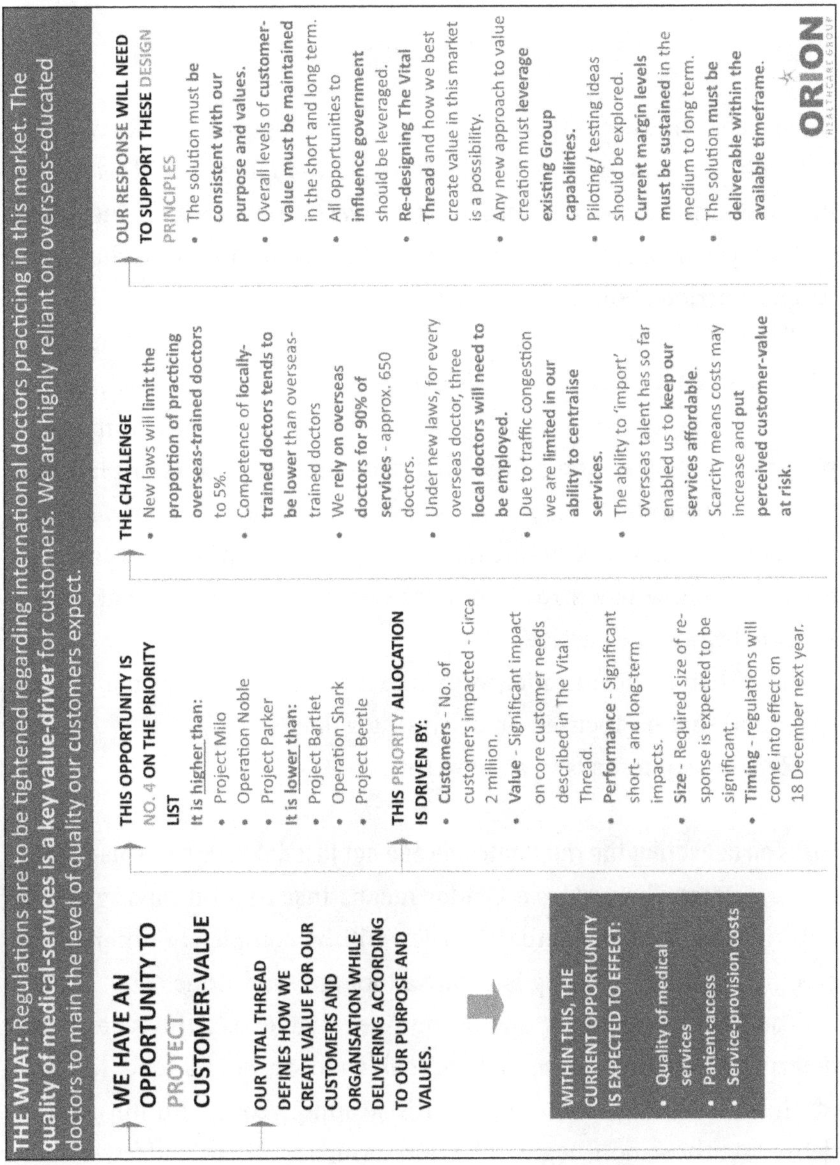

THE WHAT: Regulations are to be tightened regarding international doctors practicing in this market. The **quality of medical-services is a key value-driver** for customers. We are highly reliant on overseas-educated doctors to main the level of quality our customers expect.

WE HAVE AN OPPORTUNITY TO PROTECT CUSTOMER-VALUE

OUR VITAL THREAD DEFINES HOW WE CREATE VALUE FOR OUR CUSTOMERS AND ORGANISATION WHILE DELIVERING ACCORDING TO OUR PURPOSE AND VALUES.

WITHIN THIS, THE CURRENT OPPORTUNITY IS EXPECTED TO EFFECT:

- Quality of medical services
- Patient-access
- Service-provision costs

THIS OPPORTUNITY IS NO. 4 ON THE PRIORITY LIST

It is higher than:

- Project Milo
- Operation Noble
- Project Parker

It is lower than:

- Project Bartlet
- Operation Shark
- Project Beetle

THIS PRIORITY ALLOCATION IS DRIVEN BY:

- **Customers** - No. of customers impacted - Circa 2 million.
- **Value** - Significant impact on core customer needs described in The Vital Thread.
- **Performance** - Significant short- and long-term impacts.
- **Size** - Required size of response is expected to be significant.
- **Timing** - regulations will come into effect on 18 December next year.

THE CHALLENGE

- New laws will **limit the proportion of practicing overseas-trained doctors** to 5%.
- Competence of **locally-trained doctors tends to be lower** than overseas-trained doctors
- We **rely on overseas doctors for 90% of services** - approx. 650 doctors.
- Under new laws, for every overseas doctor, three **local doctors will need to be employed.**
- Due to traffic congestion we are **limited in our ability to centralise services.**
- The ability to 'import' overseas talent has so far enabled us to **keep our services affordable**. Scarcity means costs may increase and **put perceived customer-value at risk.**

OUR RESPONSE WILL NEED TO SUPPORT THESE DESIGN PRINCIPLES

- The solution must **be consistent with our purpose and values.**
- Overall levels of **customer-value must be maintained** in the short and long term.
- All opportunities to **influence government** should be leveraged.
- **Re-designing The Vital Thread** and how we best create value in this market is a possibility.
- Any new approach to value creation must **leverage existing Group capabilities.**
- Piloting/ testing ideas should be explored.
- **Current margin levels must be sustained** in the medium to long term.
- The solution **must be deliverable within the available timeframe.**

ORION
HEALTHCARE GROUP

The plan focuses on delivering value (not just the solution) and it is clear how existing value will be protected throughout the journey

As a leader, the *Plan* stage is one of the easier stages of The Thrive Cycle to identify. If you are talking about a macro-change, you'll usually be in some kind of strategic planning conversation. If it's an individual change, you'll probably be surrounded by lots of milestone charts and people worried about budgets and resources.

The trick to Thrive Cycle Leadership here is not to become lost in what may potentially be an overwhelming level of detail. Making sure the plans are robust and technically valid is the job of planning and project specialists. Remember that the core purpose of a plan *is to provide an organisational frame-of-reference that facilitates preparation, collaboration and communication.* It helps people to work in the same direction, know when resources are needed, and know what will be expected when they arrive.

As a Thrive Cycle Leader, your role is to make sure the plan makes sense and that it's focused on delivering value.

Here are some ways to achieve this.

Focus on delivering the right outcome and not just delivering the plan

Being a great Thrive Cycle Leader means insisting on having a plan, but knowing that the actual journey will be completely different. It's recognising that planning is iterative, not one-and-done.

Your role is to focus on the non-negotiables i.e. the factors that determine whether value will be delivered or not. I tend to think of these as being the stakes-in-the-ground. Your commitment to delivering those non-negotiables and ensuring others understand and focus on them is a critical part of the Thrive Cycle Leader's role.

Five characteristics of a good plan

THE THRIVE CYCLE LEADER ensures that a plan:

- is clear enough to enable large groups of people to collaborate
- builds momentum via quick-wins, not shortcuts
- is targeted to the audience using language, and at a level they can understand
- makes it clear what is actually expected to be delivered and when this is going to deliver value
- is clear about which achievements and dates are more important than others

Understand the landscape and its underlying terrain, not just the path you plan to follow

With all the focus on uncertainty these days, it's sometimes easy to forget that in many aspects of our lives certainty is increasing. For example, identifying health issues or predicting whether it will be raining at 6pm when the football game starts.

Navigation is another area in which we have increased certainty. If we want to drive somewhere new we get out our smartphone, or turn on the GPS, and it gives us the route. We don't need to take notice of landmarks or think through the best route, just follow the blue line and you'll reach your destination.

Thrive Cycle Leadership is not about understanding the blue line, it's about understanding the whole map, and more importantly, the terrain it represents.

To illustrate, imagine if your satellite navigation system only showed you the blue line, and not the map that lay underneath it. Would you still be able to reach your destination? Well, you probably would as long as you did exactly what the blue line was telling you.

However, what if a water main had burst on one of the roads and you had to move away from the path set by the blue line? How would you get back on track? While in reality, your navigation system would re-set, last time I checked, leadership didn't come with built-in satellite navigation, so you'd need to work out what to do.

You might start by trying to maintain the same direction. For example, stay heading north? But that wouldn't tell you when you were going to find the route again or at which point you had re-joined it. Of course, in a change-dominated environment there is one more hitch.

The roads you used to drive on are often being ripped up and re-routed.

Thrive Cycle Leadership therefore requires an ability to see the risks and the opportunities across the organisational landscape. This means having the ability to determine which areas to avoid, where the shortcuts might be and where the terrain will make the journey slow-going. As a result, if the current plan fails, you already have a framework against which you can quickly assess potential alternatives.

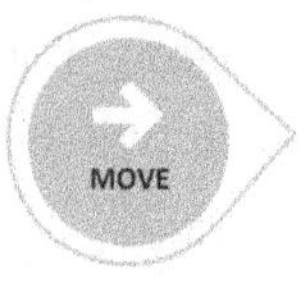

Key stakeholders understand the value to be delivered. They are motivated and empowered to do what it takes to deliver it and ensure the outcome is sustainable

Thrive Cycle Leadership during the *Move* stage of The Thrive Cycle is all about clearing a path and enabling the organisation and its people, to transition from a previous state to a new one. Most importantly, it's about ensuring the new state is the right one and that it is sustained well after the change-team has packed up and gone home.

When you find yourself at this stage of The Thrive Cycle, especially if it is a large organisational change, it may feel quite chaotic. The following ideas will help you to maintain focus in the areas that are important.

Show an unwavering commitment to your team and to the creation of value

A great Thrive Cycle Leader never goes missing in action when things go wrong. They are prepared to back their team members, particularly when calculated risks head south. This means being committed to all the people involved in the change, regardless of whether or not they report to you directly.

Be demanding of yourself and others

Being a Thrive Cycle Leader requires unwavering determination. It involves holding yourself and others to account for the commitments that have been made. If you say you're going to be there, *be there* in body and in spirit. By the way, sitting reading emails on your smart-phone is not *being there*. If others say they'll have something completed, if they don't, ask 'why not?'

Ensure trade-off decisions don't erode value-drivers

Moving an organisation involves hundreds, if not thousands, of trade-off decisions. These often have an effect upon the degree to which the desired outcome can be sustained over time.

Appreciate when you're making a trade-off decision and recognise that a change in *time*, *cost* or *quality* will impact the remaining two factors.

Empower your people by making clear what is important and providing guidance as to how trade-offs can be made. When doing so, use The Vital Thread to determine where quality is more important and where 'good-enough' is enough.

Be pragmatic and understand the rules before breaking them

Sometimes leaders say they are being pragmatic when actually they are being undisciplined. There is a distinct difference.

Being pragmatic means understanding the theory and adapting it to suit the challenges or opportunities you are faced with in real life. Thus, when a Thrive Cycle Leader decides to go outside the process, they appreciate why the process was there and what it aimed to achieve. As a result, they also know what risks they are potentially exposing themselves to when they decide to go outside the norm.

In contrast, being undisciplined means doing what is easier at the time. It is short-term behaviour without giving due consideration to the longer-term implications of a decision.

Wipe the term 'resistance to change' from your vocabulary

How many times have you heard someone say that the reason an organisational change failed came down to a 'resistance to change'? It's often said as though it's a *fait accompli*. Of course people resist change. That's just how *they* are, right?

Wrong!

In some ways, the phrase 'resistance to change' has become like the 'get out of jail free' card in the game Monopoly. It is a rather convenient 'catch-all' that is used (usually by 'leaders') when they either don't know why their organisation effected a change so badly, or they don't want to consider (or perhaps admit) they may have somehow contributed to the outcome.

'Resistance to change' moves accountability away from the people leading change and back onto their people.

In fact, after 20 years working in and around organisational change, I would estimate that 80 percent of failures that cited 'resistance to change' as the cause, were actually the result of a weakness somewhere in The Six Elements of Adaptive Success. Either it was unclear why the change had been initiated, the solution didn't solve the problem, or the leaders did not lead in the way that was required.

That's why a Thrive Cycle Leader does not accept 'resistance to change' as a 'blanket' reason for not succeeding. He or she seeks the true reason for 'resistance' then takes action to address it.

The sustainable value created by change is objectively assessed, and action is taken to strengthen The Thrive Cycle

Thrive Cycle Learning is an organisational capability we'll explore in detail when we talk about creating a Balanced Ecosystem. For now however, let's examine the Thrive Cycle Leadership behaviours that will achieve the desired outcome for this stage.

Openly reflect on the successes and failures of change

This is a hard one. It's one of those things that looks great on paper but when organisational change has finished, it can be difficult to take a step back and be objective.

When reflecting on what happened, what worked and what didn't work, Thrive Cycle Leaders look at themselves first. How effective were they during the stages in which they were involved? A Thrive Cycle Leader looks for evidence as well as opinion, and recognises that the views of stakeholders reflect as much about *their* experience as they do about what actually happened. For example, a stakeholder may provide feedback that decision-making was too slow. Thrive Cycle Leaders take into account that this perception could be the result of poor or late engagement, rather than just 'slow decision-making'.

Be holistic and look for lessons across the entire Thrive Cycle

Every organisational change starts with *Seeing* the opportunity and so, when reflecting on lessons learned, that's where you need to start. Be systematic during the review and appreciate that the factors causing an issue or opportunity may have occurred many months before the issues appeared.

In addition, these leaders ensure that the perspectives are balanced and there is an appropriate mix of self-evaluation and objective observation.

Ensure lessons and necessary changes are applied

So many organisations spend hours and thousands of dollars ensuring they complete a thorough review of 'what happened'. However, these lessons are rarely applied.

Further, appreciate that simply saying 'we must change' doesn't mean the organisation does. People come and go and gradually corporate experience fades. That's why Thrive Cycle Leaders don't simply 'note down' how the organisation should change, they champion it to ensure it actually happens.

How to assess the leadership gaps

ASSESSING THRIVE CYCLE LEADERSHIP capability within an organisation usually involves a comprehensive evaluation process. However, for the purposes of illustration, we can do it quite quickly by using The Adaptive Profile you created in Part 1.

Think about the Thrive Cycle Leadership capabilities identified in this chapter. Then, answer the following questions.

- *What score (out of 5) would you give your organisation for Thrive Cycle Leadership for each of the seven Thrive Cycle stages?*
- *Are there Thrive Cycle Leadership capabilities in which your organisation is particularly strong or weak?*
- *How might this be affecting the Adaptive Profile today and the extent to which your organisation creates value, through change?*
- *How closely do the Thrive Cycle Leadership capabilities of today match those that will be required to achieve the Target Adaptive Profile of the future?*

If your Adaptive Profile is suggesting a weakness at the *Understand* stage of The Thrive Cycle and the required leadership behaviours for that stage are also fairly low, then chances are, leadership is one of the driving issues.

Also, if the performance across The Thrive Cycle overall is low then leadership would be one of the first places I'd look.

CHAPTER CONCLUSION

We've now covered five of The Six Elements of Adaptive Success. By this point it should be starting to become clear why it is critical to focus on **all six** of them. Without the other Elements, your most capable leaders will spend most of their time fighting fires, instead of creating value. Conversely, there is little point investing in the other Elements then having leaders who lack the skills or the necessary attitude to apply them.

KEY POINTS TO REMEMBER

- Thrive Cycle Leadership enables individual change-opportunities to effectively navigate The Thrive Cycle and create value.
- Thrive Cycle Leadership is a situational role that needs to be invoked whenever leaders find themselves leading, facilitating or supporting a Thrive Cycle rotation. This is the case regardless of whether the leader is the primary Driver for the change.
- Being a great Thrive Cycle Leader means developing three core capabilities:
  - Recognise when you've entered a Thrive Cycle rotation
  - Pinpoint where you are in The Thrive Cycle
  - Apply the right mindset and behaviours to achieve the outcome for that stage
- Thrive Cycle Leadership is like wearing different leadership hats. Each stage of The Thrive Cycle requires a different hat (i.e. different mindset and behaviours).
- Building Thrive Cycle Leadership capability starts with building the capability within the Executive Team and senior leadership community.

11

The sixth element: A Balanced Ecosystem

This chapter describes the Thrive Cycle Enablers your organisation requires if it is to sustainably build, maintain and improve its Thrive Cycle capability over time.

IF YOU WANT TO BUILD A BRICK HOUSE, you're going to need some bricks. In the same way, if you want to build The Adaptive Organisation you'll need to invest in the organisational infrastructure required to achieve it. More than this, you'll need to ensure that when the parts are brought together, they form a Balanced Ecosystem.

So let's start by looking at what this actually means.

STRIKING THE RIGHT BALANCE

The Thrive Cycle requires the support of an interconnected system of seven *Enablers* (covering Customer, People, Processes and Systems) if it is to be sufficiently robust to do its job (Figure 11-1). These *Thrive Cycle Enablers* are:

- Customer relevance
- Organisational structure
- Leadership capability
- People capability
- Prioritisation
- Thrive Cycle Learning
- Thrive Cycle Management

FIGURE 11-1: A Balanced Ecosystem comprises seven Thrive Cycle Enablers.

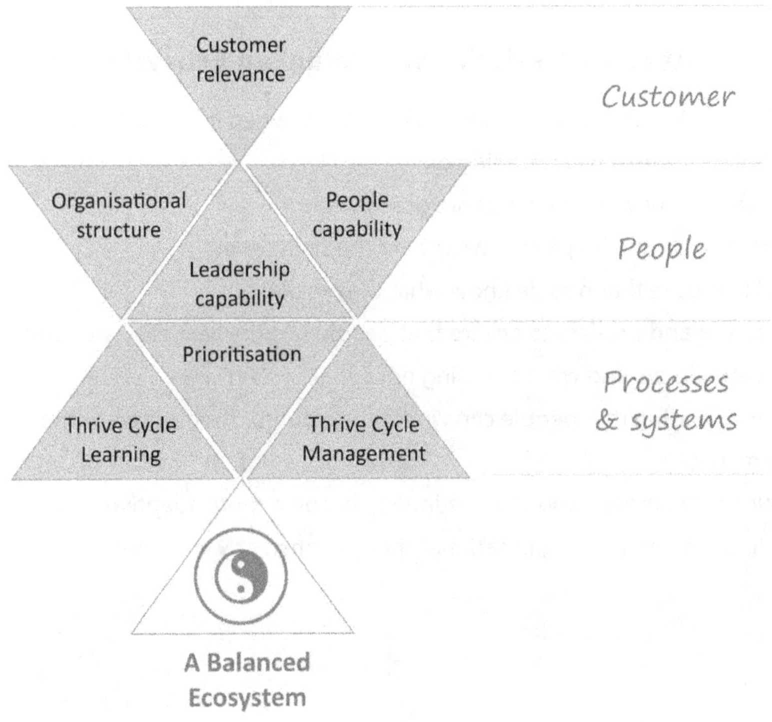

When your organisation achieves the right balance between the seven Thrive Cycle Enablers, it will be able to focus on what matters most i.e. creating value. If however, your Ecosystem is unbalanced, it will become a distraction that re-directs attention towards the process of change, rather than the outcome.

The over-arching objective when creating a Balanced Ecosystem is to build the organisational fitness required to achieve adaptive advantage. Many of the Enablers are already established business disciplines and when you reach this point, you're likely to engage some experts to help you. These may come from inside or outside your organisation.

Like any profession, experts can get pretty passionate and excited about their particular area of the ecosystem. Passion's good, but blind-passion in this space can lead to bureaucracy. Your role as the leader is to ensure your organisation's ecosystem strikes the right balance, and that one enabler doesn't over-power or undermine the others.

Eight characteristics of a Balanced Ecosystem

YOU'LL KNOW YOU HAVE a Balanced Ecosystem when it provides *enough*:

- **visibility** to know what is going on
- **triggers** to know when things are going wrong
- **insight** to be able to predict what's around the corner
- **skill** to ensure that people know what they're doing
- **structure and process** to ensure that people know where they are, where they should be, and what's coming next
- **understanding** that people can work things out for themselves, without the manual
- **drive** for the organisation to continue to become more adaptive
- **focus** to ensure that organisational change constantly creates value.

In this chapter we'll look at each of the Thrive Cycle Enablers and explore some of the factors to consider when putting them in place. Before we do however, there are a three *Golden Rules* to highlight.

RULE #1 – Consider the Balanced Ecosystem last

A low-scoring Adaptive Profile is rarely caused by the ecosystem underpinning The Thrive Cycle. It is far more likely that organisational weakness in the other Elements of Adaptive Success (e.g. failing to follow Adaptive Principles, an undefined Vital Thread or weak Thrive Cycle Leadership) has meant the Ecosystem has become dysfunctional and fragmented.

I usually recommend that a Balanced Ecosystem is the last of the Six Elements of Adaptive Success to be considered (i.e. after your organisation's position regarding the other Elements has been well understood). Otherwise you can fall into the following trap.

THE 'PICK-N-MIX' APPROACH

The 'pick-n-mix' approach treats the Thrive Cycle Enablers as though they are independent of one another. Thus, what is implemented is not an ecosystem, it's a series of disconnected solutions. The 'pick-n-mix' approach often happens when different functions select an aspect of The Thrive Cycle *they* find challenging, and then independently implement *their* 'solution'. An example might be an IT Department trying to go-it-alone implementing an 'Agile' methodology when it needs to be supported by other areas of the business.

There's something else to watch out for.

Many components of a Balanced Ecosystem *feel like* 'easy-wins'. They *look like* systems-that-you-can-buy or *appear to be* discrete processes you can bring in some consultants to implement. An ecosystem by definition is something in which the parts are interdependent. Changing one component will invariably have implications for the others and they won't always be obvious.

For all of these reasons, if your organisation is going to achieve a Balanced Ecosystem, it must start by developing a deep understanding of the other Elements of Adaptive Success and where the true needs lie.

RULE #2 – Design it before you build

A moment ago I said 'if you want to build a brick house you're going to need some bricks'. Well, before you buy the bricks and start laying them, it's good to have worked out what kind of house you want to build.

In order to create a Balanced Ecosystem that meets the needs of your organisation and supports the Target Adaptive Profile you desire, it needs to be *designed*. This requires holistic thinking that takes into account many of the factors so far described in this book. Things like:

- the current position of your organisation and its ability to adapt
- its strengths and weaknesses
- the target Adaptive Profile that it has set for the future
- the strength of the other Elements of Adaptive Success.

RULE #3 – Create a Thrive Cycle Blueprint

One of the most powerful elements of the Thrive Cycle is the continuity it creates between historically disconnected business processes (e.g. strategy, planning, execution and learning). I can guarantee that when you start looking at your Ecosystem, some of your existing processes will look like they neatly fit into one of the Thrive Cycle stages. The *See* stage could be re-labelled 'innovation', the *Understand* stage could be 'strategy and planning' and so forth. Because of this, it might sound logical to give each of those stages to the respective functional teams to design.

I strongly advise against this.

Instead bring people from the different functional areas together to create a Thrive Cycle Blueprint from end-to-end. This includes connecting the *Learn* stage back to the *See* stage. This approach will deliver significant benefits and move your adaptive agenda forward by:

- building internal knowledge and support for The Thrive Cycle
- ensuring The Thrive Cycle processes maintain continuity
- building 'horizontal' understanding as to how the organisation really works, or doesn't work, today
- creating a common goal that reduces the silos

How to develop a Thrive Cycle Blueprint

- **Step 1** Introduce The Thrive Cycle Framework and explain what it aims to achieve (using your Target Adaptive Profile).
- **Step 2** Identify the people who currently contribute to Thrive Cycle processes and have valuable insight.
- **Step 3** Decide what the overall Thrive Cycle capability needs to achieve (i.e. Set Design Principles). Use your Target Adaptive Profile to guide you.
- **Step 4** Devise a standard change-opportunity and give it a name e.g. 'Martha'. Use a realistic example and start with a changing customer need.
- **Step 5** Design the ideal change journey that 'Martha' would take through The Thrive Cycle in your organisation. Keep it high-level, ignore how things are done today and talk in terms of outcomes, not processes.
- **Step 6** Look at today's processes and the degree to which they achieve those outcomes.
- **Step 7** Identify what needs to change and give each to cross-functional teams to develop holistic solutions.
- **Step 8** Use the high-level design outcomes as a way of keeping people focused on the end-to-end, not just delivering stand-alone Thrive Cycle capabilities.

Keep these *Golden Rules* in mind as we explore the seven Thrive Cycle Enablers that will need to be combined to create your organisation's Balanced Ecosystem.

CUSTOMER RELEVANCE

You'll recall that The Vital Thread creates the essential connection between what is relevant and important to your customers, the experience your organisation delivers and how it delivers it. However, The Vital Thread can only fulfil its purpose if it accurately represents internal and external reality.

Your Balanced Ecosystem therefore needs to ensure The Vital Thread is systematically adapted and evolved such that your organisation continues to maximise customer-value. To achieve this, your Balanced Ecosystem requires a number of elements.

A Change Radar

In Chapter 9 we explored how The Vital Thread provides a way of filtering relevant information from noise. It also enables changes to be evaluated according to their potential value. Now, we need to have a way of ensuring your organisation is systematically 'looking' and 'listening' for change opportunities. In a quid pro quo, this capability is also required to ensure The Vital Thread continues to evolve and change as the world changes.

Many organisations already recognise the importance of building close relationships with their customers, investing in customer-experience and research. A *Change Radar* is a systematic process that looks for changes, identifies the ones that offer potential opportunity, and communicates them to the people who can take action.

An effective Change Radar ensures the insights being gathered through these channels are both meaningful and focused on creating customer-value. It is also a mechanism through which to collect ad hoc feedback from a range of different sources (Figure 11-2).

It is here that we can again see the value of The Vital Thread and The Change-Drivers Framework described in Chapter 9, as both provide the foundation of the Change Radar. This enables it to identify change-opportunities inside and outside the organisation, with equal effectiveness.

Let's once again come back to Orion Healthcare and revisit how its Vital Thread enables it to see change-opportunities, and to respond to them ahead of its rivals (Figure 11-3).

The Vital Thread is understood across the organisation's leadership community. This means that Orion has an army of people who are looking to identify opportunities. However, what's most important is that they are all very clear *what* they are actually looking for.

FIGURE 11-2: The Change Radar uses The Change Drivers Framework to identify opportunities

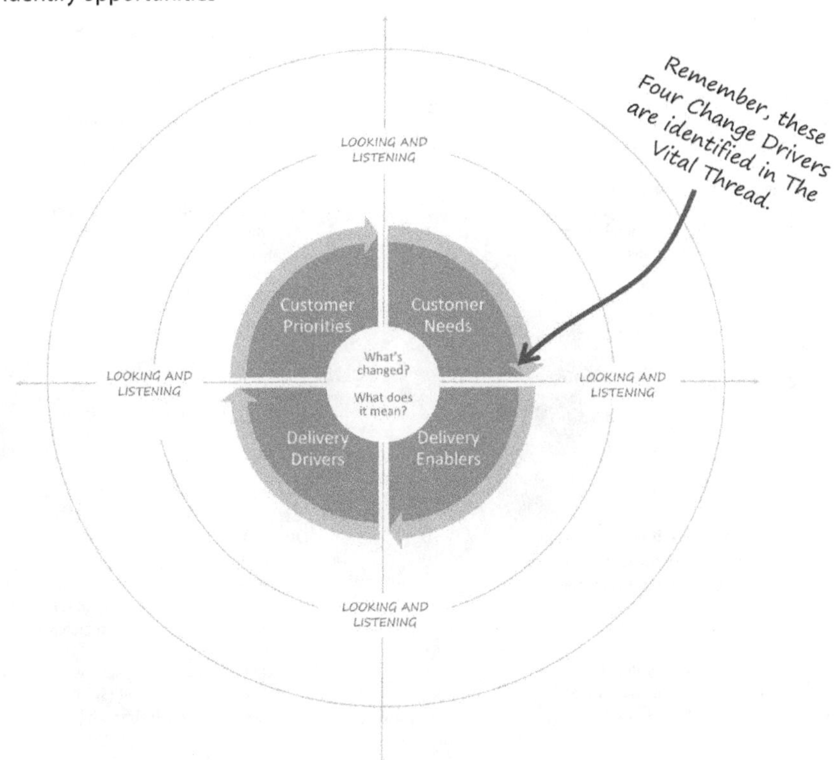

If a change is likely to influence any of the Four Change Drivers within The Vital Thread, then it signals a potential change-opportunity. This gives Orion far more channels from which to derive meaningful insights and avoid information-overload.

An Insights Incubator

An *Insights Incubator* enables the generation of ideas, but distils them to create a useful picture of the world (Figure 11-4). Most importantly,

FIGURE 11-3: The Vital Thread directly informs the Change Radar and helps Orion's people to know what kind of change they should be looking for.

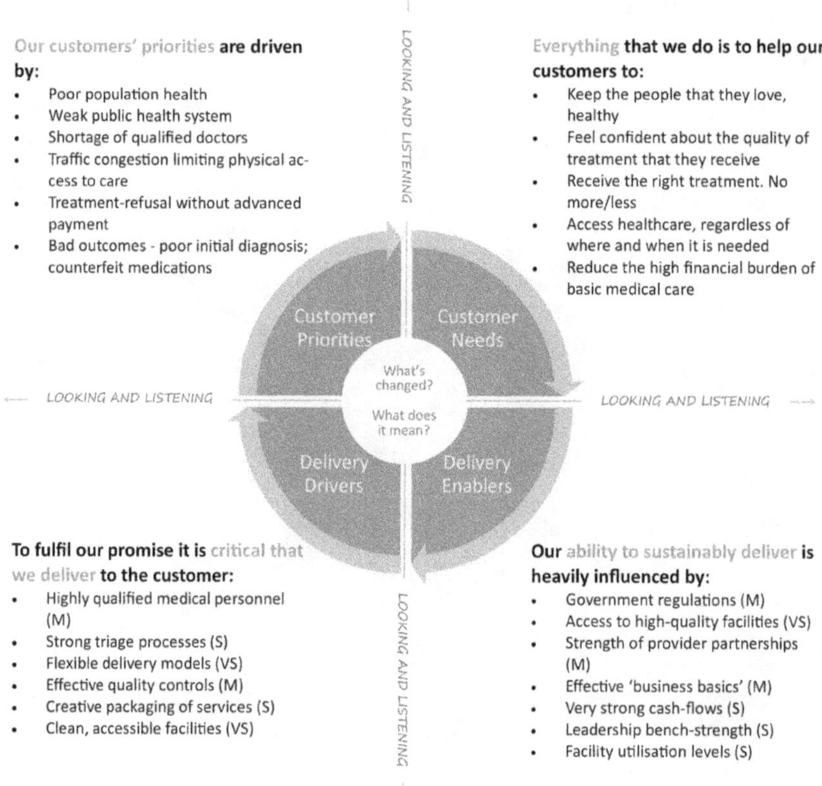

If any change affects any of these four areas, it may signal a change-opportunity for Orion Healthcare.
LOOKING AND LISTENING
Our customers' priorities are driven by:
Poor population health
Weak public health system
Shortage of qualified doctors
Traffic congestion limiting physical access to care
Treatment-refusal without advanced payment
Bad outcomes - poor initial diagnosis; counterfeit medications
Everything that we do is to help our customers to:
Keep the people that they love, healthy
Feel confident about the quality of treatment that they receive
Receive the right treatment. No more/less
Access healthcare, regardless of where and when it is needed
Reduce the high financial burden of basic medical care
Customer Priorities
Customer Needs
What's changed?
What does it mean?
Delivery Drivers
Delivery Enablers
LOOKING AND LISTENING
LOOKING AND LISTENING
To fulfil our promise it is critical that we deliver to the customer:
Highly qualified medical personnel (M)
Strong triage processes (S)
Flexible delivery models (VS)
Effective quality controls (M)
Creative packaging of services (S)
Clean, accessible facilities (VS)
Our ability to sustainably deliver is heavily influenced by:
Government regulations (M)
Access to high-quality facilities (VS)
Strength of provider partnerships (M)
Effective 'business basics' (M)
Very strong cash-flows (S)
Leadership bench-strength (S)
Facility utilisation levels (S)
LOOKING AND LISTENING

FIGURE 11-4: The Insights Incubator enables The Vital Thread to continually evolve

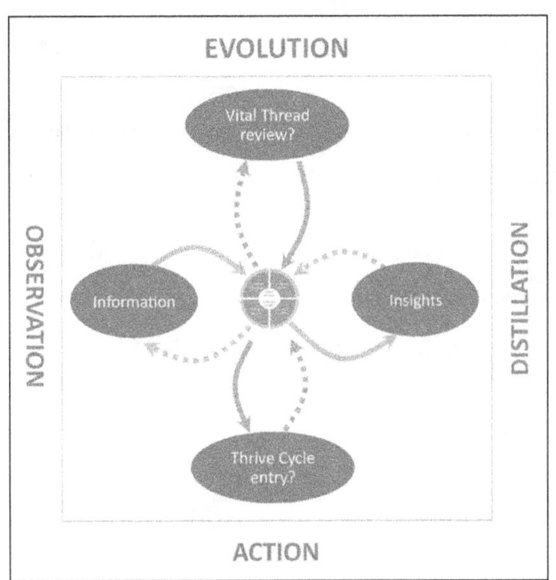

an Insights Incubator provides a tool that can be used to ensure that change-opportunities are recognised at the right time and prioritised appropriately for further exploration. It also provides the basis upon which The Vital Thread can continuously evolve.

The Insights Incubator uses the observations from the Change Radar, and identifies potential change-opportunities that may otherwise go unnoticed. It also makes it easy to contribute and build on insights. So, once the important sources have been agreed, informal and formal mechanisms need to be in place to allow insights (identifying new potential opportunities or, solutions to existing opportunities) to be not only raised but also discussed[a].

Your Insights Incubator can be used as a *litmus test* for your Vital Thread, and will tell you if it is still accurately representing your customers' reality or whether a review is required. In this context, planning becomes all about bringing the knowledge from The Change

---

a For practical strategies in this area see *Innovation as Usual* by Paddy Miller and Thomas Wendell-Wendellsborg[42].

Radar together with The Vital Thread and asking 'does anything need to change?' In this way, organisational planning becomes 'decoupled' from annual budgeting, and is more regular but less intense.

Adopting this kind of approach creates more value because it provides a single-page tool the entire organisation uses, rather than being a large document that 'lives in Finance'.

ORGANISATIONAL STRUCTURE

Thinking back to our three-legged race with thousands of people tied together, becoming more adaptive requires significant focus across the entire organisation. This can only be achieved if there is commitment from the most senior leader of the Core Organisation and his or her leadership team.

Appoint a Chief Adaptive Officer

Many large organisations have a Chief Operating Officer to ensure it delivers business-as-usual in an effective and efficient way. However, to meet the challenges of exponential change, what is also needed is a role of equal status (and influence) that can drive 'horizontal' capability.

The role is the *Chief Adaptive Officer.*

This permanent executive role exists to build The Adaptive Organisation. In other words, creating a *purpose-driven* group of people that is able to:

- *change itself* (and the infrastructure that supports it) in order to *capture opportunities* that offer the *greatest potential value*; and
- *recognise* those opportunities, regardless of whether they occur inside or outside the organisation; and
- achieve all of the above *to a standard* and *at a pace* that *creates value*; and
- gives the organisation *an adaptive advantage* over its rivals.

ABOUT THE ROLE

This is an empowered leadership role performed by someone who has the unwavering confidence of the CEO and the Board. They show advanced Thrive Cycle Leadership and set a positive example to their executive colleagues and the organisation. This person engenders rather than commands respect. They are a customer-advocate and draw heavily on their exceptional engagement and coaching skills to bring colleagues and team members on the journey.

The key responsibilities of the Chief Adaptive Officer position are:

- **Thrive Cycle Development** – Develop and evolve a strong Thrive Cycle by targeting the Six Elements of Adaptive Success.
  Note: This doesn't mean that everyone who contributes to The Thrive Cycle processes reports directly to the Chief Adaptive Officer. However, they are accountable to them for Thrive Cycle delivery.
- **Adaptive Improvement** – Set and monitor the Target Adaptive Profile, ensure that it continues to be relevant within the environmental context and establish measures to monitor progress. This includes establishing Thrive Cycle Learning capability described later in this chapter.
- **Organisational Engagement** – Engage and drive the pursuit of adaptive advantage across the Executive Team and the leadership community.
- **Thrive Cycle Management** – Ensure change is delivering value today by overseeing the organisation's portfolio of change across the organisational Thrive Cycle, spanning from before changes enter The Thrive Cycle to after they leave it.

Re-think the C-suite

It's fair to say the C-suite is a little over-crowded these days.

As organisations have increasingly recognised the importance of capabilities like human resources, information technology and risk management, respective executive roles have been added (CHRO,

CIO, CRO etc.). The Chief Customer Officer[5] (CCO) and Chief Transformation Officer (CTO) have also been recently added.

When I talk about a Chief Adaptive Officer, I am not suggesting that organisations should just add yet another senior executive role. Instead, the C-suite needs to be redesigned to place accountability for The Thrive Cycle and the creation-of-value-through-change, into a single role.

There are several existing C-suite candidates that could evolve into this role. Each of them already has components of The Thrive Cycle built into their accountabilities (Figure 11-5). They include:

- Chief Transformation Officer
- Chief Customer Officer
- Chief Strategy Officer
- Chief Operating Officer.

The focus and required capabilities of the Chief Adaptive Officer are different to these roles as they stand today. Designing the Chief Adaptive Officer role therefore requires the other roles that contribute to The Thrive Cycle (regardless of their title) to be re-designed.

Align the Executive Team

The Chief Adaptive Officer cannot create The Adaptive Organisation on their own. The other members of the Executive Team also have important roles to play.

SET TEAM-BASED, SHARED METRICS

Making the entire Executive Team accountable for delivering the Target Adaptive Profile can be a simple yet effective approach. However, if using this approach, take care to ensure the shared metrics are driving the outcome, not just 'the scores'.

I recall one organisation that wanted to improve employee satisfaction, and so put in shared metrics that were underpinned by an annual employee survey. The metrics created shared focus, but not on the factors that were underlying poor employee satisfaction. Instead,

FIGURE 11-5: For the Chief Adaptive Officer role to be effective, the C-suite must be re-designed

NEW Chief Adaptive Officer role

	SEE	UNDERSTAND	PRIORITISE	DESIGN	PLAN	MOVE	LEARN
CEO	*Accountable for overall adaptiveness but delegates responsibility to C-suite*						
CAO	✓	✓	✓	✓	✓	✓	✓
CFO	-	-	✓	-	✓	-	-
COO	-	-	✓	✓	✓	✓	-
CCO	✓	✓	-	✓	-	-	✓
CTO				✓	✓	✓	✓
CSO	✓	✓	✓	✓	✓	-	-
CRO	✓	✓	-	-	-	-	-
CMO	✓	✓		✓	-	-	-
CIO	-	-	-	✓	✓	✓	-
CHRO	-	-	-		✓	✓	✓

effort was invested in 'increasing the scores'. One team even managed to achieve a near perfect score, and yet it contained some of the least satisfied employees because the fundamental drivers of satisfaction had not changed.

When setting metrics, make them holistic (i.e. one target that all teams pursue, not one target per team). The whole idea of being adaptive is that the organisation needs to become better at working with itself. Thus, no individual leader or team should be able to achieve the performance metrics on their own.

Marking your own homework is also something to be wary of. Metrics and performance measures should ideally have some level of objectivity behind them, in addition to subjective feedback. An objective Adaptive Profile Assessment can also be useful here, bringing objectivity to an otherwise subjective topic. Later in this chapter I'll also introduce Thrive Cycle Learning and show how it can be used to develop an Adaptive Advantage Scorecard.

INTRODUCE A THRIVE CYCLE ADOPTION PROGRAM

Another way to build accountability and commitment across the Executive Team, is to have individuals 'adopt' (as in adopting a child) one of the elements of The Thrive Cycle. This person (or people, if the Executive Team is quite large) can then be the champion for driving improvements in that element over time. They will need to take time to understand what is driving performance in that area and talk to people who understand it and are affected by it.

The secret of success here is to have Executive Team members adopt a Thrive Cycle capability that is furthest away from their day-to-day role. For example, have the CIO adopt the *See* capability in The Thrive Cycle. Have the Chief Strategy Officer adopt the *Move* capability. Have the Chief Marketing Officer adopt 'Learn' and so on.

It's also important the executive concerned takes personal accountability for their element rather than delegating the responsibility to one of their team. It must be *their* knowledge, *their* understanding and *their* commitment. Otherwise, it will undermine the effectiveness of the exercise.

This approach offers multiple advantages.

It starts to build the continuity upon which The Thrive Cycle depends for success. It also enhances the depth of organisational insight around the senior leadership table. Finally, this approach enables Executive Teams and their leaders to model cross-functional and collaborative working, while enabling them to see how the day-to-day activities of their own teams contribute to, or detract from, organisational adaptiveness.

Establish an Adaptive Advantage Team

I've established several Program Management Offices during my career and people frequently ask me 'Do I *really* need a PMO?' The bridge of their nose usually crinkles-up as they ask, as if to say 'please, please, please say I don't'.

I usually answer in the following way.

Imagine you've piled all of your employees onto 30 jumbo-jets and you are going to fly them from London's Heathrow Airport to Sydney, Australia.

What sorts of questions would you want to have answered before the planes took off?

Well, you might want to confirm that Sydney was the best place to be sending them. Then, you'd probably want to know whether each plane had enough fuel, whether the pilots were suitably experienced and if the planes were mechanically fit enough to leave the ground.

Then, of course, there would be environmental considerations.

It would be a good to know the planes weren't all going to try and take off from the same runway at the same time. Once they were in the air, knowing that no other planes were planning to cross their flight-path would also be a good thing.

So what's the answer and how is this relevant to whether you have a program office or not?

At any one time, most established organisations are responding to anything from dozens to hundreds of change-opportunities. Some initiatives will be just starting, others will be in mid-flight or just coming in to land. Without some form of management capability, the organisation faces the equivalent scenario of Heathrow Airport when the entire air-traffic control team has called in sick.

My answer therefore is 'yes' and 'no'.

'Yes'... you need a group of passionate change professionals who track, monitor, improve project delivery and change management. And 'No', it's not the traditional project-by-project-dashboard-reporting-template-developing PMO that exists in many large organisations today.

What you do need instead is an Adaptive Advantage Team.

Reporting to the Chief Adaptive Officer, the Adaptive Advantage Team shares that role's objectives. The name says it all. This team exists to build long-term adaptive capability as well as ensuring that in the immediate term, organisational change creates value. Most importantly, the Adaptive Advantage Team is accountable for Thrive Cycle Management (described later in this section) and not just program management as it applies to the latter stages (i.e. *Plan, Move, Learn*) of a Thrive Cycle rotation.

Like The Chief Adaptive Officer, introducing an Adaptive Advantage Team into the senior leadership structure requires careful thought. The skill-sets in the Adaptive Advantage Team are different to the traditional PMO. While you still need project and change-management specialists, the holistic nature of the team's remit means it also requires people with backgrounds in strategy development, innovation, organisational design, people development and so on.

Maintaining the continuity of The Thrive Cycle may require the Adaptive Advantage Team to be involved in (and potentially manage) tasks that have traditionally been 'owned' by other functions. Good organisational design, effective engagement and role clarity from the very beginning are therefore essential (Figure 11-6).

FIGURE 11-6: Introducing an Adaptive Advantage Team requires careful organisational design.

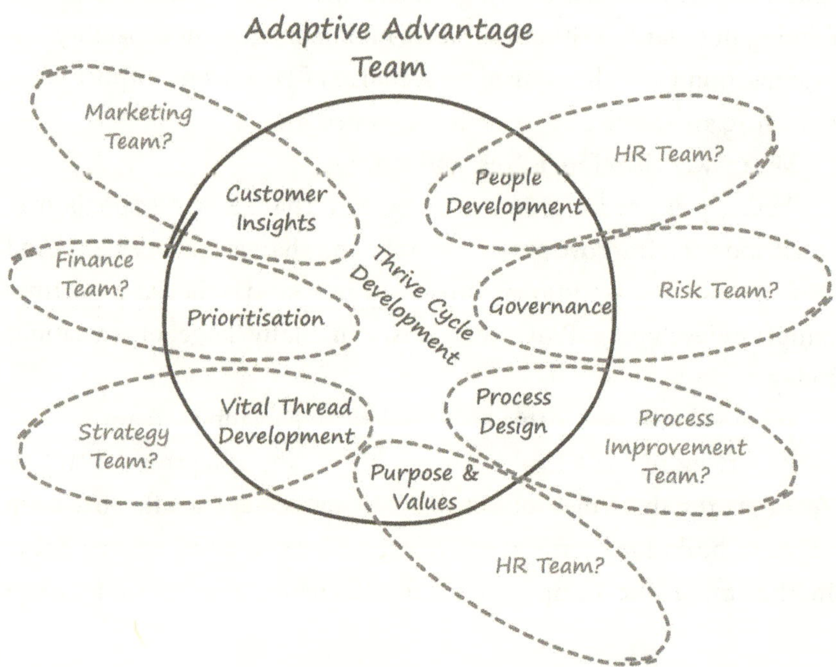

LEADERSHIP CAPABILITY

Thrive Cycle Leadership is not something an organisation wishes for and wakes up the next morning and suddenly it's there. It needs to be consciously pursued and nurtured.

Create an environment that nurtures Thrive Cycle Leadership

Having developed a sense of your organisation's Thrive Cycle Leadership capability in the previous chapter, the following describes some of the ways in which you can improve it.

INVEST IN LEADERSHIP DEVELOPMENT

It sounds like a pretty basic thing to do. However, you might be surprised how little is actually invested in something most leaders say is very important. A 2013 Economist Intelligence Unit Report found that only 11 percent of companies invested in developing the required strategy-execution skills among their executives[22].

In fairness, until now, the absence of a comprehensive framework (i.e. The Thrive Cycle) has made it hard for organisations to know what skills they should be helping their people to develop. Just having a list of attributes is insufficient. Unless leaders are taught how and when to apply them, an organisation could invest significantly and see little noticeable return.

TREAT THRIVE CYCLE LEADERSHIP AS A CORE COMPETENCY

It would be great if every leader in your organisation were a 'Master-Black-Belt' when navigating The Thrive Cycle. However, the reality is that at any one time, you will have leaders with different capabilities. Treating Thrive Cycle Leadership as a core competency means your leaders understand what *good* looks like, focus on developing these capabilities, and are overtly encouraged (and expected) to do so.

Having Thrive Cycle Leadership as a core competency also means it is clearly understood where each leader sits on a continuum ranging from moderately skilled to highly skilled. And, if a leader shows few

Thrive Cycle Leadership skills, then action is taken to help them develop.

If you find yourself in this situation and having provided development support there is still no improvement, it needs to be asked whether this leader is going to help or hinder efforts to achieve your Target Adaptive Profile. If the answer is 'hinder' then some tough decisions may need to be made.

How to use a Thrive Cycle Leadership Log

THE THRIVE CYCLE CAN BE USED as a template for developing your own leadership and that of your teams. Thrive Cycle Leadership is stage dependent, so once you know where you are in The Thrive Cycle, you can review your 'log' for that stage and remind yourself what to focus on. This gives relevant guidance in the moment when leaders need it and makes Thrive Cycle Leadership, easier.

THRIVE CYCLE STAGE	KEY LESSONS	FUTURE FOCUS
See		
Understand		
Prioritise		
Design		
Plan		
Move		
Learn		

Note also that the Thrive Cycle Leadership Log can be used as an organisational tool to track how this capability is evolving and where greater focus may be required.

FOCUS ON THRIVE CYCLE LEADERSHIP QUALITIES WHEN SELECTING OPERATIONAL LEADERS

When Amazon recruits leaders into operational roles it looks for people who can set the vision, direction and culture of their organisation[27]. In a recent advertisement, the first five lines of the role description were all about leading change, strategic thinking and becoming the most customer-centric organisation on Earth. It was only in line six that any technical requirements were described.

By way of contrast, look at the responsibilities section of the following advertisement (Figure 11-7). This similar role appeared directly below the one for Amazon.

As you can see, this role description starts with the technical management requirements. The advertisement says this is an 'opportunity to work in a fast paced and dynamic environment' and yet the listed responsibilities of the role suggest otherwise.

FIGURE 11-7: Example of a Customer Service Manager advertisement emphasising operational qualities in a changing environment

1 The environment is described as fast-paced and dynamic but...

CUSTOMER SERVICE MANAGER

As a Customer Service Manager, you will lead a Customer Service Team of three Senior Representatives and over 10 Service Representatives to deliver a remarkable customer service experience. You will have the **opportunity to work in a fast paced and dynamic environment** with a talented team of innovative professionals and the most passionate and brightest minds in (the industry). Full on-the-job training and support is provided.

Responsibilities of the role include:

Weekly rostering of team members across four locations; Responding to escalated customer queries; Reviewing and implementing customer service **policies; Documentation** of customer service processes; Implementation of upcoming; promotions and communications; Weekly service **reporting** at general meetings.

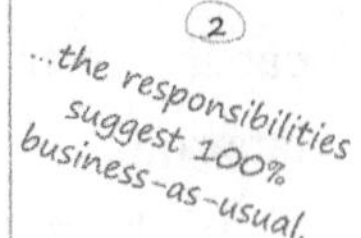
2
...the responsibilities suggest 100% business-as-usual.

Are you recruiting the right operational leaders?

THINK ABOUT YOUR OWN organisation. Take some time to look through the position descriptions for recently-advertised leadership roles in operationally-focused business areas.

- *What attributes does it look for when recruiting these kinds of leadership roles?*
- *How might this be affecting the leadership of change across your organisation today?*

ENSURE THRIVE CYCLE LEADERSHIP QUALITIES ARE BALANCED ACROSS THE STRUCTURAL HIERARCHY

We all know that the behaviour and expectations of our boss influences the way we behave at work. But how does the Thrive Cycle Leadership capability of leaders impact the same capability of those sitting below them in the hierarchy?

In my experience, great Thrive Cycle Leaders are excellent at selecting and developing great Thrive Cycle Leaders. Less capable leaders are not. The latter select leaders based upon other qualities (like technical ability) and so this cascades into a community of leaders with limited Thrive Cycle capability. When this happens, there is no natural catalyst to initiate change. After all, if you are unaware of what you're missing, why would you decide to do something about it?

Also, more senior leaders traditionally make more of the decisions during the early stages of the Thrive Cycle. Therefore, if *they* are not capable Thrive Cycle Leaders, it will have significant consequences later on.

In short, the higher-up a leader sits in the organisational hierarchy, the better they need to be at Thrive Cycle Leadership. That's because their behaviour impacts the degree to which the leaders below them will be encouraged to be adaptive.

Looking vertically down the structural layers of an organisation can also provide valuable insights. Figure 11-8 shows scores for Thrive

Cycle Leadership across three layers of the leadership hierarchy. The higher the Thrive Cycle Leadership capability is for each of the Thrive Cycle stages, the closer the line is to the outer-edge of the chart.

In a Surfer organisation you might expect to see this kind of profile. The Executive Team consistently demonstrate Thrive Cycle Leadership, no matter which stage of the Thrive Cycle they find themselves in. They then recruit and develop their own leadership teams to have similar capabilities. This cascades to the layer of team leaders.

In this way, the layers of the hierarchy both enable and enhance Thrive Cycle Leadership capability.

By way of contrast, if you were to conduct the same kind of analysis in a Sinker organisation it might look like the next chart (Figure 11-9). Here, the weak Thrive Cycle Leadership capability of the Executive Team *inhibits* improvements in the layers below. Thrive Cycle

FIGURE 11-8: The advantages of having senior executives who demonstrate strong Thrive Cycle Leadership.

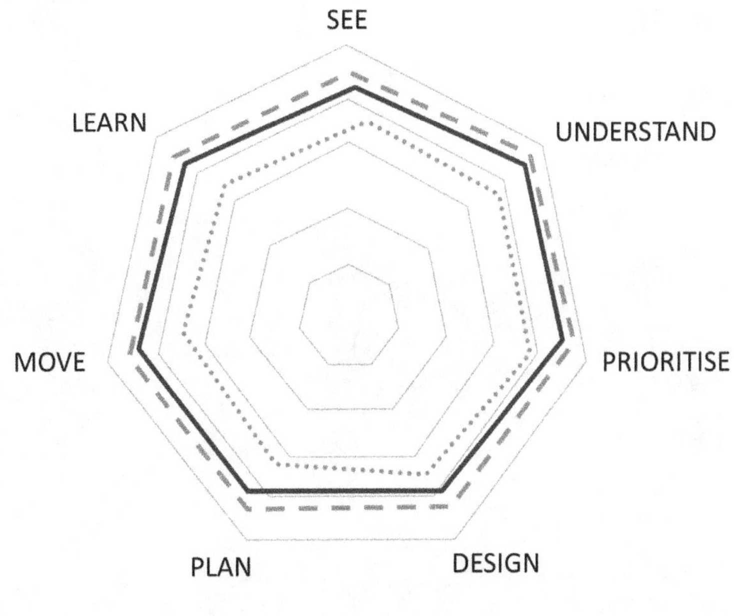

Leadership qualities are neither encouraged nor valued, and as a result, any adaptive leaders who do come along, rarely stay.

Does your organisation nurture Thrive Cycle Leadership?

NOW BEFORE WE LOOK at some of the other environmental factors affecting leadership capability, let's come back to your organisation.

- *How might your organisation's selection and recruitment of leaders be influencing its Adaptive Profile today?*
- *What impact might Thrive Cycle Leadership capability across the leadership hierarchy be having?*
- *What areas would need to be addressed if your organisation wanted to be more adaptive in future?*

FIGURE 11-9: The disadvantages of having senior executives who show weak Thrive Cycle Leadership.

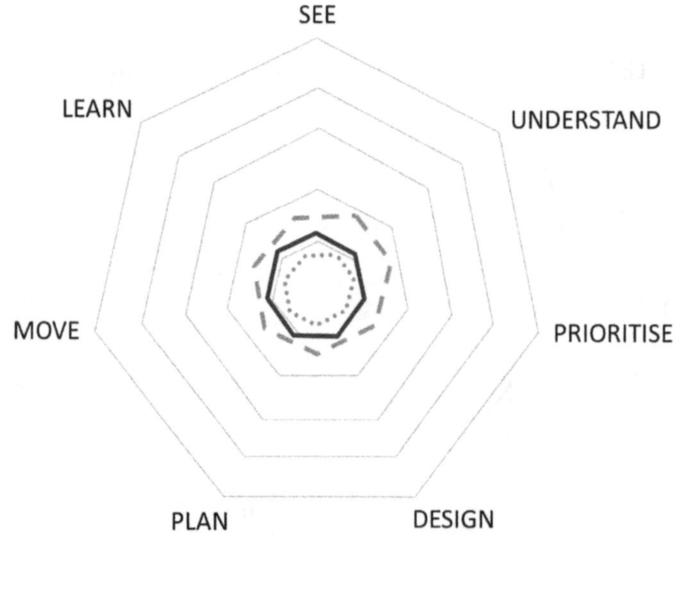

Having now understood the spread of Thrive Cycle Leadership across the organisation, let's explore some of the ways to improve it.

Use Thrive Cycle Leadership capability to drive internal promotion

Looking over a series of years at those promoted into senior leadership roles, what is the pattern telling you? Do people climb the corporate ladder because they deliver a strong operational performance, or because they are highly adaptive?

Every leadership team needs to have a mix of strong business-as-usual delivery and Thrive Cycle Leadership. If the pattern suggests that high levels of performance in both areas are rewarded through promotion, then your organisation is in a positive position. If this is not the case, it is more likely that the Thrive Cycle Leaders your organisation needs, leave because they feel unable to progress their careers.

Foster a diverse Executive Team

By Executive Team I mean the group of most senior leaders within the Core Organisation. Does it have a blend of career backgrounds or does it mainly comprise people with operational or finance backgrounds? Does it contain a mix of leaders from within the organisation and from outside? Does it include people who have lived in different countries? Different industries?

Another interesting area to explore is the number of women in senior leadership positions. A recent study found that organisations that had better financial performance in uncertain environments had more women in leadership roles. In the bottom 20 percent of performing organisations, 19 percent of all leaders were women. In the top 20 percent of financial performance, 37 percent of all leaders were women[26].

The more diverse the Executive Team, the more adaptive it is likely to be. That's because it is less likely to become trapped in the belief that there is one way of doing things.

Recognise the relationship between Thrive Cycle Leadership capability and The Vital Thread

The success of an organisation's leaders, and their Thrive Cycle Leadership capabilities, are directly linked to the strength of your organisation's Vital Thread. When it is clearly defined and consistently understood, The Vital Thread makes Thrive Cycle Leadership easier. Rather than leaving a leader to work out what is important for themselves, The Vital Thread defines it in advance.

So, what happens in an organisation in which The Vital Thread is undefined? What does that mean for Thrive Cycle Leadership?

In short, the less defined The Vital Thread, the more Thrive Cycle capable your leaders need to be.

When The Vital Thread is strong it makes all types of change easier to lead. This means a less experienced Thrive Cycle Leader can manage the easier types of change, which leaves the 'black-belt' Thrive Cycle Leaders, who are few in number, to take care of 'the hard stuff'.

If, however, the organisation does not have a strong Vital Thread, even the easy change is difficult. And as such, it takes up valuable time of the experienced Thrive Cycle Leaders who should really be focused on the big, important change. All of this means the organisation has far less leadership capability available than it would have with a strong Vital Thread.

How to assess your leadership outlook

AS YOU HAVE PROBABLY GATHERED, when it comes to Thrive Cycle Leadership, there is a lot to think about. To start with, it can help to use a simple framework (Figure 11-10). To do this, you just need to rate the following two questions (between 1 and 5). 1 = very low, 5 = very high.

- *(Vertical axis) How would you rate the overall Thrive Cycle Leadership capability within your organisation today?*
- *(Horizontal Axis) To what degree is Thrive Cycle Leadership capability nurtured within your organisation?*

Now, plot both these scores in a two-by-two matrix (Figure 11-10).

FIGURE 11-10 : Two-by-two matrix to assess leadership outlook

OBJECTIVE LEADERSHIP ASSESSMENT

High Capability

Low Capability

5 4 3 2 1

Strong Thrive Cycle Leaders who are constrained by the organisation

Strong Thrive Cycle Leaders who are supported by the organisation

Incapable Thrive Cycle Leaders who reinforce the inhibiting factors of the organisation

A supportive organisation but with few capable Thrive Cycle Leaders

1 2 3 4 5

Inhibited

Supported

ORGANISATIONAL FACTORS

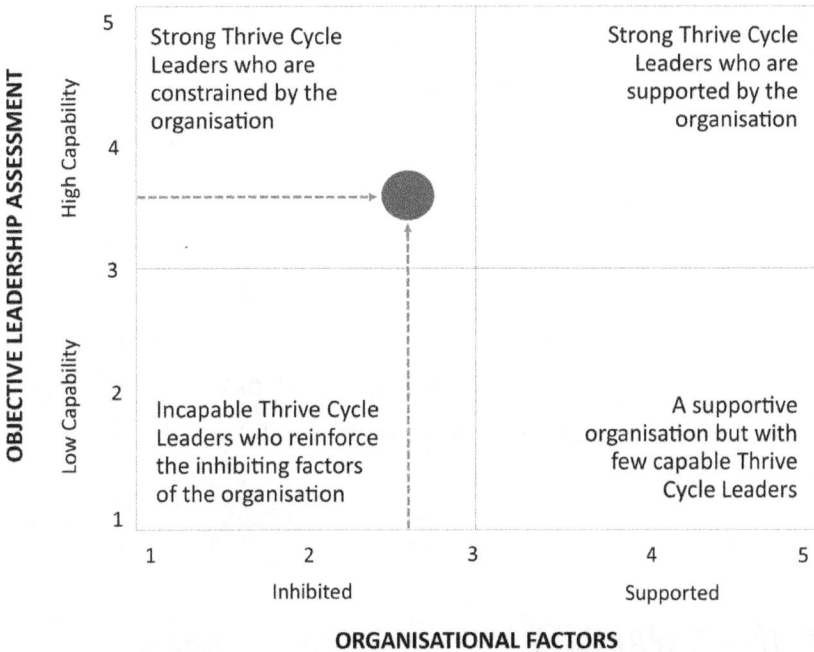

The above example suggests that organisational factors may be inhibiting Thrive Cycle Leadership behaviour. However, despite this, the overall leadership profile is moderately positive. In this scenario it is likely that over time, Thrive Cycle Leadership will reduce (rather than increase), primarily because the organisation is not providing a supportive environment.

While each organisation needs to be considered holistically, there are a number of rules-of-thumb that can be applied to each quadrant of the matrix. These have been summarised in Figure 11-11 and provide a good starting point from which to identify potential risks and opportunities.

FIGURE 11-11: Summary of risks and opportunities associated with each leadership quadrant

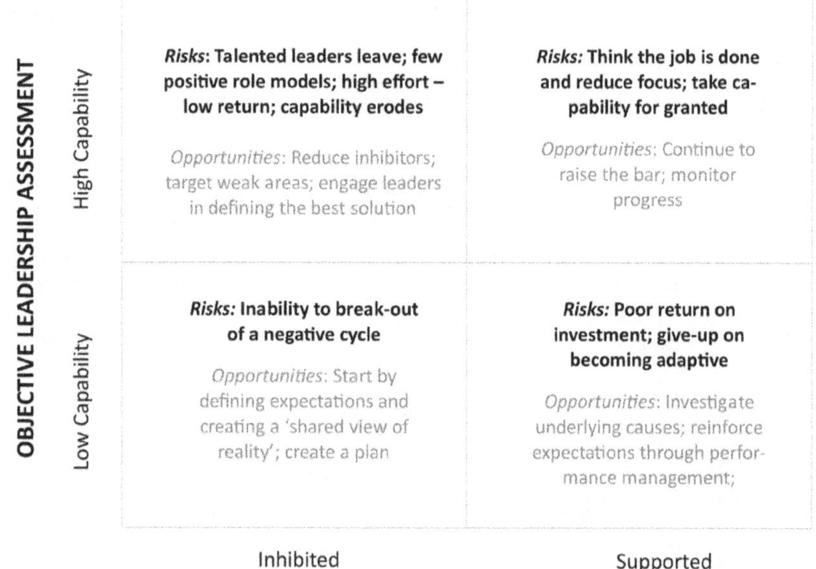

Once again, this offers a great way to kick-off a Thrive Cycle Leadership conversation within your organisation.

PEOPLE CAPABILITY

Many areas within this book focus on creating an environment that enables people to thrive during uncertainty. Of course, leadership capability as described in the previous section also has a critical role to play.

So what else does your Balanced Ecosystem need to enable your people to repeatedly and successfully navigate The Thrive Cycle?

Prepare people for change in advance

In Chapter 7 we talked about how there is frequently a disconnect between organisations' enthusiasm for becoming adaptive and their readiness to do so. Similarly, the times when many organisations realise their people need to understand change, are the times when their people are in the worst position to learn.

Let's put this in a different context. Imagine that you are walking home, having worked late one evening. It's dark and as you walk along the path you hear an unfamiliar noise behind you. You didn't think anyone else was around. Then, you hear it again but this time it seems to be closer. It sounds like heavy footsteps, walking quickly.

Now, you're scared. What happens to your body? You go into survival mode, don't you? Your heart rate increases, your brain starts to produce adrenaline (ready to fight or flee) and your thoughts start racing through all the possibilities at a million miles per hour.

Now let's hold that moment right there. You. In the dark. Scared. How open do you think you are to learning something new at this point? So, if I started yelling self-defence techniques in your ear, how confident would you feel using them if the footsteps behind you turned out to be an attacker? Not very?

Change brings with it many emotional experiences. The greater the unknown, the greater the level of fear, uncertainty, and doubt. When your people are afraid, they don't think clearly and are less likely to listen. When they feel uncertain and doubtful, they will make less effective decisions and be less confident when doing so.

This is the complete opposite to how you need your people to be if they are to successfully navigate and thrive in significant change. That's why The Adaptive Organisation builds an understanding of change into the everyday psyche of the organisation, and empowers people with knowledge in advance.

Use The Thrive Cycle Framework like a map

In the previous chapter I talked about a Thrive Cycle Leader recognising when they were in a Thrive Cycle rotation and identifying where they were. Developing this same skill across other team members helps them to recognise when they are in a Thrive Cycle rotation. This enables them to know what to expect and helps them to orient themselves when the *knowns* become *unknown.*

Be clear about the rules of the change-game

Imagine if a team walked out onto a football field and all the players, and the referee, needed to agree to the rules before they started. And imagine if they had to do this every time a team met a new opponent, or had a new referee.

How much time do you think would be spent playing the game, compared to arguing about the rules?

Very little, right?

That's because the rules of football give the players, the referee and the spectators a shared point of reference that allows them to make sense of the game. This does not guarantee the rules are always followed, nor does it mean they are consistently applied. However, it does provide a shared basis of understanding from which a good game can be played.

Transitioning an organisational change through The Thrive Cycle is like a game of football. If the organisation has an embedded set of rules that governs how organisational change is expected to play out, it enables its people to effectively participate in the game.

Grow-your-own change-facilitators

A change-facilitator is any role that assists the organisation to navigate the processes within The Thrive Cycle. They exist under many different titles: consultant, change manager, business analyst, project manager, internal communications consultant and so on.

The more, trusted home-grown change-facilitators your organisation has, the more likely organisational change will be implemented effectively.

'When the rules of the change-game are unclear, people spend more time arguing about the rules and focus less on achieving the desired outcome.'

A BETTER RESULT FOR A LOWER COST

A competent home-grown change-facilitator is more likely to understand the organisational landscape and be able to look further ahead and see potential road-blocks. A home-grown facilitator is also more likely to be versed in the ways of getting things done within the organisation and navigating the 'cultural quirks'.

An internal person is more likely to be motivated by the values and purpose of the organisation than an external contractor. Thus, while their roles may be nomadic within your organisation, they have joined and stayed for a reason. This person will also remain after the change is over and has a vested interest in making sure that value is created.

Importing temporary, external talent every time an organisational change is needed is incredibly expensive. I'm not just talking about the daily rates either. I am referring to the time it takes to bring people up to speed about the organisation, the way it works and what it is trying to achieve. So, your organisation pays more, but ends up receiving less value than if it had invested in its people.

ESTABLISH CHANGE-FACILITATION AS A VALUED AND CLEARLY-DEFINED CAREER PATH

At any one time, an organisation's portfolio of change is likely to contain initiatives of varying sizes, complexities and types. Some will be so small that they need little facilitation. Others have the potential to turn the organisation's ways-of-working upside-down.

For this reason, your organisation needs to have not just one change-facilitation skillset, but a range of capabilities. In addition, it needs to be able to match those capabilities with the type of change being effected.

Establishing change-facilitation as a career path within your organisation will give you a large resource pool from which to draw people with different but known capabilities. These people aren't just waiting around for the right change that suits their skillset. Many have business-as-usual roles and change-facilitation offers an opportunity to broaden their skills and learn something different.

Further, when an organisation understands the change-facilitation skills its people have, and also understands what each change-opportunity needs, it is bound to drive a better outcome. It means that people facilitate change which is at a level that challenges them, but is not so difficult that they drown in it. For the organisation, it means that it can be confident the person leading the change is suitably qualified and as such, more likely to create value.

The Dos and Don'ts of using external consultants

OVER THE YEARS I HAVE worked with some fantastic external consultants – highly professional, skilled people who had unique expertise which they applied to great effect. Equally, I have experienced my fair share of 'consulting disasters', which not only cost millions of dollars, but alienated pretty much every stakeholder on the program.

Maximise your organisation's investment in professional services by being discerning with choices. Within the context of delivering change, consultants (i.e. professional services firms, not individual contractors) are most effective when they are brought in to:

- provide a broader or fresh perspective on a well-defined topic
- to meet specialised short-term skills the organisation doesn't have, or doesn't have time or the appetite to develop itself
- temporarily fill gaps in an organisational capability while helping the organisation to develop that capability

Conversely, using management consultants is least effective when they are used in the following circumstances:

- Second-guessing your own people – it's guaranteed to cause disengagement
- Creating an 'instant' adaptive capability – there is no such thing
- Outsourcing Thrive Cycle Leadership – that's why your leaders are there

PRIORITISATION

Prioritisation is the way in which choices and trade-offs are made in your organisation. These decisions are triggered by some form of constraint, whether it's money, time, management capacity or resources.

As soon as I say the word 'prioritisation' I can almost hear the eyeballs of half my audience rolling in their heads. However, prioritisation is a critical component of any Balanced Ecosystem because it is often where business-change and business-as-usual come to blows. The same teams and resources are involved in delivering both elements of business. Prioritisation often means making the difficult choice between delivering today or delivering for the future.

An effective prioritisation process makes priority decisions easier and better informed. To achieve this, your organisation needs to answer the following types of questions:

- *What changes are we expecting to enter The Thrive Cycle?*
- *What Thrive Cycle rotations are already underway?*
- *What stage of The Thrive Cycle has each change-opportunity reached?*
- *What value do we expect from each rotation?*
- *What are the chances that each rotation will actually deliver that value?*
- *Where are our resources currently?*
- *What resources are needed (people, systems, funds) to secure that value?*
- *When The Thrive Cycle rotation was completed, was the value realised?*

I appreciate this is a big list. However, this is the kind of organisational insight required if prioritisation is to be effective. This means your Balanced Ecosystem will need to be able to efficiently answer these questions on an ongoing basis.

Value-Driven Metrics

You'll recall that when I introduced The Third Element of Adaptive Success – The Anchors of Certainty – I talked about creating Value-Creating Values. Well, Value-Driven Metrics build on these and enable them to be applied at an organisational level, to the change-opportunities that present themselves. These metrics not only apply to this component of The Thrive Cycle but throughout, and can be used any time a choice needs to be made between one activity and another.

Value-Driven Metrics need to be sufficiently robust to support formal approval decisions, and yet simple enough to empower leaders making real-time choices. They should be as useful to an Operations Manager (when choosing whether to release team members for user-acceptance testing) as they are to an IT Manager (working out where to allocate the next available business analyst).

Six key features of Value-Driven Metrics

VALUE-DRIVEN METRICS are most effective when:

- they are directly aligned to the Four Change Drivers described in The Vital Thread
- they articulate metrics for customer, organisational, and shareholder value
- they are balanced in their approach to measurement and use an effective blend of financial and non-financial metrics
- there is alignment across the metrics (i.e. succeeding against one doesn't inhibit succeeding against another)
- improvements in the metrics actually translate into improvements in value-creation. If they don't, you need to re-think the metrics
- there is ongoing monitoring and accountability for performance against those measures

AVOID DISCRIMINATING BETWEEN DIFFERENT TYPES OF CHANGE-OPPORTUNITY

The Adaptive Organisation ensures that its metrics take into account the ability to recognise the value being 'protected' as well as that being 'enhanced'.

When the organisation's ability to deliver *existing* value is threatened, action needs to be taken to protect it. However, these kinds of changes can become what I call 'grudge' initiatives because preventing value from being lost doesn't show as an improvement in the organisation's financial statements. Accounting formulae find it difficult to calculate a tangible financial benefit from a *potential* loss that never actually happened. Examples of these kinds of initiatives include systems replacements, some regulatory changes and disaster recovery services. These are the types of initiatives that often sit on your organisation's risk-register.

It is much easier to show the tangible benefits for change-opportunities that create tangible *new* value. For example, a new product that promises to attract 10,000 new customers should translate into a positive movement in financial statements. This type of initiative can appear to be more attractive than one that protects twice as much value.

This is one of the factors that is worth explicitly addressing when creating Value-Creating Values. Namely, how will your organisation define 'value' in such a way that it covers value that would have affected the financial statements had no action been taken?

WORRY LESS ABOUT BUDGETS AND MORE ABOUT VALUE

This topic is always guaranteed to get a good conversation going with an audience.

To my left I usually have the Finance people who want the smallest investment for the greatest and fastest return. To my right, I have the Operational people who want a solution that makes it easier to do their job and a better experience for the customer. Then, I have the 'Change-people' who are trying to balance the requirements of both.

When it comes to change and budgets there are three immortal truths.

TRUTH #1 – Responding to a change-opportunity is not like buying a car

If you were to say that you want 'a medium-sized car with a sun-roof, hybrid-motor and leather seats', after a few phone calls and online searches, you'd have a reasonable idea as to what you should expect to pay. That's because for all their unique selling points, you are starting with a concept that is familiar i.e. a medium-sized car. You know what it is, you know what it does and to some degree, how it works.

Organisational change doesn't work like that.

Most change-opportunities, and their organisational responses, are completely unique. That's because complexity, the right solution and the overall degree of difficulty are driven by factors like timing, the nature of your organisation and its current position.

Therefore, unlike a car, it is not possible to accurately predict what a change will cost your organisation to implement. Nor can it be done using costs incurred by other organisations when faced with the same challenge or opportunity.

TRUTH #2 – Most change costs more than your organisation is comfortable paying

I have yet to come across any change-opportunity that comes with a money-back guarantee. Because of this, some organisations try to constrain costs by putting an arbitrary limit on them. This is usually set by either past experience or an internal barometer that has determined 'what this kind of thing ought to cost'. Either way, this approach can be the start of a vicious cycle of overspending and compromised solutions.

TRUTH #3 – The best way to ensure that change creates value, is to decide in advance how much you'd be prepared to pay in order to realise that value

As a change-opportunity progresses through The Thrive Cycle, the organisation develops its view of the *value* it is expected to create.

This information enables the organisation to answer the following question:

- *What is the dollar limit that we would be prepared to spend in order to realise the potential value of this change-opportunity?*

If you believe that responding to a change-opportunity will attract ten-thousand more customers and this will create one-million-dollars per year in economic-value, you might be prepared to pay up to two-million-dollars to create that value. Conversely, if a change is only going to retain one-thousand customers, then you might be willing to spend one-hundred-thousand dollars realising that value.

To be clear, I am not setting out to re-write the rules of project accounting here. What I am saying is that if the organisation has some idea as to how much it would be prepared to pay in order to realise an expected amount of value, it provides a more meaningful framework within which to consider and make decisions about project plans and costs. It maintains focus on creating value, not saving money; and importantly, creates a useful benchmark that can be used to flag if a change-opportunity is at risk of eroding, rather than enhancing, value.

REMEMBER, GETTING THE METRICS RIGHT TAKES TIME AND PERSISTENCE

Like other areas of your Balanced Ecosystem, defining the *right* Value-Driven Metrics will take some time. Trying to get this kind of thing 'perfect' usually means you never actually start. Put something in place and then iterate over time.

Portfolio Management

The term *Portfolio Management* is commonly used to describe the way in which an organisation identifies, prioritises, authorises and manages change-opportunities.

As a senior leader, you don't need to know the ins-and-outs of portfolio management. That's why you have an Adaptive Advantage Team. What you do need to know, is how to recognise a good portfolio management capability when you see one.

It has the following features.

IT IS FIT FOR PURPOSE

It matches the size and sophistication of the capability with the needs of the organisation. There's nothing like having a sledgehammer process when what is needed are a few lines in a spreadsheet.

Also, effective portfolio management enables small, low-risk change to have a faster, leaner management process than big, risky, expensive change. It also recognises the difference between a 'punt on a new idea' versus a repeated almost business-as-usual change that has been done many times over.

IT ENSURES THE PRIORITISATION PROCESS IS ONGOING, NOT ONCE-OFF

Some organisations see prioritisation as a one-off event. A proposal is put forward, given a priority, the project then reaches the starting gate and it is off and running. However, in a change-dominated environment, regular prioritisation (and re-prioritisation) is necessary.

The world keeps changing and so the factors that led to a priority being assigned three months ago may not drive the same conclusions today. This is not to say that an organisation should be chopping and changing its priorities every few weeks. But it does mean the organisation needs to be willing to stop successful projects because they need to make way for others that will create more value.

IT WORRIES LESS ABOUT CONTROL AND MORE ABOUT MAXIMISING VALUE

When portfolio management is implemented in a Splasher organisation (because 'it's the latest thing to have'), it tends to adopt a headmaster, control-driven approach. Portfolio management sets the rules, and the rest of the organisation works around them. Organisational change needs to be run 'by the book' because that is the only way of having any idea of where each change actually is. This creates a rigidity that works against being adaptive.

In a Surfer organisation, however, the Compelling Sense of Purpose and the self-discipline of its leaders mean portfolio management can progress its primary purpose. That is, to ensure the organisation realises maximum value from the change-opportunities it pursues.

Everything else is just a means to this end.

IT IS CLEAR WHETHER A DECISION HAS BEEN MADE, WHAT IT WAS, AND WHY

Have you ever attended a meeting that was called to make a specific decision? Then, as you've stood to leave, you've wondered whether the decision actually was made, and if so, what it was?

Ambiguous decision-making has a number of significant consequences. If there were ten people in the meeting, there are ten versions of the outcome. They then update their teams, who update theirs, and so on. Assuming only ten people in each team, now you have a thousand versions of 'what was agreed'.

Now that's just one decision, from one meeting. Imagine what happens where there are dozens of decisions and then hundreds. Is it any wonder people become confused?

This reinforces why, when it comes to priority decisions, there can be no halfway house. It is either made or it isn't.

Also, in a world of constraints, you simply can't have or do everything. That's why prioritisation always involves two decisions, not one. The first determines what *is* going to be allocated priority, and the second decides what *is not*. Sometimes organisations forget this second one. They keep adding more initiatives to the 'top priority' list but don't recognise they have more initiatives than they have capacity to deliver.

IT BALANCES THE 'CERTAINTY VS UNCERTAINTY' RATIO

During the early stages of any change-opportunity there is maximum uncertainty. At this point little is known about how the opportunity will be responded to, how much value it will create and so on. Therefore, any approval process that is put in place needs to recognise this and reflect a similar level of flexibility with regard to expectations regarding value-realisation, timeframes and costs.

Agreeing to invest millions in something that is completely unknown, and expecting to be guaranteed a 12 percent return-on-investment is always going to end in tears. In order to address unknown, higher-risk opportunities, The Adaptive Organisation will 'chunk-down' the approval process into smaller, more manageable parts. When doing so, however, it takes care to avoid major initiatives having to unnecessarily jump through approval hoops.

IT PRESENTS A COMPLETE PICTURE OF THE INTERNAL CHANGE LANDSCAPE

Making priority decisions without first understanding what is already going on in the organisation is like promising to take the kids to their favourite ice-cream shop, then finding out that it's closed.

Having a complete picture of the change-landscape means your organisation clearly understands where every change is. This also means having an understanding of the impact the change process, and the new end-state will have on customers, your people, and the organisation as a whole. This complete picture means your organisation can be confident that, when viewed collectively, the entire change-portfolio is delivering value.

IT ONLY COLLECTS INFORMATION THAT IS USEFUL AND RELEVANT

The collection of data is a necessary evil for portfolio management capability. This usually means that someone in the organisation needs to input data into a report on a regular basis.

When doing this, there has to be a level of pragmatism and practicality. The lower risk the change, the less information is needed.

This is unless the small change is a core enabler for another huge, high-risk initiative.

Ensuring the data being collected is relevant and of sufficient quality, is also important. I can't begin to count the number of times I have seen dashboards that said that 'all was well' on a project, only to discover that three-quarters of it was below the water-line.

A Governance Framework

As soon as I use the word *governance* I can feel the eyes of the *other half* of my audience, roll back into their heads. I know… it's not very sexy but it's incredibly important when it comes to being adaptive.

Here's why.

An effective Governance Framework empowers your people to make choices at the time those choices need to be made.

It is particularly important in a change-dominated environment. That's because the 'knowns' that have previously formed the basis of decisions often revert to being 'unknowns'. This sense of 'I used to know how to do this in the old world, but now I'm not so sure' undermines the confidence of both leaders and team members. Having a well-articulated, well-understood framework enables this confidence to return. And that's good, because confidence is what will get the organisation through The Thrive Cycle.

An effective Governance Framework also limits what I call *the decision traffic jam.* This occurs when one delayed decision stops another action from progressing, which stops another decision and so on. Given the interconnected nature of established organisations, it only takes a few delayed decisions to bring hard-earned momentum to a grinding (and expensive) halt.

So what critical success factors does a Governance Framework require to create The Adaptive Organisation?

- It describes who can make what kind of decisions. Importantly, these go beyond financial sign-off authority.
- It provides guidance (usually in the form of clear principles) as

a basis upon which to make priority decisions. These should be equally relevant to small and large decisions.
- It is easy to understand and useful.

THRIVE CYCLE LEARNING

Learning from change successes and failures is something most organisations know they should do, but few are good at it.

In fact, one study found while 72 percent of executives believed that learning from failed strategy execution was important, only 40 percent said their company was good, or excellent at it. Further, 33 percent of respondents said they had no process for learning, and the majority of organisations said they relied on an 'informal' approach[22].

The traps that prevent learning

In theory, the concept of continuous improvement is pretty basic. Do something; learn from it; change something; do better next time.

So, if most organisations think learning is important, why do they fail to do it and become more adaptive over time? Once again, there are a few common traps to watch out for.

TRAP #1 – ONLY KNOWING, OR CARING ABOUT, HALF THE STORY

Without a concept like The Thrive Cycle, organisations lack a complete picture of what *really* happened to an initiative. Many post-implementation reviews start their analysis somewhere around the *Plan* stage and yet, as we've explored in previous chapters, what happens before this stage is a critical determinant as to whether an initiative succeeds or fails.

TRAP #2 – NOT WANTING TO SAY 'WE GOT IT WRONG'

Acknowledging that things could have been done better, in some organisations, is seen as admitting failure. In these organisations the aim of conducting a review can become more focused on showing why an initiative was such a raging success, rather than how it could have created even more value.

TRAP #3 – THE TIME-LAG ISSUE

The cause of an issue can occur months before its effects emerge. This time-lag means that making the right connections, and thus, the *actual* learning, is difficult to capture.

TRAP #4 – MEASURING SUCCESS ACCORDING TO PROCESS, NOT VALUE-CREATION

Did a project deliver within an arbitrary timeframe? Did it cost what we said it would cost (before we had any idea as to what was required)? Were the promised cost-savings realised (even though the project didn't really solve the problem it set out to address)? These are common ways in which organisations assess whether a change initiative was successful. Therefore, when setting out to learn from the experience, many organisations start by asking the wrong question. For example, 'Why didn't it deliver within the timeframe?' instead of asking, 'How could we have delivered more overall value to customers and the organisation, given the time we had available?'

TRAP #5 – APPLYING LINEAR THINKING TO A MULTI-DIMENSIONAL CONCEPT

Whether an individual change succeeds (i.e. creates value) or fails (i.e. erodes value) is the result of factors with multiple dimensions. That means the factors that cause success or failure in one scenario may not do so in another. This can make the lessons difficult to transfer.

TRAP #6 – RELYING UPON A SAMPLE OF ONE

Sometimes organisations treat each change initiative as though it's the only one they've ever undertaken. As a result, they take evidence from a single example and extrapolate it across the entire organisation's change ability. For reasons described in the previous point, this means the core issues and opportunities are rarely identified.

TRAP #7 – THE 'GLAD IT'S ALL OVER' FACTOR

Finally, we encounter another one of those human factors. Pursuing change-opportunities is really hard work. This means that by the time the change has been implemented, everyone is so relieved it's done, they just want to get on with something new.

♦ ♦ ♦

So, how do you overcome these traps? How do you ensure your Balanced Ecosystem enables your organisation to learn from experience and constantly pursue adaptive advantage?

The answer is *Thrive Cycle Learning.*

How Thrive Cycle Learning works

Thrive Cycle Learning refers to the way in which your organisation identifies, captures then applies lessons learnt throughout The Thrive Cycle. Thrive Cycle Learning creates insights at three levels.

LEVEL 1: STAGE LEARNING

As its name suggests, this level focuses on whether a stage within a specific Thrive Cycle rotation is achieving the outcomes it needs to. It is at this level that most of the data is gathered.

Stage Learning can be done at any time during a Thrive Cycle rotation. It follows the same review process we talked about when exploring Capability #2 of Thrive Cycle Leadership (Figure 11-12).

You'll recall that in order to work out where you were in The Thrive Cycle, you used a checklist describing the desired outcomes for each stage. When conducting Stage Learning, it's the same checklist. However, instead of having just one person's perspective, you gather feedback from many people across your organisation.

Key questions to answer at this Level include:

- *How have we progressed so far?*
- *Are we on track to deliver value?*
- *Are there any changes that need to be made?*

Gathering timely feedback in this way empowers your leaders and enables them to address issues before they become irreparable. It also helps to identify training or communication issues that may otherwise have slipped under the radar.

One of the real benefits of this approach is that it is quick and easy to do and therefore doesn't get left until the very end. Most importantly, it focuses on value-creation and not whether the process was completed.

How to get Thrive Cycle Learning right

THRIVE CYCLE LEARNING is built on the following principles:

- gather feedback from the people who were there (not those who later heard about what happened)
- minimise the time delay between the event actually happening and gathering feedback about that event
- gather lessons incrementally and apply interventions continuously
- enable people to give feedback at any time
- be transparent with process and results

FIGURE 11-12: Level 1 - Stage Learning uses incremental feedback to assess how well a change-opportunity is progressing

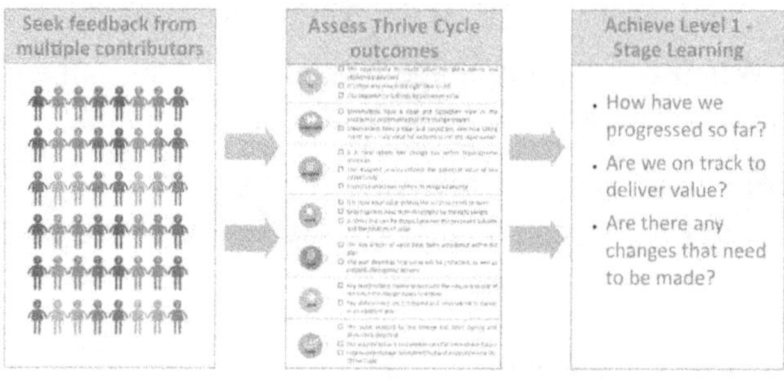

LEVEL 2: ROTATION LEARNING

Rotation Learning occurs once a change-opportunity has completed its rotation through The Thrive Cycle. It takes the cumulative view of insights gathered during Level 1 learning and looks holistically at the overall journey the change has taken.

For example, if issues were identified during the *See* stage, were they addressed or did they persist throughout the entire Thrive Cycle journey?

Rotation Learning answers questions like:

- *How well did we navigate The Thrive Cycle?*
- *How well did we learn and adapt throughout the Thrive Cycle journey?*
- *How well did the organisational environment support or inhibit success?*

Rotation Learning helps to provide the critical link between what actually happened (i.e. the business outcome) and why it happened. This level also places the change within the context of your organisation and recognises how environmental factors may have influenced the outcome.

This approach also reinforces the holistic nature of change and the importance of learning lessons throughout the entire Thrive Cycle journey rather than just at the end.

LEVEL 3: ORGANISATIONAL LEARNING

Organisational Learning holistically looks across your organisation's change portfolio and identifies the trends. These insights are created using the combined outputs from Level 2 – Rotation Learning. Similarly, Level 3 learning also provides the organisational context needed for Level 2.

Organisational Learning examines the overall health of your organisation's Thrive Cycle, as measured in real-time rather than retrospectively.

The types of questions answered at this level include:

- *Is our Thrive Cycle capability improving or deteriorating?*
- *Are there some stages of The Thrive Cycle that we do better than others?*

If issues or weaknesses within The Thrive Cycle are found at any of the three Levels of Thrive Cycle Learning, the intervention approach is the same. Once the area has been identified, the Six Elements of Adaptive Success can be used as a guide to identify what, if anything, needs to change.

The Adaptive Advantage Scorecard

Systematically engaging in Thrive Cycle Learning enables you to regularly assess how your organisation is progressing against its Target Adaptive Profile. In this way, the data can feed into an *Adaptive Advantage Scorecard* (Figure 11-13) that answers questions like:

- *What was our initial Adaptive Profile?*
- *How strong is our Adaptive Profile today?*
- *Are things improving or declining?*
- *What should we continue, stop, or change?*

FIGURE 11-13: The Adaptive Advantage Scorecard

	SEE	UNDERSTAND	PRIORITISE	DESIGN	PLAN	MOVE	LEARN
TARGET ADAPTIVE PROFILE	**3.8**	**3.8**	**4.3**	**4.1**	**4.2**	**4.2**	**4.3**
TODAY	3.1 ↑	3.4 ↑	3.4 ↓	3.4 →	4.0 ↑	2.6 ↑	2.1 ↑
WHERE WE STARTED	2.5	3.1	3.6	3.4	3.9	2.2	1.5
CURRENT IMPROVEMENT PRIORITIES	Thrive Cycle Leadership (Capabilities 2 & 3)/ Vital Thread development/ Balanced Ecosystem (Prioritisation & Thrive Cycle Learning)/ People capability (Thrive Cycle introduction)						

How to use the Six Elements of Adaptive Success to identify learning opportunities

LET'S SAY YOUR ORGANISATION conducted a Level 1: Stage Learning review. This found that 87 percent of feedback from informed participants (i.e. those who were close to the change) strongly disagreed with the statement 'stakeholders have a clear and consistent view of the threat or opportunity this change addresses'. So only 13 percent of your people know why you're organisation is doing what it's doing.

In this scenario, your organisation could use the Six Elements of Adaptive Success to pinpoint what was causing the result and thus, find a way to address it in real-time.

- **Start with Thrive Cycle Leadership** – We are talking about an individual change, so I'd always start by looking at Thrive Cycle Leadership. This Element has the most direct and immediate impact on a single change and it's progression through The Thrive Cycle. Have leaders worn the right Thrive Cycle Leadership 'hats' at the right time? Have the right questions been asked and answered?
- **Review The Vital Thread** – Is it clear how the change is supposed to create value for customers and the organisation? Does anyone know where the value is supposed to come from? Or, are you dealing with a solution that was looking for a problem?
- **If everything looks fine with these two elements, then there is probably a more systemic organisational issue.** What is Level 3 – Organisational Learning – telling you about the overarching environment? Is this issue occurring for every change that goes through The Thrive Cycle? Or, is it an anomaly?
- **Look at the Balanced Ecosystem (and its seven Thrive Cycle Enablers)** – While these may be contributing to the problem, it is unlikely to be causing it.

A key point to note here is that this kind of evaluation keeps the focus on the organisation collaboratively improving itself, not looking to blame a team or department for failure. This sense of collaboration and a prevailing idea that 'we're all in this together' are critical if the adaptive aspiration is to be achieved.

The Adaptive Advantage Scorecard is the core monitoring and governance tool for your Executive Team. Just like financial statements or sales reports, this simple tool is discussed as part of a regular agenda item at Executive Team meetings and forms the basis for aligned and targeted improvement decisions.

What's great about it, is that it's not merely a report. The factors driving the numbers are simultaneously creating learning and driving improvement (Figure 11-14).

THRIVE CYCLE MANAGEMENT

Like Finance or Human Resources, The Thrive Cycle doesn't operationally run itself. It needs to be managed. This is one of the primary accountabilities of your Adaptive Advantage Team.

The right Thrive Cycle Management approach looks different in each organisation. It depends on your Target Adaptive Profile, the size and complexity of the organisation and its current and future change landscape.

When designing your own Thrive Cycle Management approach here are the key factors to consider.

Change-methodologies and frameworks

Your organisation will require change methodologies to help individual Thrive Cycle rotations run smoothly. A good methodology is one that can be easily understood and works with, rather than against, the culture of your organisation.

A good methodology follows the 80/20 rule. It provides guidance for the 80 percent of change situations encountered within your

FIGURE 11-14: Thrive Cycle Learning enables Adaptive Advantage to be continuously measured, monitored and improved

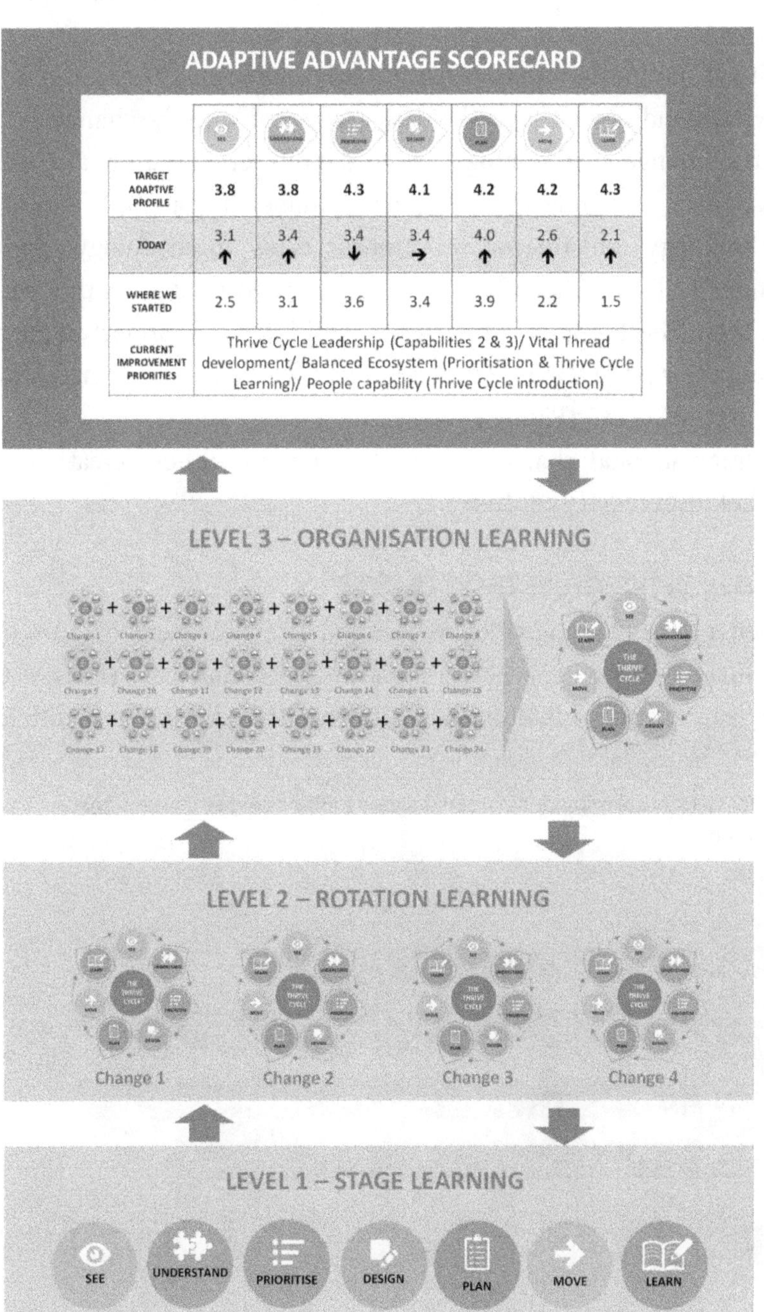

organisation. Attempting to develop standards that cover the outliers (i.e. the other 20 percent) creates complexity, and bureaucracy quickly follows.

It's also important to be able to scale the intensity of processes up or down depending on the level of risk associated with the change.

The change methodologies within your organisation also need to connect with one another. For example, if you have a project methodology, an internal communications methodology, and a Systems Delivery Lifecycle in IT, they all need to align with a set of common check-points. Otherwise, you'll have a project manager saying their project is in Phase 2, but for the IT people it's actually at the start of Stage 3 (Figure 11-15).

Organisational change is complex enough without creating this kind of unnecessary confusion.

COMMON METHODOLOGY TRAPS TO AVOID

When it comes to topics like process and discipline every organisation is different. It's funny how the same discussion can either cause people to salivate with enthusiasm, or run like heck. Because different

FIGURE 11-15: Misalignment between delivery methodologies causes unnecessary confusion.

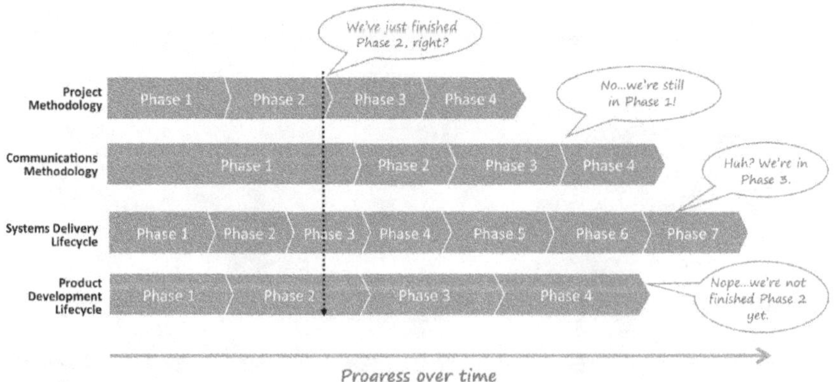

organisations have different 'appetites' in this direction, it can unwittingly lead them into a number of traps.

TRAP #1 – Process-ising everything

If your organisation likes formality and documents 'everything' then it may well want to do the same within a Balanced Ecosystem. The trouble with change is that by the time you've documented something, the subject matter has usually changed, and your documentation is instantly wrong.

Also, if you try to document every different scenario in a reference manual, it will be too big and cumbersome for anyone to read. Either way it won't deliver the outcomes a Balanced Ecosystem sets out to achieve.

The alternative is to focus more on principles and frameworks, rather than blow-by-blow procedures and policies. People are more likely to read them and it will empower them in a way that is needed when operating in a change-dominated environment.

TRAP #2 – Equating process with bureaucracy

A process is primarily a communication device that informs people how something works, or at least how it is meant to work. It also provides a starting point from which something can be improved.

Within some environments, particularly those in which things have historically been achieved through personal relationships and favours, process can be a dirty word. It can be seen as slowing things down, not making them more effective. As a result, when a process is put in to support change, it is sometimes dumbed-down or ignored. Ironically, when this happens, a process that started out being fit for purpose becomes bureaucratic, because it tries to stop people working around it.

CHAPTER CONCLUSION

Many different factors combine to create a Balanced Ecosystem and it can feel a little overwhelming at first.

Just remember that poor adaptiveness rarely stems from the Ecosystem. An imbalanced Ecosystem is far more likely to be a consequence of a weakness in one (or more) of the other five Elements of Adaptive Success. Start by understanding them and then use that knowledge to help create your design. Then work out where to start building your Balanced Ecosystem.

KEY THINGS TO REMEMBER

- When creating a Balanced Ecosystem, there are three Golden Rules.
  1. Consider the Balanced Ecosystem last
  1. Design before you build
  2. Create a Thrive Cycle Blueprint
- A Balanced Ecosystem comprises seven Thrive Cycle Enablers. They include:
  1. **Customer relevance** – Ensure that the inside of your organisation remains in-sync with what's happening in the external environment. Establish a Change Radar and create an Insights Incubator that captures opportunities and evolves The Vital Thread.
  2. **Organisational structure** – Creating The Adaptive Organisation is not a part-time job. Re-design the Executive Team, appoint a Chief Adaptive Officer and mobilise an Adaptive Advantage Team.
  3. **Leadership capability** – Create an environment in which Thrive Cycle Leadership is nurtured and valued. Treat it as a core competency for every leader, especially those in the most senior roles.
  4. **People capability** – For your people to thrive in a change-dominated environment they need to be prepared in advance. Teach them how change works, how the experience may affect them, and what to do when everything feels out-of-control. Grow-your-own change facilitation capabilities, and choose and use external consultants wisely.
  5. **Prioritisation** – A good prioritisation process makes good decisions easy to make. Use Value-Driven Metrics and remember that 'getting it right' will take time. Establish portfolio management and governance processes that are 'fit-for-purpose'.
  6. **Thrive Cycle Learning** – Many forces will prevent your organisation from learning if you let them. Thrive Cycle Learning creates insights at three levels. It enables your organisation to address issues before they are out of control, and create an Adaptive Advantage Scorecard that enables you to continuously measure, track and improve adaptive capability.
  7. **Thrive Cycle Management** – These are the processes and systems that support change through The Thrive Cycle. When making choices, ensure solutions 'fit' with your organisational culture and use a common language to make communication easier.

PART 3

Unlocking Your Adaptive Organisation

Now we've understood The Thrive Cycle capability and examined The Six Elements of Adaptive Success sitting beneath it, it's time to take action. This final section comes back to the eight fundamental questions asked in Chapter 1. It shows how you can now develop the answers and drive the change.

12

The Answers

This chapter brings us full-circle back to the eight questions I described at the beginning of the book. We'll go over each of them and I'll show how you can use what you've learned to unlock the adaptiveness within your organisation. This chapter also provides a useful summary to use when you engage others in your workplace.

AT THE START OF THIS BOOK I MADE YOU A PROMISE. Namely, that the insights and strategies I'd share would enable you to unlock the adaptive capability within your organisation and create an adaptive advantage.

You'll recall that one of the critical factors for creating The Adaptive Organisation is the ability to answer eight fundamental questions. These Adaptive Fundamentals, as I call them, provide the necessary clarity and alignment to holistically bring about change within your organisation.

You'll also recall that in order to answer these questions, we first needed a way to overcome your organisation's Adaptive Zone of Avoidance. Left in place, this blind-spot would prevent you from *Seeing* the opportunity of adaptive advantage and prevent the necessary conversations from ever gaining traction.

Fortunately, you now have The Thrive Cycle. This provides a sturdy basis from which to start any adaptive conversation. Whether you're developing organisational insight, defining adaptive advantage, engaging stakeholders, determining areas for improvement or tracking and monitoring progress, The Thrive Cycle Framework brings it all together and turns an otherwise conceptual idea into a robust, actionable priority.

So now let's come back to the eight Adaptive Fundamentals and explore how you can use the ideas from this book to answer them within your organisation.

Q1: WHAT ARE WE TRYING TO ACHIEVE?

In Chapter 2 we explored how being adaptive is different to being agile or adaptable. Having an organisation that is able to respond and move quickly is helpful but it's not enough. You need one that can also learn and do things differently when today's approach becomes irrelevant.

To build The Adaptive Organisation your leaders will need a clear, shared understanding of the desired outcome. Without it, they will lack the single focal point needed to keep the organisation moving in the same direction.

In this book we've defined The Adaptive Organisation as being a *purpose-driven* group of people that is able to:

- *change itself* (and the infrastructure that supports it) in order to *capture opportunities* that offer the *greatest potential value*; and
- *recognise* those opportunities, regardless of whether they occur inside or outside the organisation; and
- achieve all of the above, *to a standard* and *at a pace*, that *creates value*; and
- gives the organisation an *adaptive advantage* over its rivals.

This definition will enable you to move the driver for change beyond just the 'feel good factor' and make it a commercial imperative. Keeping the definition with you and constantly referring to it will ensure that building The Adaptive Organisation always comes back to creating value for customers and doing so better than anyone else. In other words, securing one of the few sustainable advantages available in an environment of constant change and building a high-performing, successful organisation.

Q2: WHY SHOULD OUR ORGANISATION BECOME MORE ADAPTIVE?

Every change needs to have a common-sense reason behind it. When you are changing an entire organisation, this reason needs to be pretty compelling if it is to align the hearts, minds and actions of your people. Achieving this will create the necessary motivation, determination and resilience to successfully complete the journey.

In Chapter 2 we looked at the positive case for change and showed how multiple studies have found adaptive organisations perform consistently better than non-adaptive ones. This is true for both short and long-term performance.

Non-adaptiveness attracts expensive and painful side-effects. It makes change costly, exhausts your best people and causes your organisation to leak value like a sieve. Further, in the future world of even greater, more complex and convergent change, the ability to adapt will be paramount and those unable to do so, will be left behind.

So that's the logical argument.

Unfortunately, big statistics, case-studies and catastrophic failures of iconic organisations are rarely enough to trigger a substantial shift in organisational behaviour and mindset. Human denial and our ability to justify maladaptive behaviour can pose a significant barrier to 'the truth'.

Organisational growth is generally a good thing, but it can foster some unhelpful habits. This includes taking the short-cut to economic-value, fragmenting the Customer-Value Continuum, and becoming locked into vertical thinking. These muffle the case for adaptive change and cause it to be drowned-out by other more immediate, urgent priorities.

So let's take a closer look at the question. It doesn't ask 'why should the average organisation become adaptive?' it asks 'why should *our* organisation become adaptive?'

Therefore, when answering it, the case for change must be directly related to *your* organisation and its circumstances. Above all it must be clear what it means to have an adaptive advantage and the benefits accompanying it.

You now have several tools to enable you to make this happen.

THE ADAPTIVE PROFILE – THE PICTURE YOU CAN POINT TO AND SAY 'WE ARE HERE'

In Chapter 3 we completed the Adaptive Audit and used it to create an Adaptive Profile. When you work on creating Enduring Commitment within your organisation, you will go through a similar process but this time you'll seek input from many different stakeholders. This will start to create a collective picture of where your organisation is today.

The chances are that when you do your first Adaptive Audit, the Adaptive Profile will be unclear with scores spread out across each of The Thrive Cycle capabilities. For example, there may be inconsistencies between the answers given by leaders and the people who execute change, or among the leaders themselves. This may be caused by inconsistent views of reality or by the fact that initially, people tend to be more informed about the areas of The Thrive Cycle in which they most often participate. This means feedback on unfamiliar areas will be less informed.

This kind of scenario is to be expected and provides a good opportunity to explore 'why the views are so different and what might be sitting behind them'. The more candid discussion you have, the clearer the Adaptive Profile position will become, so make sure you give it sufficient time.

Remember that once people are aware of The Thrive Cycle, they will notice it more and be better equipped to identify issues and opportunities to improve it.

THE FOUR ADAPTIVE ARCHETYPES – A WAY TO START CONVERSATIONS

Conversation is a powerful tool when you are wanting to build commitment to a change. The Surfer, Swimmer, Splasher, Sinker Archetypes have been created to be shared and discussed. They'll enable you and your leaders to have a non-threating discussion about your organisation, without *really* discussing *your* organisation. They also give you and your team a shared language to raise organisational self-awareness and keep adaptiveness top-of-mind. For example, referring to Surfer or Sinker-behaviour offers a quick way to identify what is, and is not supportive of The Adaptive Organisation.

ENDURING COMMITMENT – A WAY TO BUILD BELIEF IN THE CHANGE

The first Element of Adaptive Success - Enduring Commitment - is all about *the why.* The approach described in Chapter 6 will take your leaders on a journey of collaborative discovery, and create a collective view of the way things are as well as the way things should be.

The overarching objective is to move the answer to 'why should our organisation be adaptive?' from being a head-driven rationale to a heart-driven commitment. It's the internal belief that 'yes… there is a gap and it needs to be closed otherwise we will miss mind-blowing opportunities and/or suffer unthinkable consequences'.

In this way, creating Enduring Commitment makes the difference between *saying* your organisation needs to be more adaptive (but doing nothing), and *knowing* it (and taking focused action).

Q3: WHY SHOULD WE CHANGE NOW?

I've repeatedly said prioritisation is one of the most challenging jobs of a leader, and committing to create The Adaptive Organisation, and potentially not pursuing something else, is no different.

COMMITMENT – HELPING TO MAKE 'NOW' THE OBVIOUS ANSWER

This topic has been covered at numerous points along our journey and so I will simply summarise here.

The process described during the first Element of Adaptive Success – Enduring Commitment – is one of the most effective ways to answer this Adaptive Fundamental question collectively, as an organisation.

In Chapter 2 we looked at *why it's now or never* and examined how market factors like digitisation are making more traditional industries obsolete, changing consumer preferences and data overload are moving at lightning speed. We also considered how the nature of change, is itself changing. Increasing volatility, complexity and uncertainty mean that there is more 'big' change, with even bigger implications.

All of this highlights the way change has been managed in the past, will no longer be sufficient for the future.

REFLECT UPON THE PAST – LAY THE SITUATION OUT ON THE TABLE FOR ALL TO SEE

One of the exercises I asked you to do before completing The Adaptive Audit in Chapter 3 was reflect on the past and examine your internal change-landscape. You'll remember that in this exercise I asked you to consider what triggers change within your organisation. And, to what extent does change create value today?

Do this exercise with a cross-section of your leadership community. It is likely to trigger some 'lightbulb moments' and enlightening conversations. Another approach is to ask people who deliver change within your organisation to estimate the proportion of waste that occurs during organisational change. They will know because they have to navigate barriers created by a weak Thrive Cycle on a regular basis. Then, look at how much your organisation spends on strategy execution and organisational change each year. Applying the proportion of waste to the amount being spent over three or five years may give you a useful statistic.

In Chapter 2 I shared a study that had found almost 11 percent of investment in organisational change was wasted. What is 11 percent of your strategic change budget? What's the economic and human opportunity-cost of leaving things the way they are?

Using analogy or physical examples to bring the facts to life can be another useful strategy. For example, I once brought a pile of small stones into an Executive meeting, piled them onto the board table and used them to show how inadequate prioritisation (i.e. too many rocks in the jar) was undermining the value and success of mission-critical change in the organisation.

Stories can also be really powerful. I once had a project in which an automated phone-payment system was rejecting 80 percent of calls. When Executive enthusiasm to reallocate scarce resources was lacking I said '...this means that when five customers call us to pay for their $2000 product, four of them make it all the way through three selection menus, enter their credit card details and then... clunk... we hang-up on them'. The payment system was fixed.

Whatever approach you use, make sure you create 'a sense of urgency'[35] and not blind-panic. You need people to be focused and committed to 'building The Ark' not running around screaming 'We're all gonna die!'

Q4: WHAT DOES THE ADAPTIVE ORGANISATION LOOK LIKE FOR US?

If you're going to inspire people to move the entire organisation to a new and better place, there needs to be a common understanding as to what is waiting for them on the other side. Having reached this chapter you now have the knowledge and tools to do this.

THE THRIVE CYCLE – A COMMON REFERENCE POINT AND LANGUAGE THAT HELPS PEOPLE TO 'GET IT'

In Chapter 1 we looked at the concept of time and how human beings have created a framework of language and tools to make it concrete and useful. The Thrive Cycle Framework achieves the same outcome for the concept of being adaptive. Therefore, as soon as people understand The Thrive Cycle capability exists and that it depends on your organisation mastering the Six Elements of Adaptive Success, they can use this knowledge to have a structured conversation.

When answering this fourth Adaptive Fundamental question, The Thrive Cycle Framework will enable you to move beyond the generic description of The Adaptive Organisation (presented in Chapter 4) to one that describes *your* Adaptive Organisation, using the Target Adaptive Profile in Chapter 6. But for any of this to make sense, your people must first understand The Thrive Cycle. It's therefore the logical place for you to start.

THE FOUR ADAPTIVE ARCHETYPES – CLARIFIES BY STATING WHAT THE ADAPTIVE ORGANISATION DOES NOT DO

The clearer you can make the picture of The Adaptive Organisation, the easier it will be for your people to understand what they are setting out to create. This clarity will enable them to be more focused, spend less time understanding what they're trying to achieve, and more time actually achieving it.

All of the characteristics attributed to Surfers, Swimmers, Splashers and Sinkers are real. They occur within real organisations and I have seen first-hand how they directly contribute to adaptive success or failure. Sharing these Archetypes within your organisation will increase clarity by describing what The Adaptive Organisation is, and what it's not. This in turn will help people to identify and thus challenge non-adaptive characteristics which may otherwise have passed unnoticed.

Q5: WHERE ARE WE TODAY?

Successful change must start with an agreed picture of where the organisation is today. This not only helps with identifying why change is required, it is a critical step for understanding what change is needed and the size of the gap.

THE ADAPTIVE PROFILE – ALIGN PEOPLE FIRST, THEN REFINE MEASUREMENT

Chapter 6 described in detail how to develop an initial starting-point by using a self-assessment tool (i.e. the Adaptive Audit). When you first start out, this approach, along with other independent data will provide a good initial view of your organisation to 'get the ball rolling'. It will sound a bit strange, but gaining stakeholder agreement using imperfect data is better than not gaining agreement using perfect data.

Once you've started to build commitment to creating The Adaptive Organisation, and you've started addressing the Six Elements of Adaptive Success, you can then focus on measuring Adaptive Performance more accurately and systematically. When talking about The Balanced Ecosystem in Chapter 11, I introduced the concept of Thrive Cycle Learning. This approach uses incremental-learning to build an on-going view of your organisation's Thrive Cycle capability. The three levels of learning enable The Adaptive Advantage Scorecard to be created. This forms the basis of an ongoing review and improvement program.

It's important to note that full Thrive Cycle Learning capability will take time to develop. I recommend starting with regular self-assessed Adaptive Audits (say two or three a year). Then, once you have your Adaptive Advantage Team in place, gradually evolve your Thrive Cycle Learning capability and build a real-time, Adaptive Advantage Scorecard.

Q6: WHAT IS THE GAP BETWEEN TODAY AND OUR DESIRED FUTURE?

The Adaptive Profile depicts the strength of The Thrive Cycle within your organisation. The Target Adaptive Profile depicts how strong the Thrive Cycle capability needs to be if your organisation is to achieve an adaptive advantage in its chosen markets (Figure 12-1).

On paper, *the gap* is the distance between your organisation's Adaptive Profile and the Target Adaptive Profile its Executive Team (with input from the Board and other stakeholders) has set for the organisation. In 'the real-world' however, the gap is the difference between how effective your organisation's Thrive Cycle capability is today versus how effective it needs to be.

FIGURE 12-1: The Target Adaptive Profile we set in Chapter 6

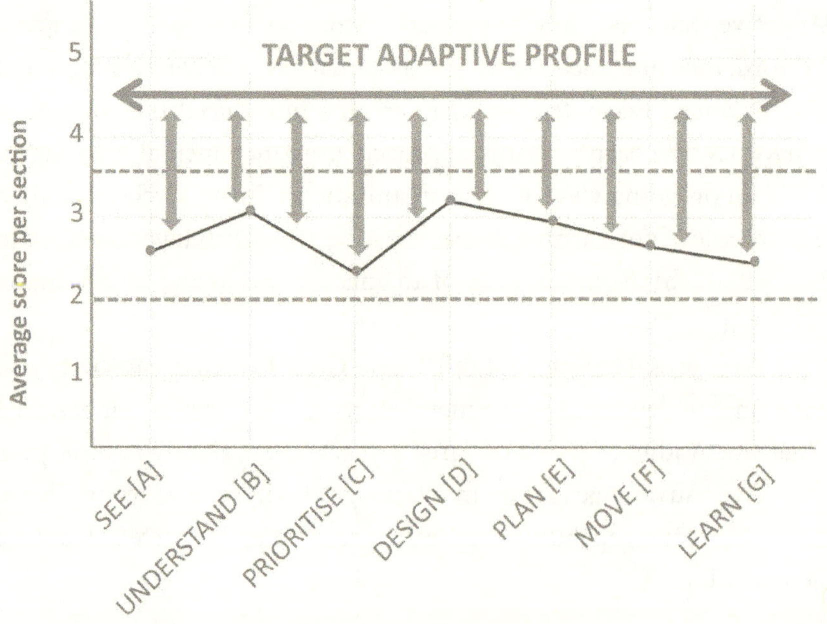

THE ADAPTIVE PROFILE – WORK FROM LEFT-TO-RIGHT TO UNDERSTAND THE STORY BEHIND THE NUMBERS

As you look at the picture showing your organisation's Target Adaptive Profile and its current Adaptive Profile, it can feel quite daunting, especially if the gap is quite large.

Remember, even though an Adaptive Profile takes the form of a straight line we're actually talking about a cycle in which each part builds on the part that came before it (like a spiral staircase). The insight comes from seeing the full picture, not just the single points on a line.

Start with *See*, and think about what the data is telling you. Which areas are stronger than others? Then, move towards the right of The Profile, and do the same thinking for the other Thrive Cycle capabilities. However, before you move onto the next, think about how the capabilities to the left are influencing the current one.

For example, if you are thinking about *Design*, consider how the capabilities of *See*, *Understand* and *Prioritise* are impacting the *Design* capability within your Thrive Cycle. Capture these thoughts somehow (e.g. – writing them in words or use a mind map). This will give you the *real* story and bring meaning to the dots on the page.

I suggest doing this before you start looking for ways to address the gaps.

START WITH DESIGN PRINCIPLES – FOCUS ON THE OUTCOME AND RECOGNISE THAT THERE ARE MANY POSSIBLE SOLUTIONS

In Chapter 10, I shared that one of the core roles for a Thrive Cycle Leader is to insist upon setting Design Principles prior to looking for solutions. When building The Adaptive Organisation, the same applies.

Use the Target Adaptive Profile and think about what kind of criteria your Thrive Cycle Blueprint would need to meet before you start designing it. Answer questions like:

- *How quickly do we need to be able to respond to new changes?*
- *How many Thrive Cycle rotations does our organisation need to be able to manage at the one time? 10? 50? 250?*

- *How long should it take for different kinds of change to progress from See to Plan? A week? A month? 6 months?*

Setting these criteria upfront will ensure that the solution you end up with actually delivers the kind of adaptive organisation you need.

Q7: WHAT'S CAUSING THE GAP AND WHERE SHOULD WE FOCUS?

The strength of The Thrive Cycle within your organisation is determined by the strength of its Six Elements of Adaptive Success (Figure 12-2).

If these are all strong, The Thrive Cycle will be strong and your organisation's Adaptive Profile will be high. If, however, the Six Elements of Adaptive Success are weak, your organisation's Thrive Cycle will be weak, resulting in a low Adaptive Profile.

Therefore, when it comes to working out what's causing your current Adaptive Profile and working out how to improve it, the Six Elements of Success hold the key.

I appreciate there's a lot of content in Part 2 so in a moment I'll briefly review each of the Elements and show you how they will enable you to answer the above question. I'd also encourage you to go and read Part 2 again. Having the full picture will place each of the Elements in context and highlight the relationships between them.

I also find it useful to think about the Six Elements of Adaptive Success in pairs (Figure 12-3).

THE FIRST AND SIXTH ELEMENTS – THE BOOKENDS

Enduring Commitment and The Balanced Ecosystem are *The Bookends* of the Thrive Cycle Framework. Enduring Commitment ensures your organisation recognises The Thrive Cycle as a necessary organisational capability for achieving adaptive advantage. Enduring Commitment also creates clarity by developing a meaningful goal for your organisation to pursue.

FIGURE 12-2: The Thrive Cycle capability is underpinned by the Six Elements of Adaptive Success

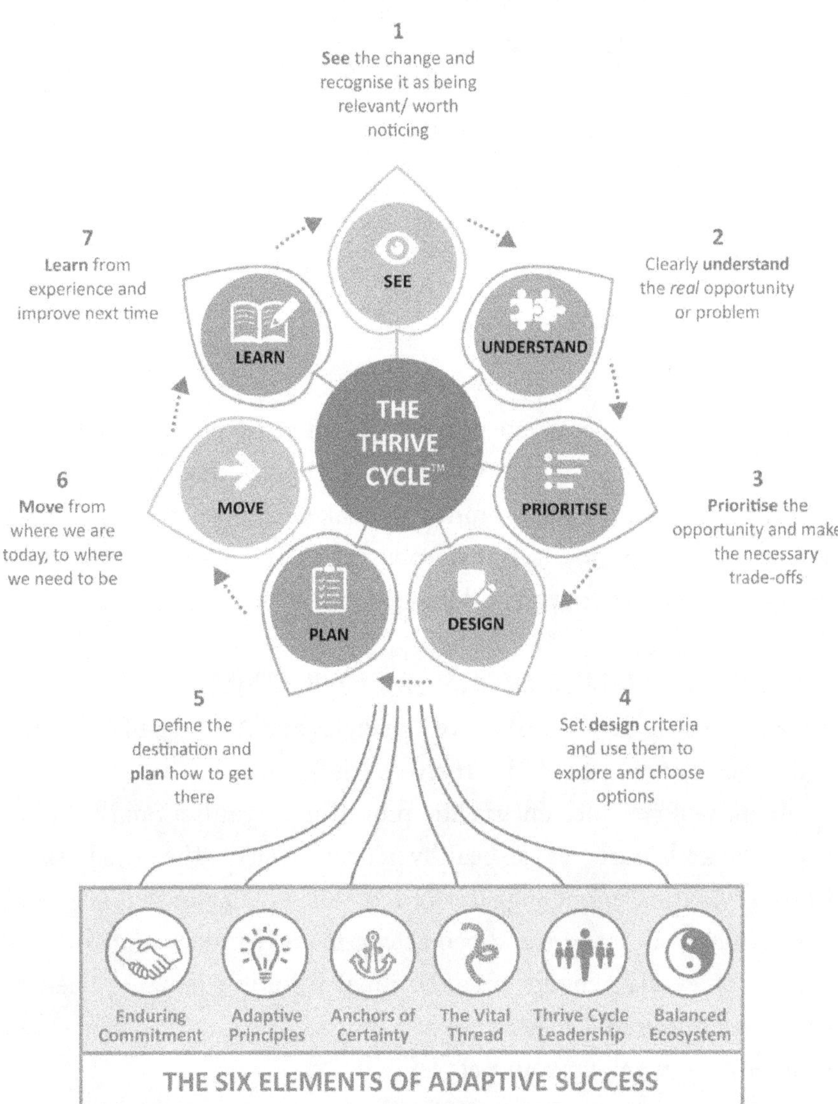
The Thrive Cycle Framework
1
See the change and recognise it as being relevant/ worth noticing
2
Clearly understand the real opportunity or problem
3
Prioritise the opportunity and make the necessary trade-offs
4
Set design criteria and use them to explore and choose options
5
Define the destination and plan how to get there
6
Move from where we are today, to where we need to be
7
Learn from experience and improve next time
SEE
UNDERSTAND
PRIORITISE
DESIGN
PLAN
MOVE
LEARN
THE THRIVE CYCLE™
Enduring Commitment
Adaptive Principles
Anchors of Certainty
The Vital Thread
Thrive Cycle Leadership
Balanced Ecosystem
THE SIX ELEMENTS OF ADAPTIVE SUCCESS

FIGURE 12-3: The Six Elements of Adaptive Success can be thought of in pairs

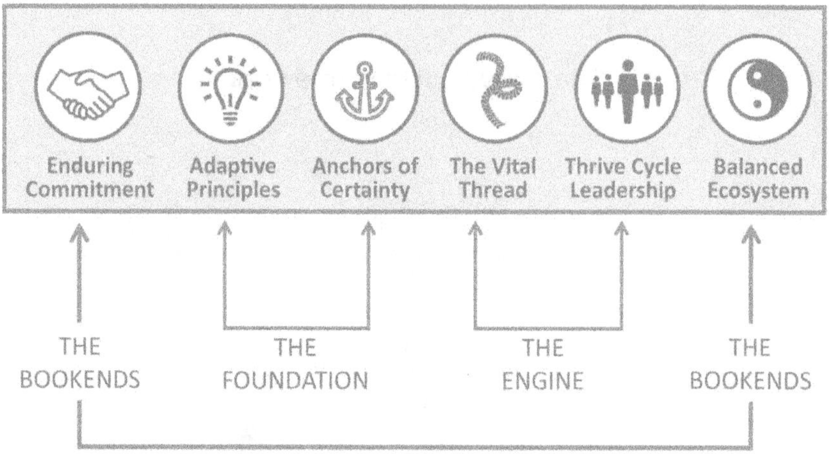

The Balanced Ecosystem provides the necessary infrastructure to embed Thrive Cycle capability into the fabric of your organisation. In short, while Enduring Commitment makes sure your organisation cares whether or not it *has* a robust Thrive Cycle, the Balanced Ecosystem makes sure you build one and continue to improve it.

THE SECOND AND THIRD ELEMENTS – THE FOUNDATIONS

The next two elements – Adaptive Principles and Anchors of Certainty – are The Foundations of The Thrive Cycle.

Adaptive Principles ensure the prevailing organisational mindset supports and nurtures a healthy Thrive Cycle. The Anchors of Certainty, as their name suggests, provide an invaluable reference point from which your leaders and people can make decisions and embrace change. They also ensure organisational thinking remains open to new possibilities and fosters aligned decision-making, resilience and positive energy among your people.

THE FOURTH AND FIFTH ELEMENTS – THE ENGINE

The Vital Thread and Thrive Cycle Leadership make The Thrive Cycle *go round.* The Vital Thread does this by ensuring continuity and alignment of opportunities entering, then progressing through a Thrive Cycle rotation. By doing this, the Vital Thread ensures changes avoid getting in each other's way and the overall change portfolio of your organisation collectively delivers value.

Thrive Cycle Leadership drives and supports the change through each rotation. It keeps change moving, people motivated and ensures your organisation and its people successfully transition to the new world. More importantly, Thrive Cycle Leadership ensures that adapting to change is always about creating more value for customers and the organisation.

So, let's briefly revisit all Six Elements of Adaptive Success and how they strengthen the Thrive Cycle capability of your organisation.

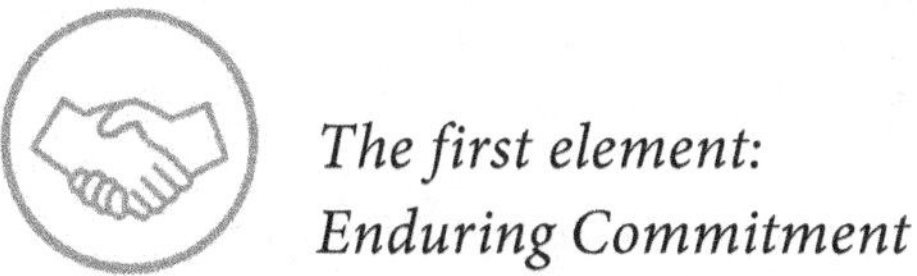

The first element:
Enduring Commitment

Enduring Commitment ensures your organisation has a clear sense of what being adaptive means, and how it will create an advantage in its chosen environment. Enduring Commitment also ensures being adaptive is not left to chance; rather, it is something that is measured and monitored, and at an emotional level, actually *matters.*

This element provides your initial starting point. Without it you have no basis upon which to assess the gap, no Target Adaptive Profile and insufficient motivation and enthusiasm to deliver the required outcome.

If this element is weak, your organisation and, more specifically its leaders, will struggle to even talk about becoming adaptive, let alone build sufficient alignment to create an adaptive advantage.

Creating Enduring Commitment will require you to go on a journey and take your people with you (Figure 12-4). It's as much about building engagement as it is about setting a clear goal to pursue.

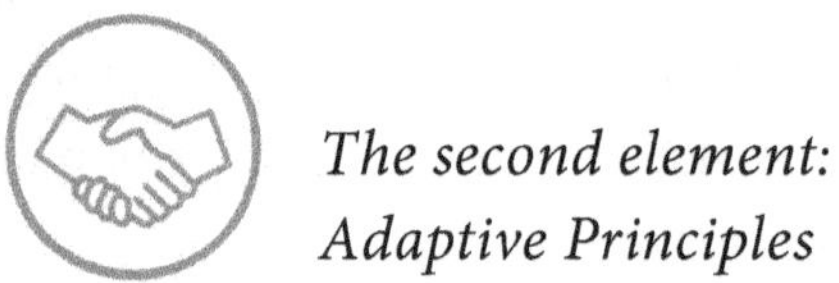

The second element:
Adaptive Principles

Adaptive Principles nurture then maintain an adaptive mindset across your organisation. Reinforcing these principles within the culture means commitment will be sustained and a focus on being adaptive will continue beyond the tenure of individual leaders.

THE FIVE ADAPTIVE PRINCIPLES	
PRINCIPLE #1	**Put Customer-Value first** – This ensures that change is ultimately about creating or protecting customer-value. If organisational change is not doing this, it's usually eroding it.
PRINCIPLE #2	**Intimately understand where and how value is created** – If you don't know how you create value today, how can you know whether a change will increase or erode customer-value and thus, economic-value?
PRINCIPLE #3	**Believe that adaptive advantage is worth the effort** – Subscribing to this principle helps overcome 'unhelpful organisational habits' like vertical-thinking, taking the short-cut to economic value and pursuing pseudo growth. This principle also overcomes the perils of 'If it ain't broke, why fix it?' and 'waiting for the right time' (which never arrives).
PRINCIPLE #4	**Understand every change and treat it with respect** – This means recognising that changes vary in terms of predictability, speed, nature and sexiness. The same commitment is needed regardless of the type of change.
PRINCIPLE #5	**Ensure the net-effect of change is positive** – Changes are rarely independent of each other so the collective impact and value created by all change needs to be considered.

FIGURE 12-4: Reminder of the process behind Enduring Commitment

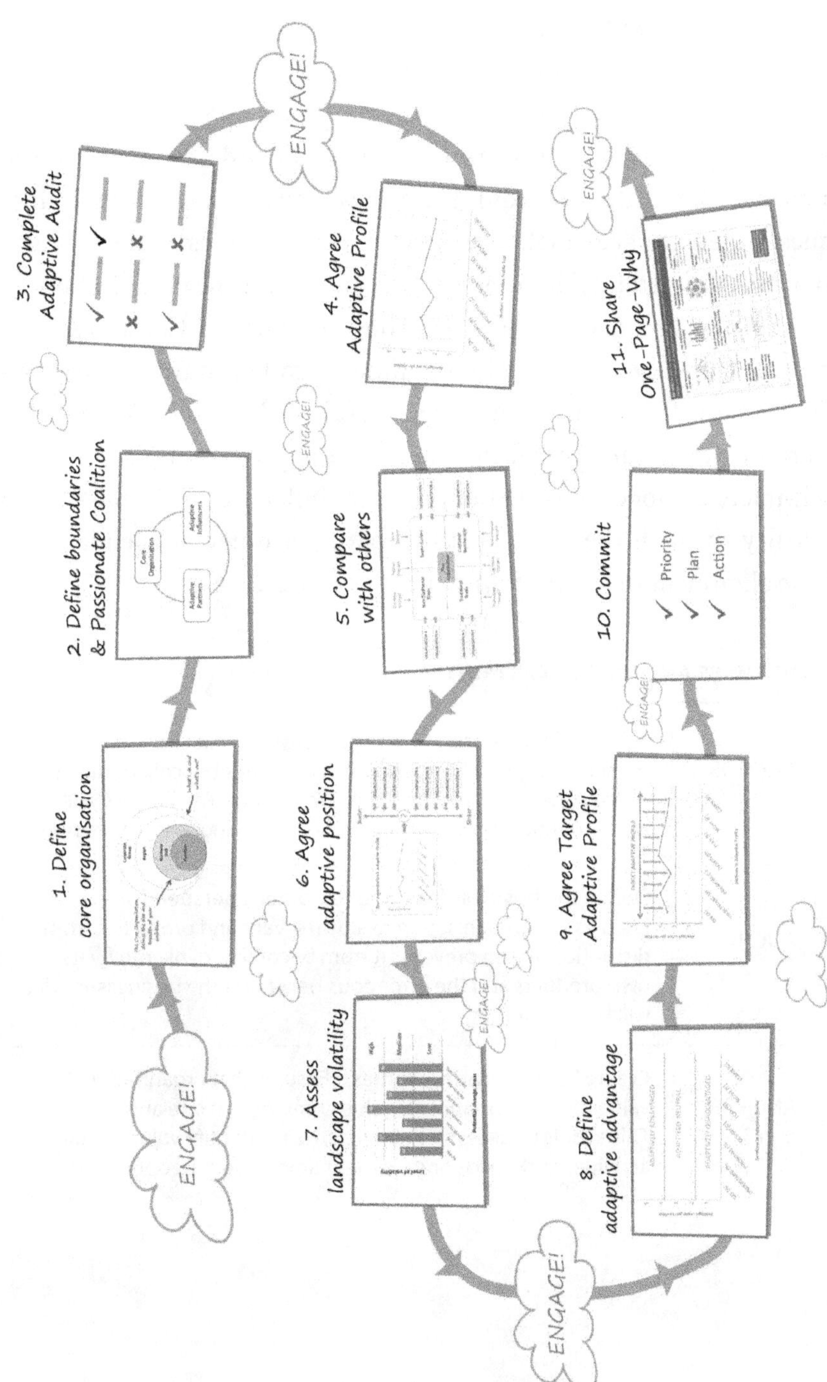

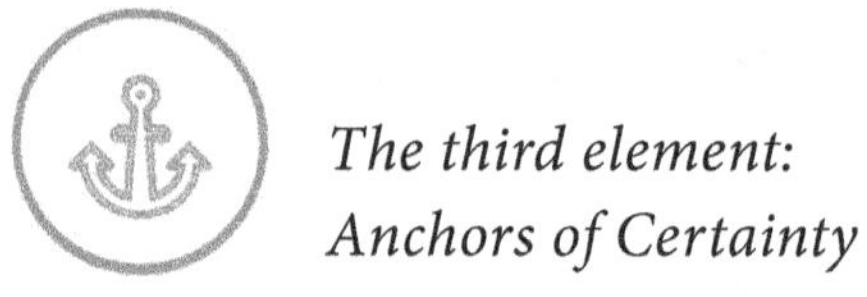

The third element:
Anchors of Certainty

A core capability of any organisation is making decisions. However, a change-dominated environment brings many former 'knowns' into question, and this can make even the simplest decisions harder to make. In this way, 'certainty' becomes like an anchor for the organisation.

When your organisation has strong Anchors of Certainty, your people will feel empowered and willing to go beyond their position-description to make change successful. When the Anchors of Certainty are weak other factors become the primary motivators (e.g. self-interest, money, jurisdiction, political influence). This makes each journey through the Thrive Cycle a battle of different agendas with little alignment in terms of direction or value creation.

THE THREE ANCHORS OF CERTAINTY	
ANCHOR #1	**A compelling Sense of Purpose** – Ensures that changes are pursued for the right reasons. It also creates the collaborative energy needed to navigate change through The Thrive Cycle and engenders resilience, trust and the willingness to take risks.
ANCHOR #2	**Define the business from the customer's perspective** – Enables your organisation to stay relevant and protects it from disruption. It also prevents it from becoming blinkered by its own products and the erroneous belief that the business-model will last forever.
ANCHOR #3	**Create Value-Creating-Values** – Ensures that organisational values and the creation of value complement one another. This avoids unnecessary conflicts, helps identify value-eroding activities and builds engagement among your people.

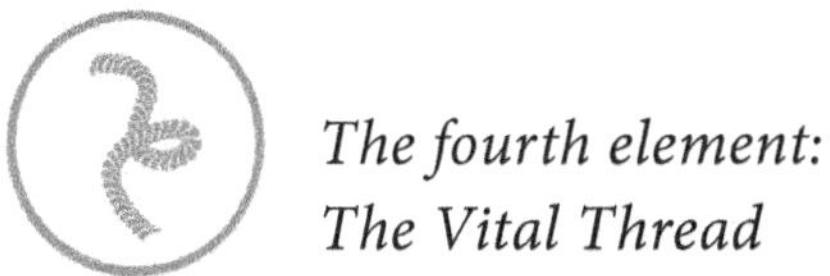

The fourth element:
The Vital Thread

The Vital Thread is an organisational tool that meaningfully connects your organisation's external world with its internal world. In Chapter 9 we met Orion Healthcare and saw first-hand how a strong Vital Thread enabled them to achieve alignment when the Government changed the rules regarding overseas doctors.

The Vital Thread is a must-have if you are going to create The Adaptive Organisation, and ensures that continuity is maintained throughout every Thrive Cycle rotation.

THE VITAL THREAD SUPPORTS THE ADAPTIVE ORGANISATION BY...
• helping its leaders and people to remain aligned and deliver maximum value while moving through The Thrive Cycle • ensuring the heavy thinking has been done before the big opportunities materialise. This enables the organisation to focus on realising the potential of the opportunity, rather than 'getting on the same page' • enabling priority decisions to be made without creating false certainty and bringing an underlying consistency to the organisation's change agenda • putting short, medium and long-term value back on the same value-continuum • offering your people and leaders a lifeline they can hold onto, such that they can maintain focus and confidence when plans turn out to be wrong • enabling your organisation to authentically and consistently answer the question 'Why?' and overcome many of the underlying causes of resistance

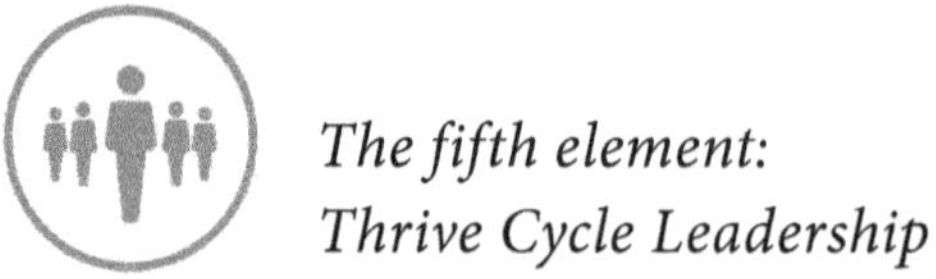

The fifth element:
Thrive Cycle Leadership

In Chapter 10 we explored Thrive Cycle Leadership and showed how applying the right leadership mindset and behaviours at the right time enables change to progress through The Thrive Cycle. We also looked at how Thrive Cycle Leadership is essential if your people are to successfully transition to the new future state.

Being a great Thrive Cycle Leader requires three core capabilities. When Thrive Cycle Leadership is absent, the negative effects accumulate making the journey slower, more costly and the outcome significantly less satisfactory.

All leaders within your organisation need to recognise and develop *all* three capabilities if they are to effectively perform their role and thus, create value for customers and the organisation.

THE THREE CAPABILITIES OF THRIVE CYCLE LEADERSHIP	
CAPABILITY #1	**Recognise when you've entered a Thrive Cycle rotation** – this creates a mental trigger to invoke Thrive Cycle Leadership.
CAPABILITY #2	**Recognise where you are in The Thrive Cycle** – this enables you to know what mindset and behaviours are required.
CAPABILITY #3	**Understand and apply the right mindset and behaviours for that stage of The Thrive Cycle** – this gives the change and your people the best chance of progressing smoothly through The Thrive Cycle and successfully creating value.

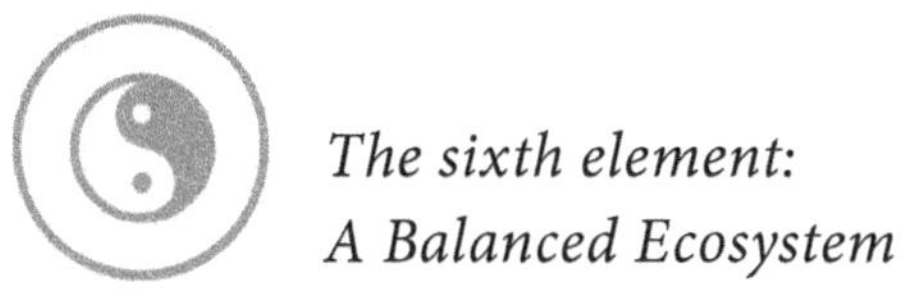

The sixth element: A Balanced Ecosystem

A Balanced Ecosystem comprises seven Thrive Cycle Enablers. Together they ensure the pursuit of adaptive advantage is embedded within your organisation and there is a constant focus on improving The Thrive Cycle capability.

The seven Thrive Cycle Enablers and their contribution toward a Balanced Ecosystem are as follows.

THE SEVEN THRIVE CYCLE ENABLERS	
THRIVE CYCLE ENABLER #1	**Customer relevance** – Ensures alignment between what the organisation thinks creates value, and what actually creates value for customers. It does so by continually evolving The Vital Thread and ensuring the organisation, its proposition and operational capability work effectively together to create value. *Highlights: The Change Radar; Insights Incubator; Ongoing Vital Thread Review.*
THRIVE CYCLE ENABLER #2	**Organisational structure** – Makes adaptive advantage an organisational priority and ensures it receives ongoing focus (both top-down and bottom-up) *Highlights: Appoint a Chief Adaptive Officer; Re-think The C-Suite; Introduce an Adaptive Advantage Team.*
THRIVE CYCLE ENABLER #3	**Leadership capability** – Ensures Thrive Cycle Leadership is a valued and developed competency and that it is nurtured within your organisational environment. *Highlights: Invest in leadership development; Build Thrive Cycle Leadership into recruitment and selection; Balance Thrive Cycle Leadership across the hierarchy; Use The Vital Thread to make leadership easier.*

THRIVE CYCLE ENABLER #4	**People capability** – Ensures your people have the knowledge and resilience to thrive within an uncertain environment. *Highlights: Prepare your people in advance; Teach them the rules of the change-game; Make change-facilitation a valued capability; Use consultants wisely.*
THRIVE CYCLE ENABLER #5	**Prioritisation** – Ensures clear priority choices are made for the right reasons and the consequences are understood. *Highlights: Value-Driven Metrics; Implement effective portfolio management capability; Develop robust governance.*
THRIVE CYCLE ENABLER #6	**Thrive Cycle Learning** – Ensures the organisation's Thrive Cycle capability is tracked and consciously improved over time. *Highlights: Apply three levels of learning (1 – Stage, 2 – Rotation, 3 – Organisation); Create an Adaptive Advantage Scorecard and use it to monitor progress and maintain commitment.*
THRIVE CYCLE ENABLER #7	**Thrive Cycle Management** – Ensures the Thrive Cycle has the operational processes and support tools to logistically work and cope with the required demand. *Highlights: Using change-management frameworks; Aligning methodologies.*

How to 'unpack' your Adaptive Profile and work out where to focus

EACH POINT ON YOUR ORGANISATION'S Adaptive Profile today is being impacted by the Six Elements of Adaptive Success. The next logical question is 'which ones are impacting which parts of The Thrive Cycle?' The following steps will help you to answer it.

Step 1 – Review the Foundation Elements

How strong are the Adaptive Principles and Anchors of Certainty within your organisation? If they are weak, they will be inhibiting your entire Thrive Cycle capability across every stage. Changes will 'clash' with one another, short-term economic-value will more likely be driving change, and your people will have no shared basis upon which to make decisions.

Conversely, strong Foundation Elements will give direction without relying on strict control. People will be better equipped to navigate The Thrive Cycle and feel empowered to do so.

Step 2 – Review The Engine Elements

Start with The Vital Thread – How clearly is it defined within your organisation and how much does what you have today guide people through each stage of The Thrive Cycle? Are there certain stages where its absence or presence is having a particular impact?

Remember, if your Vital Thread is weak it will weaken Thrive Cycle Leadership across your organisation. With this in mind, review the attributes of Thrive Cycle Leadership. Are there certain stages where Thrive Cycle Leadership is demonstrated more or less effectively than others?

Step 3 – Review The Bookend Elements

Look at The Balanced Ecosystem – how many of each of The Thrive Cycle Enablers exist within your organisation? When you look at all of these Enablers, how well do they fit together? Is it really an Ecosystem or a series of independent interventions with no overarching design?

Without drive, goal clarity or measurement, the journey through The Thrive Cycle is random and unpredictable. Does your organisation demonstrate an Enduring Commitment to building an adaptive advantage? Is it pursuing a clear goal and does it measure progress on a regular basis? Without consistency there can be no adaptive advantage.

Step 4 – Map the Elements against your organisation's Adaptive Profile

A heat-map (Figure 12-5) provides a useful way to explore how the Six Elements of Adaptive Success are contributing to your organisation' s Adaptive Profile. Thinking holistically, is each Element a) Enhancing [🡅] b) Inhibiting [🡇] or c) Maintaining [🡆] each stage of The Thrive Cycle capability.

FIGURE 12-5: Use a heat-map to understand what's driving your organisation's Adaptive Profile.

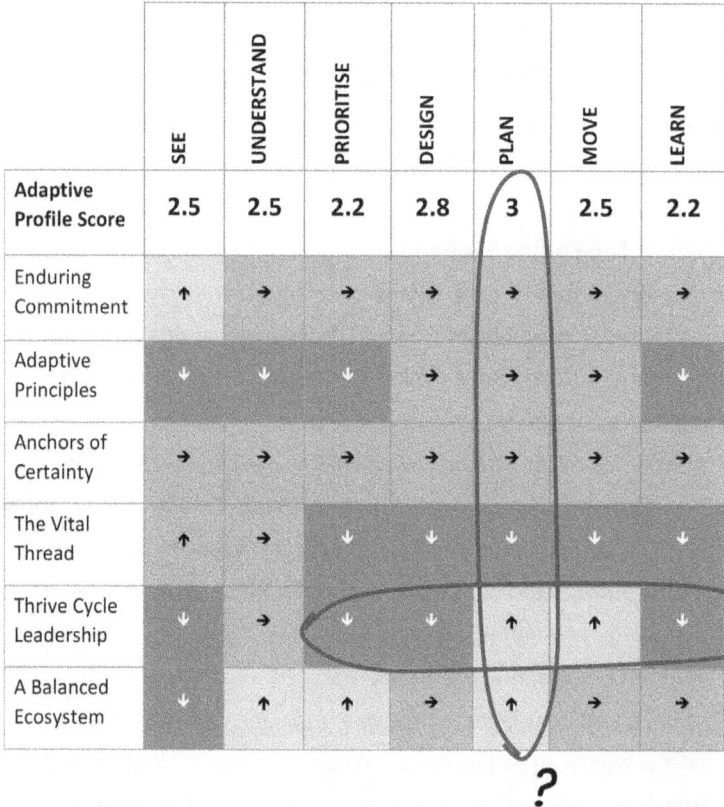

	SEE	UNDERSTAND	PRIORITISE	DESIGN	PLAN	MOVE	LEARN
Adaptive Profile Score	**2.5**	**2.5**	**2.2**	**2.8**	**3**	**2.5**	**2.2**
Enduring Commitment	↑	→	→	→	→	→	→
Adaptive Principles	↓	↓	↓	→	→	→	↓
Anchors of Certainty	→	→	→	→	→	→	→
The Vital Thread	↑	→	↓	↓	↓	↓	↓
Thrive Cycle Leadership	↓	→	↓	↓	↑	↑	↓
A Balanced Ecosystem	↓	↑	↑	→	↑	→	→

?

?

Developing this kind of map using the collaborative efforts of informed stakeholders can help to identify where focus is needed most, while also building engagement.

Q8: WHERE DO WE START?

The path you choose to follow when creating The Adaptive Organisation will be influenced by many factors – your ambition, position of influence, the sense of urgency and the size of the challenge. The more you learn about your organisation, the better you will understand the gaps and the more refined your approach will become.

For all these reasons, the roadmap for your organisation will be something that evolves. Remember this and avoid the temptation to 'lock it in' too soon (or you may be locking-in the wrong approach). Planning in phases will give structure and direction, while also allowing the plan to develop.

All this said, what you need right now is a way to get things started. That's what the following roadmap will enable you to do (Figure 12-6).

Phase 1 – Listen. Talk. Learn.

- **Desired outcome:** To generate interest in creating The Adaptive Organisation and gain the commitment of key stakeholders to invest time exploring the idea further.

Before you do anything, you need to understand the lay-of-the-land. What's the current appetite for building The Adaptive Organisation? What's a priority at the moment? What's the history regarding strategy execution and organisational change?

From your organisation's perspective, you need to establish a basis upon which to start the adaptive conversation and build interest in talking about, let alone building, The Adaptive Organisation. Key activities during this phase could include:

- building your fact-base
- sharing The Thrive Cycle and asking people what they think it looks like in your organisation
- conducting a mini-Adaptive Audit and using it as a conversation starter. e.g. Survey 20–40 participants and use the findings as a means of creating 'lightbulb moments' with leadership colleagues
- working out your initial stakeholder strategy. Who really matters and who can help?

FIGURE 12-6: A four-phase roadmap to get you started

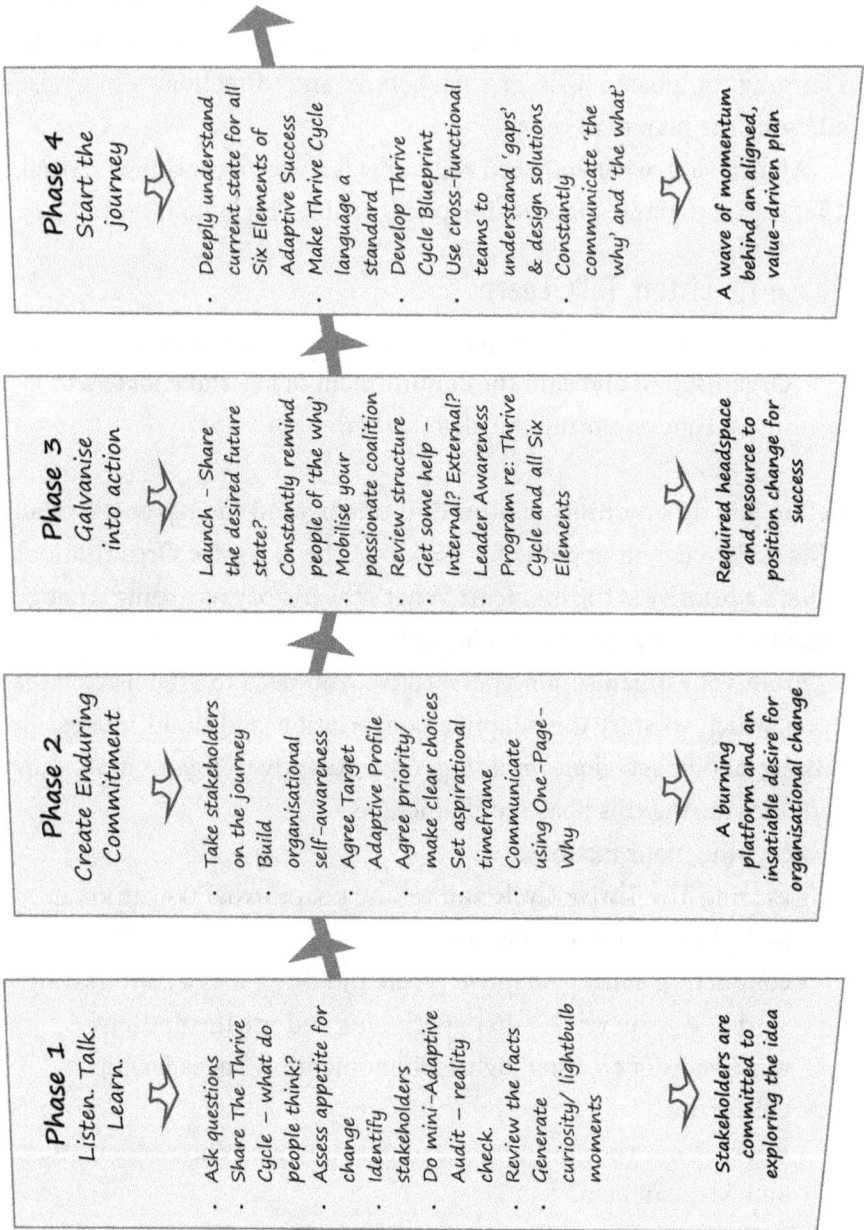

Phase 1
Listen. Talk. Learn.

- Ask questions
- Share The Thrive Cycle – what do people think?
- Assess appetite for change
- Identify stakeholders
- Do mini-Adaptive Audit – reality check.
- Review the facts
- Generate curiosity/ lightbulb moments

Stakeholders are committed to exploring the idea

Phase 2
Create Enduring Commitment

- Take stakeholders on the journey
- Build organisational self-awareness
- Agree Target Adaptive Profile
- Agree priority/ make clear choices
- Set aspirational timeframe
- Communicate using One-Page-Why

A burning platform and an insatiable desire for organisational change

Phase 3
Galvanise into action

- Launch - Share the desired future state?
- Constantly remind people of 'the why'
- Mobilise your passionate coalition
- Review structure
- Get some help – Internal? External?
- Leader Awareness Program re: Thrive Cycle and all Six Elements

Required headspace and resource to position change for success

Phase 4
Start the journey

- Deeply understand current state for all Six Elements of Adaptive Success
- Make Thrive Cycle language a standard
- Develop Thrive Cycle Blueprint
- Use cross-functional teams to understand 'gaps' & design solutions
- Constantly communicate 'the why' and 'the what'

A wave of momentum behind an aligned, value-driven plan

Phase 2 – Create Enduring Commitment

- **Desired outcome:** To establish a strong foundation of organisational self-awareness, alignment and commitment toward creating The Adaptive Organisation. This includes agreement regarding where the organisation is today, the Target Adaptive Profile and most importantly, the priority.

Follow the process I've described in Chapter 6 and combine data with rich conversation. Have the debates and candid conversations and work to build consensus. You may want to engage someone to help facilitate the process. Before you do, make sure you're clear about your objectives, and the engagement outcome you're looking for. Also, before looking externally, consider whether there may be internal people who can help. Activities may include:

- conducting a full Adaptive Audit and using the findings as the starting point for the 'Enduring Commitment' process
- engaging and educating stakeholders about The Thrive Cycle framework and developing a common language
- setting your organisation's Target Adaptive Profile
- establishing a high-level plan and next steps.

REMEMBER, IF AT FIRST YOU DON'T SUCCEED...

While it would be great if you could just do a ten-minute presentation and everyone in the leadership community would be on-board, it's probably not going to happen like that. The more likely scenario is that you will need to build your passionate coalition one conversation at a time. Knowing this when starting out, will make it easier when you encounter resistance.

Phase 3 – Galvanise into action

- **Desired outcome:** To have the logistical requirements in place to start pursuing adaptive advantage as an organisational priority.

How you achieve this outcome will depend on your starting point and your position of influence. If you hold 'the top-job' in your Core Organisation, you may decide to restructure, appoint the equivalent of a Chief Adaptive Officer and hand the mantel over to them to run with it. If you are a member of the leadership team, you may need to convince the head of your Core Organisation to appoint you into the Chief Adaptive Officer role.

Alternatively, you might decide to engage a consultant to better understand what needs to be done and come up with 'a plan for the plan'. All approaches are equally legitimate.

Activities during this phase may also include:

- communicating the objective of The Adaptive Organisation (as defined in this book)
- introducing a Thrive Cycle Education Program for leaders – using it to engage others
- securing professional services support or establishing your own Adaptive Advantage Team (or a hybrid of the two).

REMEMBER, BUILDING THE ADAPTIVE ORGANISATION IS NOT A PART-TIME JOB

Part of the Galvanise phase is obtaining financial commitment for professional services support, as well as any new roles or restructuring. Broader communication will also be important along with maintaining engagement among your key stakeholders.

Phase 4 – Start the journey

- **Desired outcome:** To ensure 'Building The Adaptive Organisation' enters your organisation's Thrive Cycle as a high-priority change-opportunity and to start building momentum through an actionable, aligned, value-driven plan.

I appreciate finding out that we are only *now* entering The Thrive Cycle may be a little deflating. However, the truth is that the first three phases of the roadmap are the ones that will 'unlock' your organisation. Having your leadership colleagues and the broader organisation *See* the opportunity and develop an *insatiable need* to do something about it will make all future activities exponentially easier and more successful.

Once you've achieved this level of commitment, the shared ambition needs to be actively pursued in the *right* way. This means progressing through The Thrive Cycle by:

- **understanding** what's driving your Adaptive Profile and analysing the Six Elements of Adaptive Success within your organisation. Where are the strengths and weaknesses?
- **prioritising** by assigning the required budget and resources
- **designing an approach** that will address the gaps between today's Adaptive Profile and the desired target. Develop your Design Principles and create your Thrive Cycle Blueprint. Engage cross-functional teams to help you
- **planning** how to deliver the change e.g. what's the best approach? Timeframes? Who's accountable for what? Don't try to plan two years in detail. Have a big-picture high-level plan then do shorter, more detailed near-term phases
- **moving** towards the desired future state and tracking progress
- **learning** by tracking progress and pursuing continuous improvement.

Throughout, make sure you look for quick-wins to build momentum. For example, you may decide to develop your organisation's first Vital

Thread early in the journey. This activity will not only deliver a critical requirement for The Adaptive Organisation, but also provides a good opportunity for people to engage with the change in a meaningful way.

Whatever quick-wins you identify, remember to watch out for the traps I've described in this book and make sure they really are quick-wins and not ill-informed short-cuts.

CHAPTER CONCLUSION

The Adaptive Organisation is not *a project* that happens off to the side and reports in every so often. While its execution will eventually need planning and structure, first you need the whole-hearted engagement and leadership of the entire Executive Team *and* your community of senior leaders. The sooner your colleagues understand what it is you're trying to achieve, and why it's a good thing to do, the sooner they can help. This is where you need to start.

Over time, it's likely your organisation will use several mechanisms to bring about change. Sometimes you'll use formal programs, other times changes will be made as part of continuous improvement processes. Regardless of the combination, you must have an overarching view as to where the gaps are and how successfully they are being filled. Create an Adaptive Scorecard and use it.

Finally, remember the creation of The Adaptive Organisation is a long-term ambition. There will be quick-wins and incremental gains but for the 'big stuff', it is better to focus on two or three changes at a time and do them well.

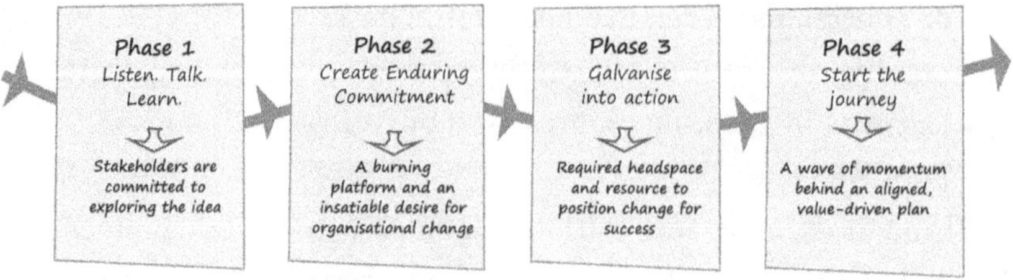
Phase 1
Listen. Talk. Learn.
Stakeholders are committed to exploring the idea
Phase 2
Create Enduring Commitment
A burning platform and an insatiable desire for organisational change
Phase 3
Galvanise into action
Required headspace and resource to position change for success
Phase 4
Start the journey
A wave of momentum behind an aligned, value-driven plan

KEY POINTS TO REMEMBER

- To build the solid foundation and level of leadership commitment required to create The Adaptive Organisation, your organisation needs to clearly answer the eight Adaptive Fundamentals. They are:

1. **What are we wanting to achieve?**
   Use the definition of The Adaptive Organisation to establish a clear goal.

2. **Why should our organisation become more adaptive?**
   Share examples and statistics from other organisations and create 'lightbulb moments' by following the process to create Enduring Commitment.

3. **Why should we change now?**
   Analyse your organisation and lay the current situation out on the table. Use analogies, stories and case-studies to bring the change-opportunity to life.

4. **What does The Adaptive Organisation look like for us?**
   Your Target Adaptive Profile must be meaningful and relevant to your organisation and its circumstances. Use the four Adaptive Archetypes to develop your own picture, rather than starting with a blank page.

5. **Where are we today?**
   Once again, the first element – Enduring Commitment – directly answers this. Involve the right stakeholders and contributors, follow the process and personally engage people throughout. Be resilient – you may not hit the jackpot first time. Just keep going!

6. **What is the gap between today and our desired future?**
   Understand the story behind the numbers, put it into words or a picture. Make sure you have your Design Principles worked out.

7. **What's causing the gap and where should we focus?**
   Think of the Six Elements of Adaptive Success in pairs. The Bookends, the Foundations and the Engine. Start by understanding the Foundations within your organisation, then see if you have the right Engine. Finally, look at the Bookends and see whether your organisation currently has the commitment and ongoing support your Thrive Cycle requires.

8. **How do we start?**
   You know your organisation and so ultimately, you need to decide the best long-term approach. In the meantime, the four-phase roadmap will get you started.

13

You're it!

In this final chapter we'll explore your role as the Driver behind The Adaptive Organisation. We'll look at what it will take to play this role effectively and share some practical ideas to help you along the way.

EVERY CHANGE NEEDS a *Driver*, and when it comes to creating The Adaptive Organisation, that Driver is now you.

So what will it take to play this role effectively and what kinds of strategies can you use to ensure the right outcomes are achieved.

LEAP INTO THE DRIVER'S SEAT

The role of the Driver is in addition to the ongoing role you'll be playing as a Thrive Cycle Leader. Your job is to create the energy and focus necessary to build momentum, motivate people and ensure that positive change actually occurs. You're going to need a never-ending supply of passion and enthusiasm.

You also need to understand The Thrive Cycle and be able to confidently talk about it. It's your job to introduce The Thrive Cycle into your organisation, and get others talking about it as well.

Being the Driver means doing these things all the time and not just when you feel like it. You never know who's watching and it only takes one thoughtless comment or behaviour to undermine months of hard work.

ENGAGE THE NON-BELIEVERS

There may be times when, no matter how much your vision makes good logical sense, other factors and agendas will get in the way. There will be people in your organisation who may be skeptical and need further convincing. Others may give you a flat 'no'.

It's true. Some people are just 'difficult' and disagree for disagreement's sake. Big mouths with big ambitions and even bigger egos. While most organisations have these kinds of stakeholders, in my experience they are in the minority.

Most of the time when people don't want to buy-in to a change it's because they either don't understand it, or believe it's threatening something they need or want. It could be money, power, trying to get the job done, work-overload, protecting their team or getting a promotion. They object because they believe what you're proposing stands between them and their objective.

Don't be discouraged by dissent. Expect it and see it as a challenge. While it may be tempting to mentally stamp 'DIFFICULT' on the stakeholder's forehead, seek to understand their perspective and find a way to work with it.

Twelve ways to engage the non-believers

STAKEHOLDER ENGAGEMENT is one of the most challenging and time-consuming tasks of the Driver role. While there is no magic formula, here are twelve things you can do when facing this situation.

- **Be clear in your own mind as to why change is necessary** and what will happen if things remain the same. Test, practice and refine your 'pitch'.

- **Ask them to help you solve the problem**. Instead of presenting the answer, lay the issue out on the table then engage them by exploring different ways to solve it. Doing this often opens up possibilities you hadn't thought of.
- **Widely share independent data** that shows what you're proposing is the right thing to do and that lots of others are already doing it. As anyone in marketing knows, people find it easier to agree to something if they're not the first ones to try it.
- **Assess how much this person really matters** in terms of what you are wanting to achieve. To what extent can they influence the outcome? If they matter a lot, you need to invest time and engage them. If they matter a little bit, then I'd suggest 'give it a go', then move on.
- **Assess your power-base**. Find out what you have that they might want and use this as leverage. Using stand-over tactics or threats is never a good idea. It pushes dissent underground, which is where it causes the most damage.
- **Be clear what role they need to play** during and following the change. Use this outcome to guide your approach.
- **Find out what matters to them** i.e. what do they care about both professionally and personally? Then, show how building a more adaptive organisation will directly make those things better (i.e. easier, more successful, less costly).
- **Be patient.** It can be frustrating when you can see that a change is a no-brainer, and someone important just doesn't *get it*. It's tempting to jump-in and ram it down their throat. I've been there. I've done it. Trust me – this never works and is more likely to cause much bigger alignment issues down the track.
- **Find out who they listen to** or whose opinion they care about. Then, influence that person.
- **Never ignore or go-around a powerful stakeholder**. When someone is 'being difficult' it can feel like it's easier to cut-them-out of the equation e.g. exclude them from emails, not invite them to meetings etc. While

this provides relief in the short-term, it will create an exponentially larger problem for you later on.

- **Don't start by asking them to 'buy the car'**, start by asking them to consider how having a car would make their life better. Being adaptive is a pretty big concept, so it may help to seek agreement in bite-sized chunks that are less daunting.
- **Recognise when you've reached the point of diminishing returns.** There may be times when you've tried everything but with no result. You need to think about how this situation will affect the likelihood of the change succeeding? It may be time to make some tough decisions? *Do* – Assess the situation objectively, be brave and take action. *Don't* – Ignore it, hope it will just resolve itself or compromise the outcome of the change, just to keep that person happy.

BE TRULY COMMITTED

A former colleague shared a great example of Driver behaviour with me the other day. She reported to the Chief Strategy Officer in a multinational corporation, and described how her boss insisted on spending one and a half hours with every new leader when they started. He did so to engage them intellectually and emotionally in his vision for the organisation and to discuss the role they needed to play.

Larry Bossidy, the CEO who transformed AlliedSignal, spent 30-40 percent of his time developing his leaders. He did so for two years[7]. That's a pretty significant chunk of time for a CEO to spend on a single task. However, that's the kind of commitment it takes when you're driving significant organisational change.

BE RESILIENT

Moving an entire organisation, even just a small distance, is a big task. One day everything looks like it is speeding along, and the next, it can feel like everything has fallen apart. Be ready for set-backs and help your team to be ready for them. It makes it easier to float over them when they arrive and saves valuable energy for the important stuff.

How to build resilience in your team

ONE OF THE SECRETS to being a great Driver is to recognise (and accept) that fear and uncertainty does strange things to people. In order to cope, they sometimes revert to unhelpful behaviours, and as a Thrive Cycle Leader and the *Driver*, it's your job to get your team through it.

I remember leading the final stages of a post-merger integration. We were moving a two-million strong customer-base from the systems of one company onto the systems of another. If you've ever been involved in this kind of change you'll know it's a bit like trying to fit all your furniture into someone else's house (while their furniture is still there). There were about twenty major systems and the entire migration needed to happen within a 24-hour period.

As go-live approached, tensions were at an all-time high, as the unintended consequences of decisions made months earlier haunted the program on a daily basis. Scope was being cut and compromises were being made.

No one likes to make mistakes and this was particularly true when two-million customer accounts were at risk. This scenario provided the perfect environment for mud-slinging, as nervous stakeholders attempted to show why whatever was happening wasn't their fault.

Back 'in the trenches', the delivery and operational teams were working fourteen to sixteen-hour days and constantly felt like they were under attack. Many team members felt victimised and frustrated that they were having to clean-up after people who weren't being held to account. Team members wanted to point fingers and say 'it's their fault not ours'.

In many ways the team members were right – it wasn't their fault. However, it was their job to deliver and 'throwing the mud back' wasn't going to achieve the required outcome.

So we coined a phrase to use when these moments occurred. *Just suck-it-up and move on.* Using this made the situation less intense and gave people a light-hearted way of letting the frustration wash over them, rather than being sucked into it. I could say to people 'Folks, I've got a suck-it-up moment for us' and instead of getting caught in a non-productive discussion regarding whose fault it was, we could move quickly into problem-solving mode.

Here's the key message.

As the Driver of change, if you spend your time trying to get every decision-maker to admit they caused an issue, you'll never achieve the outcome. The best advice I can give is to choose your battles and ask yourself 'what difference will it make?' If the only answer is that 'it will make you feel better' and won't actually improve the chances of success, then it might be time to *suck-it-up and move on.*

BE BRAVE

Being the Driver means being prepared to risk looking foolish in the interests of achieving the best outcome.

Risk-taking is a popular business topic, particularly with regard to organisations and being willing to act on market opportunities. However, this kind of organisational behaviour starts with having people who are prepared to take personal risks. This means if you want your people to take personal risks, you need to go first.

But what is a personal-risk, and why are we sometimes reluctant to take them?

What would you say if we were having lunch in a formal restaurant, and I asked you to stand-up and sing the childrens' song *Row, Row, Row Your Boat* as loudly as you could? You'd most likely respond with a resounding 'no'. In fact, most people would, even if they were certain they'd never visit the restaurant again, never see any of the patrons and there would be no ongoing repercussions.

So why is that?

Most of us have innate defense mechanisms to protect us against physical and emotional harm. We naturally pursue things that make us feel good, and avoid things that make us feel bad. Embarrassment makes us feel bad and often, we'll do everything we can to avoid it. However, as the Driver of change, you can't afford to avoid it.

Step-up and step-into it.

What to do if you make a mistake

I'M OFTEN ASKED by leaders 'If I make a mistake, should I acknowledge it?'

As a leader you are accountable for your actions, the actions of your team and the ensuing consequences. Therefore if a mistake has consequences that threaten the desired outcome, then it's better to acknowledge it, take corrective action, and move on.

Note that I'm not saying you should publicly 'fall on your sword' and send a self-flagellating letter-to-the-masses saying how sorry you are that you 'stuffed-up'. You are still the leader and your credibility is paramount. This means remaining confident (not arrogant) and being transparent about what's happened and why.

Doing the following will help you minimise, acknowledge and recover when you get it wrong.

- **Base your decisions and actions on sound rationale** – Use objective judgement, the available data and take into account specific circumstances. Recognise the assumptions you're making and check whether they have a solid foundation. If it's *a guess* (and sometimes it will be), understand why it's a guess and make it as 'educated' as possible.
- **Identify what's changed and understand why a previously good idea has become an issue** – Intuition has its place in decision-making but when you make a mistake, saying 'it just felt like the right thing to do at the time' is rarely an acceptable explanation. Instead, ask yourself 'what's changed since the original decision which now means that it was a mistake?' Were the assumptions wrong? Has new information become available?

- **When engaging others, use the following formula** to explain what's happened and move the focus toward taking positive action. Be authentic, transparent and outcome-oriented.
  - **Situation** – what's happened?
  - **Complication** – why is this a problem?
  - **Implication** – what does it mean?
  - **Plan** – what are we planning to do about it?
  - **Appreciation** – Acknowledge the human impacts of the mistake.
  - **Action** – What do we need to do right now?

CONFIDENTLY EMBRACE THE UNKNOWN

Several years ago a show called *Thank God You're Here* ran on Australian television[56]. In this 'improvisation' gameshow, each week new comedians and actors would appear as guests and be required to enter a blue door onto a stage facing a live audience. When they entered the stage, the guest would find themselves in a surprise situation with other costumed cast members, and be expected to improvise their way through a five minute performance. The role they were meant to play was only revealed to them when they arrived on stage.

The show offers significant parallels with being the Driver at the front of The Adaptive Organisation. You will often feel like a guest on *Thank God You're Here*. You'll need to find your way through unexpected scenarios, when you don't know all the answers and you are not sure what you're supposed to do.

This can be unnerving and can erode your confidence, especially if you're used to relying on your technical expertise. Some of the following strategies may help.

PRACTICE QUICK-THINKING

Actively practice thinking on your feet and engage your team in fast-paced exercises where there is no time to plan what is going to be said.

You could start every team meeting with a three minute word game or create your own version of theatre-sports. Or, have people present a news item based only on a newspaper headline.

This may feel a bit strange at first but after a while, you'll be surprised how much more comfortable (and thus, more confident) you and your team will be when faced with unexpected scenarios and ambiguity. You'll also have some good laughs.

LEARN TO LET GO OF CONTROL

The period of time between realising you don't know an answer and then working out what the answer is, gives rise to one of the most uncomfortable feelings around – *uncertainty.*

Most of us like to be in control but when there is uncertainty, you have limited control, and what you're left with is knowledge, experience and attitude. So as the person who is leading the charge toward The Adaptive Organisation, how do you practically work through this? How do you lead when you feel like you don't have all the answers?

Start by building self-awareness and noticing when you are in a place of uncertainty. Become conscious of what it feels like and what happens to your body when you are in that situation. Once you have this awareness, train yourself to mentally *let go of control.*

Now, I appreciate that saying this is a bit like telling someone about to undergo a double root-canal procedure to 'relax'. So let me explain what I mean.

When I talk about letting go of control I mean having a sense of being calm, focused and fully in control of yourself, without being in control of your environment. An actor might use the term *being centred* or an athlete might refer to *being in the moment.* Others may also refer to it as being in a state of *mindfulness.*

It doesn't matter what you call it, having the ability to let go of control 'on-demand' is incredibly powerful. It's like having a force-field around you and provides freedom and confidence to act. And, like most skills, it's something that improves with practice.

Three ways to let go of control

A BIT LIKE RELAXATION, learning to let go of control is a very individual thing. I might go for a walk to relax whereas you might prefer to read a book or practice deep-breathing. Ultimately you need to find a way to let go of control that works for you. Try things out and accept that you may need to try a number of different approaches before finding the right one.

Here are a few ideas to get you started.

When I first started doing this I used to picture a desert covered with constantly shifting sand. Then, I'd imagine I was balancing on a narrow plank of wood. I'd mentally 'surf' the sand until I found the right balance and I'd focus on what it felt like. After some practice, I didn't need the image anymore and was able to engage the feeling of 'being physically and mentally balanced' whenever uncertainty arose. In particularly difficult situations, I could recall the image to help me re-balance.

One leader I know used to reduce the significance of the uncertainty by comparing their current scenario to a far more extreme situation. Having thought through the more extreme possibility, when he returned to the real-life situation, it seemed far less scary and easier to handle.

Yet another colleague used to imagine she was a fly on the wall – observing what was going on rather than being part of the uncertain situation. She found doing this gave her the distance she needed to stay calm, think clearly, and be objective.

CHAPTER CONCLUSION

Tom Peters once said '... any idiot with a high IQ can invent a great strategy. What's really hard is fighting against the unwashed masses and pulling it off'[40].

Being the Driver for any change takes persistence and the willingness to keep going, even though you encounter resistance. It's your role to help people to 'get on board' and sometimes they'll need more help than you think they should. Leading when you don't know all the answers isn't easy. People will want them yet there will be times when you just don't have answers to give. When this happens, embrace it and think of it as a challenge. This will make it easier to remain confident and do what's required.

Despite its onerous reputation, being at the front-and-centre of a major change can be incredibly satisfying and lots of fun. There is nothing like the physical energy and buzz that surrounds a committed team whose members are striving to make a meaningful difference. The atmosphere can be so electric it makes the hairs on the back of your neck stand on end.

This said, it won't always be plain sailing. There will be times when it will feel like it's a case of three-steps forward, two-steps back, and you'll question whether it's all worth it.

Go for walk, work out at the gym or go for a coffee. Recharge. Do whatever you need to and create some space between you and the change. Then, climb back into the Driver's seat, put your foot on the accelerator and rev the engine.

When you succeed, it will have been worth the effort.

KEY POINTS TO REMEMBER

- The role of the driver is to bring the idea of The Adaptive Organisation to life, build momentum, maintain focus and positive energy.
- Leap into the Driver's seat and make the role your own.
- Engage the non-believers and seek to understand their perspective.
- Be truly committed and allocate the time that's needed to personally bring people on board.
- Be resilient and build resilience in your team.
- Be brave and willing to make mistakes.
- Confidently embrace the unknown by practicing quick-thinking and learning to let go of control.

A final thought…

Picture an organisation where change is something that is embraced and not feared; where the ability to adapt is the norm and not the exception; and where change is something that energises people, rather than exhausting them. That's the organisation you and I have set out to create.

You've read this book because you believe your organisation could be so much more than it is. It could provide so much more value to its customers; achieve superior economic performance; and create an environment in which people thrive on change and love coming to work every single day.

At the very start of our conversation, I said I believe any organisation can become adaptive. And now you have the knowledge, strategies and tools to be able to lead your organisation with the energy, passion and confidence required to make it adaptive.

However, this will only happen if you put the key in the lock and turn it.

Unlocking your Adaptive Organisation doesn't have to involve a massive gesture or a loud fanfare. You don't need a business-case or approval to start. You just need to *See* the opportunity, recognise its potential and do something about it.

You have the toolkit so now it's time to use it. Share The Thrive Cycle concept, use data to create insights, build your passionate coalition and inspire action. Take on the challenge from this moment, and as you do so, remember:

'It does not matter how slowly you go so long as you do not stop.'

—Confucius

I wish you every success.

ADDITIONAL SUPPORT

Visit The Thrive Cycle Learning Centre at
www.thethrivecycle.com

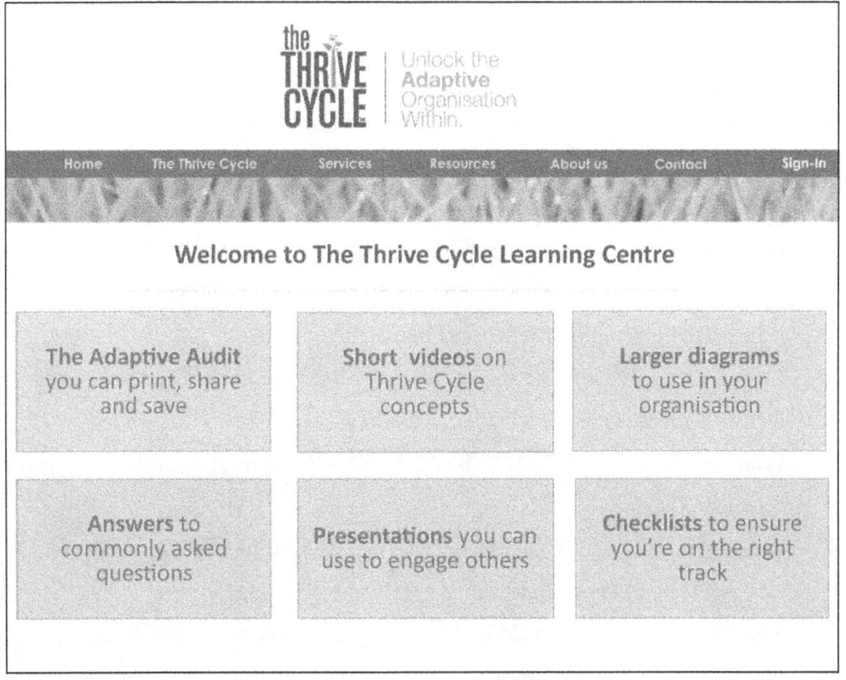

REFERENCES

1. African Development Bank. (22 May, 2015). [Video] - High Level Event II - *Leadership for The Africa We Want - 2015 Conference - Kagali*, p. https://www.youtube.com/watch?v=zbGZaykJ5iU.
2. Bartlett, J., & Miller, C. (2011). *Truth, Lies and The Internet - A report into young people's digital fluency.*
3. Barton, D., & Wiseman, M. (December, 2013). Why Big Investors are crucial to ending the plague of short-termism. *McKinsey - Insights & Publications - Website: http://www.mckinsey.com/insights/leading_in_the_21st_century/focusing_capital_on_the_long_term.*
4. Birshan, M., Gibbs, E., & Strovink, K. (November, 2014). Re-thinking The Role of The Strategist. *McKinsey Quarterly.*
5. Bliss, J. (2015). *Chief Customer Officer 2.0: How To Build Your Customer-Driven Growth Engine* . New Jersey: Wiley.
6. Bonchek, M. (20 April, 2012). Business Lessons from The Titanic. *Harvard Business Review.*
7. Bossidy, L., Charan, R. & Burck, C. (2002). *Execution: The Discipline of Getting Things Done.* Chatham, Kent: Random House.
8. Bradbury, T., Graves, J. (2012). *Leadership 2.0.* San Diego: Talentsmart.
9. Brown, T. (2009). *Change by Design: How Design Thinking Transforms Organisations and Inspires Innovation.* New York: HarperCollins.
10. Burrows, T. (2003). *Taj Burrow's Book of Hot Surfing.* Sydney: Rolling Youth Press.
11. Caixiong, Z. (5 May, 2015). Robots Go It Alone at Factory with No Asssembly Workers. *China Daily Newspaper - USA.*

12. Cambridge Dictionaries Online. (28 September, 2015). Definition of Organisation. *Cambridge Dictionary Website http://dictionary.cambridge.org/dictionary/english/organization.*
13. Chan Kim, W., & Mauborgne. (2005). *Blue Ocean Strategy: How to Create Uncontested Market Space and Make The Competition Irrelevant.* Boston: Harvard Business School Publishing Corporation.
14. Collins, J. C., & as, J. (1996). Building Your Company's Vision. *Re-reprinted in "On Strategy", 2011, Harvard Business Review Press*, 77-102.
15. Dean, D., DiGrande, S., Field, D., Lundmark, A., O'day, J., Pineda, J., & Zwillenberg, P. (19 March, 2012). The Internet Economy in the G-20 - The $4.2 Trillion Growth Economy. *BCG Perspectives - Boston Consulting Group.*
16. deBono, E. (1985). *Six Thinking Hats.* Boston: Little, Brown and Company.
17. Deloitte. (2013). *2013 - Culture of Purpose: A business Imperative - 2013 Core Beliefs and Culture Survey.* Deloitte.
18. Drucker, P. (2001). *The Essential Drucker.* New York: HarperCollins.
19. Duhigg, C. (2012). *The Power of Habit: Why We Do What We Do in Life and Business.* New York: Random House.
20. Economist Intelligence Unit. (2005). *Business 2010 - Embracing The Challenge of Change.* London: Sponsored by SAP.
21. Economist Intelligence Unit. (2008). *The role of Trust in Business Collaboration.* New York: Sponsored by Cisco.
22. Economist Intelligence Unit. (2013). *Why Good Strategies Fail - A Lesson for The C-Suite.* London: The Economist Intelligence Unit Limited.
23. Economist Intelligence Unit. (May 2014). *Gut & Gigabytes - Capitalising on the art and science in decision-making.* PWC .
24. EMC. (2014). *The Digital Universe of Opportunities: Rich Data and the Increasing Value of the Internet of Things.* EMC Digital Universe with analysis by IDC.
25. Ernst and Young. (2011). *The Digitisation of Everything - How organisations must adapt to changing consumer behaviour.* London: Ernst and Young.

26. Global Leadership Forecast 2014-2015. (2014). *Working Within The VUCA Vortex.*
27. Goodwin, D. (2011). Amazon's 4 Pillars of Success: A Preview of Jeffrey Eisenberg's Keynote Address. *Pubcon SFIMA Summit.* Lauderdale, Florida.
28. Groysberg, B., & Connolly, K. (16 March, 2015). The Three Things CEOs Worry About Most. *Harvard Business Review.*
29. Gunther-McGrath, R. (2013). *The End of Competitive Advantage - How to Keep Your Strategy Moving As Fast As Your Business.* Boston: Harvard Business Review Press.
30. Heifetz, R. (1994). *Leadership Without Easy Answers.* Boston: Harvard University Press.
31. Horney, N., Pasmore, B., & O'Shea, T. (2010). Leadership Agility: A Business Imperative for a VUCA World. *People and Strategy, Vol. 3, Issue 4,* 32-38.
32. IBM. (2010). *Capitalising on Complexity: Insights from the Global CEO Executive Study.* London: IBM.
33. IFLA Trends Report (2013). *Riding the Waves or Caught in The Tide.* International Federation of Library Associations.
34. Kotter, J. (1996). *Leading Change.* Boston: Harvard Business School Press.
35. Kotter, J. P. (2008). *A Sense of Urgency.* Boston: Harvard Business Review Press.
36. Kotter, J., & Heskett, J. (2011). *Corporate Culture and Performance.* Toronto: Maxwell McMillan International.
37. Kruszelnicki, K. S. (9 December, 2008). Chameleon Belief Blends into Background. *Website: ABC Science - http://www.abc.net.au/science/articles/2008/12/09/2441246.htm.*
38. McKinsey & Company. (September, 2014). Lou Gerstner on corporate reinvention and values. *McKinsey Quarterly.*
39. McKinsey and Company. (March, 2010). Building Organisational Capability Survey Results. *McKinsey Insights and Publications - www.mckinsey.com.*

40. McKinsey and Company. (31 March, 2015). An Interview with Tom Peters. *McKinsey Quarterly.*
41. Merrick, E. (2010). *Exploiting Complexity and Enhancing Adaptability: Creating opportunities for communication solutions in health services.* Sydney & Melbourne: Joint venture between University of Technology Sydney & The University of Melbourne.
42. Miller, P., & Wedell-Wedellsborg, T. (2013). *Innovation As Usual - How to help your people bring great ideas to life* Harvard Business Review Press.
43. Moss-Kanter, R. (2009). *Super Corp.* New York: Crown Business.
44. Oesterwalder, A., & Pigneur, Y. (2010). *Business Model Generation: A Handbook for Visionaries, Game Changers and Challengers.* Wiley and Sons.
45. PMI Pulse of The Profession. (February 2014). *The High Cost of Low Performance - 2014.* Newtown Square, PA USA: Project Management Institute.
46. Porter, M. (1996). What is Strategy? *Reprinted in "On Strategy", 2011*, 1-37.
47. Porter, M. (2008). The Five Competitive Forces That Shape Strategy. *Reprinted in "On Strategy", 2011, Harvard Business Review Press*, 39-76.
48. Rapert, M. I. (2002). The strategic implementation process: Evoking strategic consensus through communication. *Journal of Business Research*, 301-310.
49. SAP. (28 July, 2015). Predicting The Next Disruption. *The Australian Business Review.*
50. Senge, P. (1990). *The Fifth Discipline - The Art and Practice of of The Learning Organisation.* New York: Doubleday - Random House.
51. The Wachowski Brothers. (1999). *The Matrix.* Warner Brothers Studios.
52. Welch, J. (2001). *Jack: Straight from The Gut.* New York: Warner Business Books.
53. Welch, J., & Welch, S. (2005). *Winning.* Hammersmith: HarperBusiness.
54. Williams, T., Worley, C. G., & Lawlers, E. E. (15 April, 2013). The Agility Factor - Columbia Business School. *Strategy + Business.*

55. Wooldridge, B., & Floyd, S. (1990). The strategy process, middle management involvement, and organisational performance. *Strategic Management Journal - Vol. 11 - 3*, 231-241.
56. Working Dog Productions. (2006-2009). *Thank God You're Here - Australian Television Series.* Melbourne.

INDEX

www.ingramcontent.com/pod-product-compliance
Lightning Source LLC
Chambersburg PA
CBHW021028210326
41598CB00016B/945

* 9 7 8 0 9 9 4 4 7 5 1 0 7 *